D1381651

Gender Inequalities in the 21st Century

Gender Inequalities in the 21st Century

New Barriers and Continuing Constraints

Edited by

Jacqueline Scott

Professor of Empirical Sociology, University of Cambridge, UK

Rosemary Crompton

Emeritus Professor of Sociology, City University London, UK

Clare Lyonette

Research Fellow, Institute for Employment Research, Warwick University, UK

Edward Elgar

Cheltenham, UK • Northampton, MA, USA

Published by
Edward Elgar Publishing Limited
The Lypiatts
15 Lansdown Road
Cheltenham
Glos GL50 2JA
UK

Edward Elgar Publishing, Inc.
William Pratt House
9 Dewey Court
Northampton
Massachusetts 01060
USA

A catalogue record for this book
is available from the British Library

Library of Congress Cataloguing Control Number: 2009938413

Mixed Sources
Product group from well-managed
forests and other controlled sources
www.fsc.org Cert no. SA-COC-1565
© 1996 Forest Stewardship Council

ISBN 978 1 84844 438 6 (cased)

Printed and bound by MPG Books Group, UK

Contents

**PART III   THE CHALLENGE OF INTEGRATING FAMILY
AND WORK**

PART IV   UNDERSTANDING INEQUALITIES

PART V   CONFRONTING COMPLEXITY

Contributors

Sameera Ahmed is Assistant Professor in the Department of Journalism and Mass Communication at Sohar University, Oman. She has previously taught at Manchester Metropolitan University (Department of Politics and Philosophy). She has worked on a number of research projects examining labour market issues for minority ethnic women; housing needs (Housing Market Renewal – HMR); and media viewing habits. Her research interests include Muslims and the media; young people's viewing habits; and developments in Arab media. Her latest publications include *The British Media and Muslim Representation: The Ideology of Demonisation* (Islamic Human Right Commission, 2007), 'Shifting geographies of minority ethnic settlement: Remaking communities in Oldham and Rochdale' in J. Flint and D. Robinson (eds), *Community Cohesion in Crisis?* (Policy Press, 2008).

Fran Bennett is a senior research fellow at the Department of Social Policy and Social Work, University of Oxford (half-time). She is a member of the Within Household Inequalities and Public Policy project of the ESRC's Research Network on Gender Inequalities in Production and Reproduction. She has previously had posts with the Child Poverty Action Group and for Oxfam, and continues to work for NGOs and others when not teaching or researching at the University. Her research interests include poverty, social security policy and gender inequalities, with a particular focus on income. She is co-editor of the *Journal of Poverty and Social Justice* (formerly *Benefits*). With Professor Jonathan Bradshaw, she is the UK independent expert on social inclusion for the European Commission.

Gunn Elisabeth Birkelund is Professor of Sociology at the University of Oslo. Her research interests include social stratification and labour market research with a specific focus on changing gender relations and, lately, also on ethnicity. Together with Arne Mastekaasa she has recently edited a book on ethnic inequality in education and work. She has published articles in *European Sociological Review*, *Research in Social Stratification and Mobility*, *Demographic Research*, *Comparative Social Research*, *Work, Employment and Society*, *Social Science & Medicine*, *American Journal of Sociology*, *American Sociological Review*, *Acta Sociologica*, as well as

Norwegian academic journals. She has held a number of administrative positions, and is presently a member of the Executive Committee at the Inter-University Centre, Dubrovnik.

Rosemary Crompton is Professor Emeritus at City University, London. She has also taught at the Universities of Leicester, Kent and East Anglia. She has researched and published widely in the areas of gender, class and employment. Her most recent books are: *Employment and the Family* (Cambridge University Press, 2006) and the third edition of *Class and Stratification* (Polity, 2008).

Angela Dale is Professor of Quantitative Social Research at the University of Manchester and also heads one of the 'value-added' arms of the ESRC's Economic and Social Data Service – that responsible for large-scale government surveys. From 2002–08 she was Director of the ESRC Research Methods Programme. Her recent research has focused on women's employment, with particular respect to ethnic differences and strategies for combining work and family life; change between generations; and the role of qualifications, particularly higher qualifications, in women's facilitating economic activity and protecting against unemployment.

Jerome De Henau is a Lecturer in Economics at the Open University. He is currently working on an ESRC-funded project on intra-household inequalities and public policies across Europe and Australia. His main research issues are gender, family policies, tax and benefit policies, labour and household economics. He has recently co-authored three chapters of a book edited by Daniela Del Boca and Cecile Wetzels, *Social Policies, Labour Markets and Motherhood* (Cambridge University Press, 2007).

Fiona Devine is Professor of Sociology and Head of the School of Social Sciences at the University of Manchester. She was previously Head of Sociology. She has served as a member of Council of the ESRC and acted as Chair of its International Advisory Committee. Her research interests include social stratification and mobility; work and employment; and politics and participation with a comparative UK–US perspective. She is the author of *Class Practices* (Cambridge University Press, 2004) and *Doing Social Science* (Palgrave, Macmillan, 2009, with Sue Heath).

Anne Lise Ellingsæter is Professor in Sociology at the University of Oslo. Her research interests include family policy, gender and work, fertility patterns and social time. Among her recent work are the co-edited volume *Politicising Parenthood in Scandinavia. Gender Relations in Welfare States* (Policy Press, 2006); and '"Old" and "new" politics of time to care: three

Norwegian reforms' (*Journal of European Social Policy*, 2007); 'Closing the child care gap: The interaction of childcare supply and mothers' agency in Norway' (*Journal of Social Policy*, 2007); 'Leave policy in the Nordic countries: a "recipe" for high employment/high fertility?' (*Community, Work & Family*, 2009).

Mary Evans taught Sociology and Women's Studies at the University of Kent until 2006. On her retirement from Kent she became a Visiting Fellow at the Gender Institute, the London School of Economics. Her interests have always been in narratives (both fictional and non-fictional) and she has written extensively on feminist theory and a number of authors, including Simone de Beauvoir and Jane Austen. She has recently completed a study of detective fiction (*The Imagination of Evil*, Continuum, 2009). Her future projects include work on the collective subject and gender, nation and religion.

Jonathan Gershuny is Professor of Economic Sociology at Oxford University, Professorial Fellow, St Hugh's College, Oxford, and Director of the ESRC-funded Centre for Time Use Research. He was Chair of the British Academy's Sociology, Social Statistics and Demography Section (S4) from 2006–09, the Director of the Institute for Social and Economic Research, University of Essex from 1993–2006, and he continues as the Principal Investigator for the Multinational Time Use Study. His research interests are in the relationship between the activities of individuals' daily lives and historical change in social and economic structure. Recent publications include 'Gender convergence in the American heritage time use study' (*Social Indicators Research*, 2007), and 'Web-use and net-nerds: a neo-functionalist analysis of the impact of information technology in the home' (*Social Forces*, 2003).

Man Yee Kan is a British Academy Postdoctoral Fellow and Research Councils UK Academic Fellow in the Department of Sociology, and a Junior Research Fellow of St Hugh's College, University of Oxford. She completed a doctoral degree in Sociology at Oxford in 2006 and previously worked as a senior research officer at the Institute for Social and Economic Research, University of Essex. Her current research interests include the domestic division of labour, the gender wage gap, work schedules and work–life balance, and empirical and methodological issues in time use research.

Nicky Le Feuvre is Professor in the Sociology of Work at the University of Lausanne, Switzerland. She was previously director of the SAGESSE interdisciplinary Gender Research Centre at the University of Toulouse II – Le Mirail, France, where she was involved in a series of cross-national comparative research projects on the feminisation of managerial and professional occupations. Her research interests include gender theory, social policy and the sociology of work and employment in cross-national perspective. She is currently involved in an EU 6th framework project entitled FEMCIT (Gendered Citizenship in Multicultural Europe: The Impact of Contemporary Women's Movements), with responsibility for the 'Economic citizenship' module.

Clare Lyonette is a Research Fellow at the Institute for Employment Research at the University of Warwick. Her former positions include Research Officer at City University, where she worked with Rosemary Crompton on the Class and Gender, Employment and Family project of the Economic and Social Research Council's Research Network on Gender Inequalities in Production and Reproduction. She also recently worked at the Relationships Foundation on a project to prepare and write a report 'Unsocial hours: unsocial families. Working hours and family well-being'. Her research interests include work and family issues, work–life conflict and stress, careers, and gender-role attitudes. She co-edited *Women, Men, Work and Family in Europe* (Palgrave Macmillan, 2007) and has written several papers for publication in peer-reviewed journals.

Arne Mastekaasa is Professor of Sociology at the University of Oslo's Department of Sociology and Human Geography. He has published about fifty articles in a broad range of international journals, and is currently working primarily within the fields of stratification, education, work and labour markets. Recent large research projects are 'Educational careers: attainment, qualification, and transition to work' and 'Friends or foes – understanding the role of firms and workplaces for worker health'. He is also a former chairperson of the Norwegian Association of Sociologists and a former co-editor of the journal of the Scandinavian Sociological Association, *Acta Sociologica*.

Jane Nolan is a Nuffield Foundation New Career Fellow in the Department of Sociology at the University of Cambridge and a fellow of Magdalene College. She was formerly a Research Associate on the Economic and Social Research Council's Research Network on 'Gender Inequalities in Production and Reproduction'. Her current research is examining the role of Western banks in the reform of financial institutions in mainland China. She has published on a wide range of topics including work–life balance, job insecurity and work intensification, gender and equality of opportunity in the Chinese labour market, kinship networks in the UK, gender and age identity, and new technologies and the gendered division of labour. Her work has appeared in international scholarly journals, including *The International Journal of Aging and Human Development* and *Gender Work and Organization*.

Anke C. Plagnol is a Senior Research Associate for the ESRC Research Network on 'Gender Inequalities in Production and Reproduction' (GeNet). She is a Postdoctoral Research Associate in the Department of Sociology at the University of Cambridge. She received her Ph.D. in Economics from the University of Southern California in 2007. Her research interests include subjective well-being, gender equality, life course studies and applied microeconomics.

Ingrid Schoon is Professor of Human Development and Social Policy at the Institute of Education. Her research interests are focused on issues of human development across the life course, in particular the study of social inequalities in attainment, health, and well-being; the intergenerational transmission of (dis)advantage; the study of risk and resilience; and the realisation of individual potential in a changing socio-historical context. She has published widely, including over 100 scholarly articles and reports, one co-edited book (with Rainer K. Silbereisen) entitled *Transition from School to Work* (2009), and one monograph, *Risk and Resilience* (2006), both published by Cambridge University Press.

Jacqueline Scott is Professor in Empirical Sociology at the University of Cambridge and a Fellow of Queens' College. She directs the Economic and Social Research Council's Research Network on 'Gender Inequalities in Production and Reproduction'. Her former positions include Director of Research at the ESRC Centre for Micro Social Change at the University of Essex, where she was involved in the original design and implementation of the British Household Panel Study. Her research interests include life-course research; gender-role change; attitudinal research; and ageing and well-being. She has recently co-edited the *Blackwell Companion to the Sociology of Families* (2004); the Sage Benchmark Series on Quantitative Sociology (2005) and *Women and Employment: Changing Lives and New Challenges* (Edward Elgar, 2008).

Sirin Sung is a lecturer in Social Policy in the School of Sociology, Social Policy and Social Work, at the Queen's University Belfast. Her main research interests include gender and social policy; gender and employment; work–life balance policies; and gender and benefits in both East Asian countries and the UK. Her recent publications include 'Women reconciling paid and unpaid work in a Confucian welfare state: the case of South Korea' (2003), in *Social Policy and Administration*, and 'Dealing with money in low–moderate income couples: insights from individual interviews' (with F. Bennett, 2007), in *Social Policy Review*.

Tracey Warren is a Reader in Sociology at the University of Nottingham. Her research interests lie in the sociologies of work and employment, time use and social divisions. More specifically, these include social inequalities in work time; income, wealth and economic well-being; the transmission of economic dis/advantage; work–life reconciliation in European countries; and time wealth/poverty. She recently co-authored *Work and Society: Sociological Approaches, Themes and Methods* (Routledge, 2008), and has published her work in a range of journals including the *British Journal of Sociology*; *European Societies*; *Feminist Economics*; *Gender, Work and Organization*; *Sociology, and Work, Employment and Society*.

Janette Webb is Professor of Sociology of Organisations and Director of the Graduate School of Social and Political Science at the University of Edinburgh. She is also a Non-Executive Director of NHS Health Scotland, and a member of the Royal Society of Edinburgh's Committee of Inquiry: 'Facing Up To Climate Change'. She has previously held academic posts at the Universities of Aston and Kent, and has been awarded research grants from ESRC, DTI, EOC and Higher Education funding bodies. Her research interests include gender relations and social divisions; markets and the organisation of economic life; power and authority; and the legitimation of inequality. Recent publications include *Organisations, Identities and the Self* (Palgrave Macmillan, 2006) and articles in *Social Politics* (2009) and *Sociological Research Online* (2007). She is currently developing new research on business and climate change.

Acknowledgements

We gratefully acknowledge support for this research from a grant by the Economic and Social Research Council (RES-225-25-1001) which funds the ESRC Research Priority Network on Gender Inequalities. We also thank City University for its support for the conference 'Gender, Class, Employment and Family' on which this book is based.

Introduction: what's new about gender inequalities in the 21st century?

Jacqueline Scott, Rosemary Crompton and Clare Lyonette

With the demise of the male breadwinner family, there has been something of a 'paradigm shift' in gender relations. But will this shift bring more or less equality? Major labour market changes, particularly in respect of women, together with dramatic changes in parenting and partnership, and greater recognition of gender equality issues in the policy arena, have served to break apart the traditional gender-role division. The expectation on the part of policy makers today is that women will be fully 'individualised' in the sense of economically autonomous, although policies are often ambiguous on this score. Social reality is more mixed; women are still disproportionately in part-time employment, and still do the bulk of unpaid care work.

The post-war welfare state in Britain in the 1940s was established on the assumption that men went out to work and women stayed at home. Both the system of work and the system of benefits depended on this male breadwinner model (Williams 2004). However, the model came under pressure to change in the 1960s and 1970s, partly in response to equality issues that were voiced by activists of the Women's Movement. It was also prompted by changing labour market opportunities and the recognition that most families required two wages to meet their housing needs and consumption aspirations. Certainly by the 1990s it was clear that the idealised picture of a male provider and female carer no longer captured the realities of people's lives.

However, shifts in gender equality have been very uneven across different sectors of society. There are marked differences by social class, ethnicity and age in the way gender inequalities are manifest. The persistence of gender and class inequalities, in particular, pose a challenge for those who argue that people's lives are becoming more 'individualised' and that the traditional social ties, relations and belief systems that used to shape people's lives are losing their significance. The claim made by Ulrich Beck and Elizabeth Beck-Gernshein, for example, is that things that once gave

1

a framework and rules to everyday life, including family unit, class and gender roles are continuing to crumble away. They go on to assert that 'For the individual, this brings historically new free spaces and options: he can and should, she may and must, now decide how to shape their own life within certain limits at least.' (2007: 502). Moreover, they claim that the other side of this individualisation dynamic is that institutions, including the labour market, the education system, the legal system and so on promote and demand an active and self-directed conduct of life.

To some extent the individualisation thesis can be seen as a correction to the overly deterministic materialist explanations of human behaviour that were common in earlier eras (Wrong 1961). Yet it is possible to swing too far the other way and, as the evidence in this book suggests, there are grounds for scepticism about the extent to which individual 'agency' and capacities for 'self-construction' have replaced structural constraints of all kinds. The discourse of individualism, however, has been extremely influential in both Europe and North America, and has many resonances with neoliberal thinking that has enjoyed such prominence in recent decades. Yet, although it is certainly the case that important changes have occurred in the way employment, class and family are being reconfigured in modern societies, the continuing influence they exert over people's everyday life experiences remains powerful. As far as women are concerned, one of the most significant elements of the way traditional practices are embedded in our social institutions is the persistence of the ideology of domesticity, in which the work of caring and nurturing is normatively assigned to women.

This introductory chapter is in four sections. First, we consider briefly the way that gender patterns in paid and unpaid work are changing across Europe and North America. Employment and family life are intrinsically intertwined but there remain pronounced differences in the work–family lives of men and women. Yet, in policy rhetoric, work–family conflicts are often framed in gender-neutral terms that ignore the persistence of the gender imbalance in paid and unpaid work. Second, we examine how the concept of gender alone is not sufficient for analysing inequalities, and, crucially, other differences such as class, race, ethnicity and age modify people's employment and family experiences. We focus particularly on the way that class interacts with issues of gender equality and we refute the claim that class no longer matters. Third, we examine longer-term trends in gender equality. We suggest that two contrasting stories can be told. One emphasises how much has been achieved in the struggle for greater equality over time, particularly in terms of the expansion of education and employment opportunities for women. The second emphasises the distance there remains to go in achieving gender equality and the slow pace of change, particularly in terms of the shifts in the amount of caring and unpaid work that is undertaken by men. Both stories can be justified by the evidence and, by considering both the optimistic and pessimistic accounts, we adopt an appropriately nuanced position for considering gender inequalities in the twenty-first century. The final section discusses the origins of this book and provides a brief overview of the book and how it illuminates the new barriers and continuing constraints that characterise gender inequalities in the twenty-first century.

CHANGES IN PAID AND UNPAID WORK

In recent decades, both in Britain and in Europe, policies have explicitly been designed to raise employment participation amongst women. Thus, for example, in Lisbon in March 2000, the Heads of Governments of the European Union subscribed to the goal of raising the employment rate of women to 60 per cent by 2010.

Table I.1 shows the progress made by women in the total employment rate since 1960 across Europe, as well as in North America (Boeri et al. 2005). A glance at performance rates in 2000 as well as the 'Lisbon distance', the percentage difference between the female employment rate in 2000 and the 60 per cent target, shows that the gaps are still substantial in Mediterranean countries, and in Belgium, France and Ireland. The gender employment gap, defined as the differences in employment rate between men and women, is falling in all countries. On average the gender gap has nearly halved since 1980, from 30 per cent (not shown in the table) to 16.6 per cent by the year 2000. This reduction in the gender employment gap is continuing. Moreover, in 2009 in the global recession, at least in the USA and UK, the rate of job loss for males is far exceeding that for females, thus potentially narrowing the employment gap further. Employment forecasts in such uncertain economic times are fraught with difficulties. However, the UK Commission for Employment and Skills (2009) predicts that, for men, the employment rate is expected to rise gradually through to 2010 and beyond, but for women the employment rate may fall. However, this gender difference is mainly because the age of state pension for women will be increased by stages from 60 in 2010 to 65 by 2020. Thus the increase in the female working age population may well exceed an increase in employment.

There is also a marked gender pay gap that is proving remarkably resilient despite the legal efforts in different countries that seek to ensure that men and women receive the same rates of pay, for comparable work. In Table I.2 we can see the gender–wage ratio in terms of median hourly wage

Table I.1   Female employment rates: 1960–2000 persons aged 15–64

		1960	1980	2000	Men 2000	Lisbon distance*
Nordic						
	Denmark	42.7	66.3	71.2	80.4	11.2
	Finland	54.9	65.0	64.3	69.7	4.3
	Norway	26.1	58.4	73.4	88.1	13.4
	Sweden	38.1	67.6	72.1	76.2	12.1
Anglo-Saxon						
	UK	43.1	54.5	65.2	79.3	5.2
Mediterranean						
	Greece		30.7	40.4	70.2	−19.6
	Italy	28.1	33.2	39.7	68.5	−20.3
	Spain	21.0	28.4	40.3	70.3	−19.7
Rest of Europe						
	Austria		52.4	59.3	78.1	−0.7
	Belgium	29.6	35.0	51.1	69.8	−8.9
	France	42.9	50.0	53.1	68.1	−6.9
	Germany	35.0	34.8	58.1	73.5	−1.9
	Ireland		32.3	52.2	74.0	−7.8
	Netherlands		35.7	62.1	81.1	2.1
	Portugal		47.1	60.1	75.9	0.1
North America						
	United States	39.5	53.9	68.0	80.4	
	Canada		52.3	65.1	75.2	
Average			46.9	58.6	75.2	

Note: * Lisbon distance is the percentage difference between women's employment in 2000 and 60 per cent.

Source: Boeri et al. (2005: Table 2.1).

for three age groups (Boeri et al. 2005). The table shows that, with the exception of Italy, Denmark and Germany, the hourly female–male wage ratio is around 10 percentage points higher for younger women than for older women. Both age or life-course and birth cohort effects are at work here. First, younger women tend to show a greater similarity to young men in terms of labour market experiences. Second, for recent generations the education gap has narrowed substantially. The UK does not fare well in this cross-national comparison. Although the wage ratio among the youngest in the UK shows only an 8 per cent gap, this rises to 33 per cent for those aged 45–54 and is the worst gender wage-ratio among these 14

Table I.2   The gender–wage gap ratio by age (median hourly wages) for 1998

		25–34	35–44	45–54
Nordic				
	Denmark	92.8	92.5	90.5
	Finland	91.1	81.9	76.0
Anglo-Saxon				
	UK	92.0	70.5	67.1
Mediterranean				
	Greece	100.0	88.3	79.7
	Italy	98.5	97.3	92.4
	Spain	94.8	95.0	82.8
Rest of Europe				
	Austria	84.1	84.8	72.6
	Belgium	96.1	96.1	88.1
	France	95.1	86.0	86.1
	Germany	85.9	82.9	80.6
	Ireland	91.1	79.5	71.3
	Netherlands	98.6	84.6	76.9
	Portugal	86.8	83.9	81.6
North America				
	USA	83.3	74.7	70.4
Average		92.2	85.6	79.7

Source: Boeri et al. (2005: Table 5.2).

countries. It remains to be seen whether the wage ratio increases for the youngest cohort as they reach mid-life. Continuous employment is likely to reduce the gender pay gap, for those women who take minimal time out of the labour market to care for children or elderly family members. There are important class differences here, and professional/managerial women are more likely to be in continuous employment than women with routine and manual employment (Crompton 2006). However, there is strong evidence from longitudinal studies in the UK that women who take time out for caring work are paying an increased penalty over time, in terms of decline in occupational status (Dex et al. 2008). Thus while caring remains gendered, the gender pay gap will persist.

As Lewis (2008) and others have pointed out, the policy regimes of many industrialised countries were designed and devised around the model of a male breadwinner family where the man worked full-time and the woman cared for the family and was not expected to be employed. This male breadwinner behaviour, in its pure sense, is hardly visible in industrialised countries of the twenty-first century because of the huge increases in women's employment that have taken place. Of course, many women do take time out of the labour force to have and care for children, even though these periods have been getting successively shorter over recent generations (Macran et al. 1996). For policy purposes the male breadwinner model still exists, albeit in a modified form. A common modification is for the male partner to be in paid work and full-time hours and the female partner to be in paid work but part-time hours.

A range of models that address work–family balance, around childbearing and childcare, together with the associated policies and example countries is set out in Table I.3 (Scott and Dex 2009). These policies are also associated with different models of gender relations and normative assumptions relating to masculinity and femininity (Crompton 1999; Gornick and Meyers 2003). Policies have grown up in very different ways in different countries, and the logic underlying the policies can vary considerably. In principle there are two extremes that policy regimes can adopt: they can either support adults, undifferentiated by gender, as paid workers; or they can acknowledge that men and women are likely to offer different levels of contributions to the labour market. No policy regime takes the extreme adult worker position, but the USA comes pretty close to this in only offering women rights to unpaid maternity leave since 1996. Scandinavian countries are often heralded as being more focused on providing equal opportunities to women and men, but policies also allow women's employment contribution to be different from men's in having longer parental leave, and long periods of part-time work following childbirth. When policies allow or encourage women to behave differently in terms of their employment participation or their hours of work, gender differences are tacitly endorsed. This 'difference' is often a reflection of gendered normative assumptions relating to women's and men's responsibilities for caring and domestic work. For example, the Netherlands is shown here as encouraging both mothers and fathers to work part-time, in order to share paid and unpaid work more equally. However, such encouragement is a very long way from achieving gender equality. Although the Netherlands has by far the highest rates of male part-time workers in Europe (about 13 per cent), women account for three-quarters of the part-time work force.

In order to link specific country policies with different time use patterns, Table I.4 shows the mean time in minutes per day that men and women spend on different types of paid work and unpaid work, for the UK, the USA, Sweden, West Germany and the Netherlands. These data are taken from time diaries of a longitudinal cross-national sample (Gershuny 2000). *Paid work* is contrasted with *Core domestic work* (referring to housework

Table I.3　Range of models of work–family balance

Model/author	Description	Associated policies	Example countries
Adult worker model family Comes in two forms:	Men and women are responsible for participating in the labour market.	Stimulate provision of formal childcare services, possibly subsidised.	Model encouraged in EU.
a) supported	Focus on getting lone parents and low earners into work.	In work-benefits, tax credits acting as subsidy to low-paying employers. Tax relief or subsidy for childcare if women in paid work.	UK since 1999, more so since 2003.
b) unsupported	Gender-neutral, equality defined as sameness.	Earned income tax credits to make sure it is economic to work. No support for workers, except what is provided in the market. Little support in leave or pay for childbearing or income replacement while childbearing and child-rearing.	USA
Gender participation model, sometimes called the Nordic model, or 'gender-differentiated supported adult worker model' (Lewis, 2008)	Gender equality promoted, but makes allowances for difference.	Generous cash support for parental leave, services for child care and elderly dependents, but also for women to have extensive periods of leave (three years if two	Sweden. To a lesser extent in other Scandinavian countries. To a lesser extent in Germany.

Table I.3   (continued)

Model/author	Description	Associated policies	Example countries
		children born in quick succession) and rights to work part-time until child is eight.	
Gender equality based on a woman's model of equality (Knijn, 2004)	All workers encouraged to reduce their weekly paid working hours to be part-time.		The Netherlands

Source: Scott and Dex (2009).

and cooking) and *Other unpaid work* (childcare, shopping and odd jobs). It is clear that women in all these countries do a greater share of unpaid work than men. However, two other facts about the gender division of work are worth noting. First, adding up women's and men's paid and unpaid work leads to near equality in the amounts of total work done by men and women, or men doing slightly more total work than women (the only exception being West Germany). Such figures suggest that claims of women's 'double shift' (Hochschild 1989) may be exaggerated. Second, the average amounts of domestic work and paid work vary by country as well as by gender, with relatively high total work hours in the United States, Sweden and West Germany and lowest total work hours in the Netherlands.

We argued above that policies that make allowance for gender differences in employment practice are likely to reinforce gender differences in domestic work. In Sweden it is clear that women are spending more time on core domestic work than men, despite an explicit policy commitment to gender equality. Nevertheless there is some evidence that policies supporting equality have some effect. The figures reported in Table I.4 show Swedish men having the highest number of minutes for men of core domestic work (56 minutes) of these countries and Swedish women spending the least time (143 minutes). Thus although, even in Sweden, equality of unpaid domestic work seems an elusive goal, it does seem that supportive policies can help nudge behaviour in the direction of greater equality.

Table I.4   Mean time spent per day on different types of work, in minutes

Country:	UK	USA	Sweden	West Germany	The Netherlands
Core domestic work					
Men	28	33	56	11	29
Women	177	182	143	238	188
Other unpaid work					
Men	83	97	117	84	84
Women	111	142	146	132	124
Paid work					
Men	367	406	379	418	325
Women	178	187	262	168	94
Total work					
Men	478	536	552	513	438
Women	466	511	551	538	406

Source: Gershuny (2000: ch. 7).

Is gender equality what people want? In the UK, fathers report being largely content with the hours they work even when their work hours are as much as 60 hours per week (O'Brien 2005). Mothers like part-time paid work; they like flexibility in their working hours; they are generally happy with care policies that acknowledge that women are different and treat them differently (Scott and Dex 2009). The case for preferences driving decisions about paid work has been argued by Hakim (2000), mainly in the context of the UK. However, preference theory is problematic, as Crompton (2006) argues, because 'preferences' are shaped and constrained by the context in which they are made. It is also the case that, as Nussbaum (2000: 114) argues, 'preferences' are not necessarily the best guide for policy making. She suggests that we also need 'to conduct a critical scrutiny of preference and desire that would reveal the many ways in which habit, fear, low expectations and unjust background conditions deform people's choices and even their wishes for their own lives'. It is certainly the case that the so-called 'choices' parents make about who is the primary earner and who takes time out to look after the children are still being made on a playing field that is not level or equal between men and women. There are a range of policies that support the male partner working longer paid hours than the female, and there remains, as we have seen, a marked gender pay gap. It seems unlikely that equality in either employment or family care will come from people's preferences, so long as employment and family norms reinforce the existing gender divide.

CLASS AND GENDER EQUALITIES

How does the class divide bear on questions of gender equality? The assertion that 'class' is no longer a concept relevant to the analysis of 'late modern' societies has been made so often as to be almost banal. The idea that in 'reflexive modern societies' the individual is author of his or own biography is one that has been repeatedly expressed. However, claims asserting the 'death of class' are greatly exaggerated. The importance of parental occupational status for children's educational outcomes has increased rather than decreased in the UK over the second half of the twentieth century (Schoon 2006). Beliefs that the UK is a meritocratic society have always been wishful thinking. How people speak, how people dress, their exposure to particular types of music and culture remain associated with social class. These 'soft skills' of conversation and taste are crucial for self presentation and 'know how' which, when combined with educational advantages and employer stereotypes, help perpetuate material class inequalities. Class and gender (along with other differences such as age and ethnicity) intersect to structure advantages and disadvantages in ways that reproduce existing social hierarchies in the life opportunities of new generations.

In this book we pay particular attention to how gender divisions are cross-cut by class divisions. In the UK, on average, women receive lower returns than men within all occupational class groupings, but the class differences between women are also considerable, and the educational attainment and employment prospects of adults and children are polarised by class as well as by gender. However, there is individual variation within social class groups and there has been an increasing interest in how some individuals 'beat the odds', overcoming early family disadvantage to achieve success in later life, in terms of educational qualifications, employment attainment, personal and family fulfilment, and quality of life.

Class matters. Women's decisions to go back to work may be different for different classes, with working-class women more likely to work because they need the money. Patterns of childcare choices are also class-related, with lower social groups more likely to rely on relatives, while professional and managerial parents 'choose' the more expensive market-based care. Even the ability to achieve a work and life 'balance' has a significant social-class, as well as a gender dimension. Women from higher social classes have many more opportunities and fewer constraints than do lower-class women to achieve their preferred balance of employment and family care. Less privileged women often do not have the luxury of putting into practice their preferences concerning the ideal family employment mix. One reason is that they lack the resources that benefit the middle class – both in terms of financial resources and in terms of knowledge of how to 'play the system'; on the other hand, professional and managerial women who work full-time have markedly higher levels of work–life conflict than women in other classes.

There has been increasing recognition that there are a rather complex set of cross-cutting influences that modify experiences of gender inequalities. The claim is that an adequate representation of gender inequalities must simultaneously include class, racial, ethnic and other differences. However, it is not always possible or appropriate to focus on complex interactions, which the concept of 'intersectionality' implies. Yet this concept poses a useful critique to the naive forms of gender analysis that assume that male and female categories dominate all other forms of difference, and that boundaries between categories are static and universal. Instead, it is necessary to bear in mind that discrimination and inequalities will interact in certain ways that depend on the context and are specific to time and place (McCall 2005).

In this book we take it as axiomatic that context matters and that gender inequalities are specific to time and place. Gender inequalities in the twenty-first century are taking new forms that are partly shaped by the economic and socio-political and cultural climate of the global society in which we live. Different countries have very different levels and trajectories of inequalities. This applies to many different aspects of inequality including household income, employment opportunities, family circumstances, responsibilities for caring, work–life balance, or quality of life more broadly. Moreover, within-country inequalities are being played out in a rapidly changing context of labour market shifts, changing class divisions, ageing populations and new patterns of migration.

IS THE GLASS HALF FULL OR HALF EMPTY?

In looking at changes in gender equality across time, two stories can be told. On the one hand, it can be argued that huge strides have been made over the past half century in terms of opportunities for women. There is much evidence that supports the positive story. The proportion of women in the labour market has grown markedly; the pay gap has narrowed; notions that a woman's place is in the home have eroded further; women have overtaken men in the numbers pursuing higher education. It is not just that increasing proportions of women are now gaining degrees, but it is also the case that female graduates now work in a much wider range of occupations than was the case 25 years ago. Women are increasingly represented in the professional and managerial classes and at least some 'glass ceilings' are being cracked.

But there is also a story that is far less rosy. Gender segregation in the workplace persists in terms of there being male and female typical jobs – with economic penalties attached to working in the feminised sector. There is also evidence of continuing imbalance in women's and men's representation in top managerial positions. Moreover, even when women get to the top, they still get paid less than men. The gender pay gap, although much reduced, seems peculiarly resistant to elimination. Moreover, as the Fawcett Society report (2005) noted, in the UK, women still experience 'sticky floors', meaning that they get stuck at the bottom of the pay ladder, clustered in low-paid jobs. So-called women's work such as caring, cleaning and catering is not valued, has limited opportunities for training and promotion, and is not paid well. There is still a gender pay gap of some 18 per cent for full-time workers and 40 per cent for those women working part-time. Moreover, some 'glass ceilings' remain stubbornly intact. The lack of acceptance that senior jobs can be done on a flexible basis combines with discrimination to stop women with family responsibilities reaching senior positions. Moreover, even when they make it to the top, women's salaries are markedly lower than those of men.

One reason why there has been so much change in some aspects of gender equality, while there has been so little change in others, has to do with the asymmetry in the speed of gender role change. As Esping-Andersen (2005) noted,

> when one studies life-course behaviour over the past, say 50 years, one is struck by a massive gender-asymmetry: all the while that women have adopted a new life-course, men have barely changed at all. We see a masculinisation of female biographies, in terms of educational attainment, postponed marriage and family formation and lifelong attachment to employment. This in turn underpins changing household structure, more fragile families, and declining birth rates. It also underpins the changing employment structure, as the disappearance of the housewife leads to the externalization of personal and social service activities. Possibly, women are reaching the limits of life-course masculinisation and, possibly, a new positive equilibrium will require that men embark upon a parallel feminization of their life-course (2005: 271).

It is possible for men to embark on a parallel feminization of their life course, but is it likely? There is some evidence to support the claim that the process of gender role change can be described as 'lagged adaptation' (Gershuny and Bittman 2005), with men slowly and somewhat unevenly increasing their contribution to unpaid work when their wives or partners return to employment following the birth of a child. Certainly, Esping-Andersen is right in depicting issues of gender equality as about the relationship between women and men. Too often discussions of gender equality seem to implicitly assume that such concerns apply to only half the human race, whereas gender applies to us all. In this book we examine different aspects of gender inequalities in the twenty-first century. We consider new barriers that have emerged in the past few decades that slow or prevent progress in gender equality. We also identify some of the continuing constraints that face women and men, employers and employees, policy makers and practitioners who are working to achieve a more egalitarian society.

ORGANISATION AND OVERVIEW

This book builds on a collection of original papers given at a successful international conference that was held at and sponsored by City University in March 2008 on Gender, Class, Employment and Family (Lyonette and Crompton 2008). The conference was co-sponsored by the Economic and Social Research Council's (ESRC) Research Priority Network on Gender Inequalities in Production and Reproduction (GeNet). Some of the contributors to this volume are part of this Network, which consists of nine interlinked research projects that are together pursuing the common goal of examining the way men's and women's work and family lives are changing and how policy can intervene effectively to promote change towards greater equality (Scott 2004).

This book is organised in five parts. Part I contains three chapters that look at family and labour market change. Schoon considers the persisting importance of class and gender in becoming an adult. Comparing British cohorts born in 1958 and 1970 she finds continued reproduction of gender and class inequalities in aspiration, education and employment. Devine examines the way class reproduction works in terms of occupational inheritance and occupational choices. Using in-depth interviews with doctors and teachers, Devine finds little evidence of occupational inheritance, but a marked difference in terms of how parents viewed the desirability of the two occupations for sons and daughters. Dale and Ahmed explore ethnic differences in women's employment in the UK and focus particularly on Pakistani and Bangladeshi women. Using both official statistics and interview data they conclude that educational qualifications are of overriding importance in these ethnic minority women's decisions to enter the labour market.

Part II deals with occupational structures and national regimes. Webb focuses on recent changes in women's and men's paid work in the UK, USA, Sweden and Japan, which exemplify different forms of advanced capitalism. She argues that gender and markets are mutually constitutive and the resulting social differences have different meanings in different societies. Warren examines the penalties of part-time work across Europe and finds that the association between part-time and low-level occupation is not universally applicable. Le Feuvre contrasts feminising professions in Britain and France and finds that the career patterns that are the most attractive to the vast majority of women in both countries are those that pose the least threat to traditional gender divisions of unpaid care-work.

The challenge of integrating family and work is tackled in Part III, with Kan and Gershuny considering the thorny question of how couples divide domestic labour and how men's and women's contributions to routine and non-routine domestic labour change with the move to partnership and parenthood. They find that while routine housework remains mainly 'women's work' throughout the conventional life course, care and non-routine domestic work are less gendered in nature. Crompton and Lyonette explore the way that mothers' employment and childcare 'choices' of couples are subject to very different opportunities and constraints depending on their occupational status. They demonstrate the persisting material inequalities associated with class. Scott, Plagnol and Nolan examine how perceptions of what matters regarding quality of life differ by gender and life stage. They find that the different caring and breadwinning roles of men and women lead to important differences in the way they perceive quality of life.

Understanding inequalities is the theme of Part IV. Bennett, De Henau and Sung examine the intra-household allocation of resources and control in the UK and show that different systems of money management are associated with which partner makes the main financial decisions in heterosexual couples. Birkelund and Mastekaasa examine how women's labour market participation leads to a reduction of earnings inequalities among households in Norway.

The final section, Part V, addresses the complexities generated by both the universal, but changing and variable, normative constructs of femininity as well as the conflicts between different 'feminisms' that these differences can generate. Ellingsæter examines the way different Nordic 'woman-friendly' policies are powerful ways of institutionalising changing social norms relating to 'good motherhood'. She suggests that the hardline implementation of lengthy breastfeeding can sacrifice the autonomy of mothers and the care-giving potential of fathers for a perceived, but not necessarily real, benefit to the child. Such perceived conflicts of interest present new barriers to the achievement of material gender equality, and open, yet again, the unresolved conflict between 'equality' and 'difference' feminism (Fraser 1994). Evans describes how normative constructions of 'the feminine' shape both the unpaid and paid work of women, both equally necessary to society. Fashion is to a considerable extent dependent on the shaping of femininity. As a commodity it is class differentiated and produces an ever greater range of demand and desire. As such, it is a central element of the engine of capitalist production and reproduction. Yet, at the same time, women of all classes remain largely responsible for the vital, and unpaid, work of caring.

Taken together, the chapters in this book demonstrate that there are not only new barriers, but also continuing constraints to the achievement of gender equality in the twenty-first century.

REFERENCES

Beck, U. and E. Beck-Gernsheim (2007), 'Families in a runaway world', in J. Scott, J. Treas and M. Richards (eds), *The Blackwell Companion to Families*, 2nd edn, Oxford: Blackwell.

Boeri, T., D. Del Boca and C. Pissarides (eds) (2005), *Women at Work: An Economic Perspective*, Oxford: Oxford University Press.

Crompton, R. (ed.) (1999), *Restructuring Gender Relations and Employment*, Oxford: Oxford University Press.

Crompton, R. (2006), *Employment and the Family: The Reconfiguration of Work and Family Life in Contemporary Societies*, Cambridge: Cambridge University Press.

Dex, S., K. Ward and H. Joshi (2008), 'Changes in women's occupations and occupational mobility over 25 years', in J. Scott, S. Dex and H. Joshi (eds), *Women and Employment: Changing Lives and New Challenges*, Cheltenham, UK and Northampton, MA, USA: Edward Elgar.

Esping-Andersen, G. (2005), 'Final remarks', in T. Boeri, D. Del Boca and C. Pissarides (eds), *Women at Work: An Economic Perspective*, Oxford: Oxford University Press.

Fawcett Society (2005), *Are We There Yet? 30 Years of Closing the Gap between Men and Women*, London: Fawcett Society.

Fraser, N. (1994), 'After the family wage', *Political Theory*, **22**, 591–618.

Gershuny, J. (2000), *Changing Times: Work and Leisure in Postindustrial Society*, Oxford: Oxford University Press.

Gershuny, J. and M. Bittman (2005), 'Exit, voice and suffering: do couples adapt to changing employment patterms?', *Journal of Marriage and Family*, **67**, 656–65.

Gornick, J. C. and M. K. Meyers (2003), *Families that Work*, New York: Russell Sage Foundation.

Hakim, C. (2000), *Work-lifestyle Choices in the 21st Century: Preference Theory*, Oxford: Oxford University Press.

Hochschild, A. (1989), *The Second Shift, Working Parents and the Revolution at Home*, London: Piatkus.

Knijn, T. (2004), 'Challenges and risks of individualisation in the Netherlands', *Social Policy and Society*, **2**(1), 57–66.

Lewis, J. (2008), 'Work–family balance policies: issues and development in the UK

1997–2005 in comparative perspective', in J. Scott, S. Dex and H. Joshi (eds), *Women and Employment: Changing Lives and New Challenges*, Cheltenham, UK and Northampton, MA, USA: Edward Elgar.

Lyonette, C. and R. Crompton (2008), 'Report on an international conference on gender, class, employment and family', *Equal Opportunities International*, **27**(8), 709–14.

Macran, S., H. Joshi and S. Dex (1996), 'Employment after childbearing: a survival analysis', *Work Employment and Society*, **10**(2), 273–96.

McCall, L. (2005), 'The complexity of intersectionality', *Signs: Journal of Women and Culture and Society*, **30**, 1771–802.

Nussbaum, M. (2000), '*Women and Human Development*', Cambridge: Cambridge University Press.

O'Brien, M. (2005), *Shared Caring: Bringing Fathers into the Frame*, Manchester: Equal Opportunities Commission.

Schoon, I. (2006), *Risk and Resilience. Adaptation in Changing Times*, Cambridge: Cambridge University Press.

Scott, J. (2004), 'Gender inequality in production and reproduction: a new priority research network', *GeNet Working Papers*, No. 1, available at: www.genet.ac.uk/workpapers/GeNet2004p1.pdf, accessed 13 May 2009.

Scott, J. and S. Dex (2009), 'Paid and unpaid work: can policy improve gender inequalities?', in J. Miles and R. Probert (eds), *Sharing Lives, Dividing Assets: An Interdisciplinary Study*, Oxford: Hart, pp. 41–60.

UK Commission for Employment and Skills (2009), 'Ambition 2020: World Class Skills and Jobs for the UK', http://www.ukces.org.uk, accessed 29 May 2009.

Williams, F. (2004), *Rethinking Families*, London: Calouste Gulbenkian Foundation.

Wrong, D. (1961), 'The over-socialized conception of man in modern sociology', *American Sociological Review*, **26**, 183–93.

PART I

Family and Labour Market Change

1. Becoming adult: the persisting importance of class and gender

Ingrid Schoon

This chapter investigates changes in gender differences of young people's educational and occupational aspirations and differences in the assumption of work and family-related adult roles. It has been argued that since the 1970s transitions into adulthood have become destandardised and more individualised, that is more variable and protracted, less norm-conforming and collectively patterned, and more strongly influenced by individual decision making and choice (Beck 1992; Giddens 1991). Much of the current debate regarding the destandardisation of the life course reflects ongoing speculations about the way in which transitions are changing – yet there is still a lack of systematic empirical evidence about how the life course has changed, if at all – and how it has differentiated across social groups (Elder and Shanahan 2007; Macmillan 2005), with one of the critical research gaps concerning changes in women's transitions and careers.

In the following I review findings based on two British birth cohorts, following the lives of over 20 000 men and women born in 1958 and 1970 respectively, to assess continuity and change in transitions to adult roles and to examine the antecedents for the transition pathways taken. Comparison of the two birth cohorts provides a unique window into the major socio-demographic changes that affected most developed Western countries during the second half of the last century. The 1958 cohort was born just at the end of a boom period, during a time of extraordinary economic growth and social transformation, while the 1970 cohort was born at the beginning of a major recession following the 1973 oil crisis and lasting until the 1990s. Comparing the transition experiences of men and women in the two cohorts enables a better understanding of the changing nature of life course transitions, and the role of gender, class and individual agency in fuelling these changes. Has there been an increasing individualisation of transition experiences, characterised by increasing importance of individual aspirations and motivation? And has there been an increasing destandardisation of life course patterns, as indicated by greater variability, and a reduced influence of social class and gender on transition pathways taken?

The findings from the cohort studies suggest that the destandardisation of life course transitions has been less extensive than is generally discussed in the literature, as is the role of individual aspirations in shaping transition outcomes. There are persisting gender and class inequalities in the aspirations expressed by young people as well as in their transition experiences. Despite rising expectations and aspirations for the future (especially among women), increasing participation of women in the labour market and expanding educational opportunities, social and gender inequalities have not disappeared, suggesting the continued reproduction of gender and class inequalities in aspiration, education and employment. The processes by which these inequalities are perpetuated are discussed.

TRANSITIONS IN CHANGING TIMES

The transition to adulthood is characterised by the assumption of new social roles, such as leaving full-time education, entry into paid employment, settling down with a partner, and becoming a parent. Ongoing debates about this transition period emphasise the need for new, more global and pluralistic views regarding the nature of transitions, moving away from previously normative timetables or 'scripts of life' (Buchmann 1989; Elder and Shanahan 2007). Up to the 1960s transition experiences of young people have been characterised by a normative linear timetable of events, involving a sequence of leaving school at compulsory school leaving age, starting work, getting married, leaving home and having children, although some authors have doubted whether post-war transitions were indeed as straightforward as the argument suggests (Goodwin and O'Connor 2005).

Following the youth and student rebellions during the late 1960s and early 1970s, it has been argued that people began to experiment with new ideas and lifestyles, bringing with them pervasive value changes (Inglehart 1977). These were manifested in demographic variations such as delayed marriage and childbirth, the rise of non-marital unions, divorce and remarriage, and ideational claims to autonomy and self realisation. Across most Western societies the average age of primary employment, marriage and family formation has been pushed back from the early to the late twenties or even into the early thirties (Arnett 2000; Bynner 2001; Shanahan 2000), and the transition into independent living became disassociated from the traditional markers of adulthood, such as getting married. The women's movement was another crucial force in reshaping the lives of both women and men, encouraging women to pursue education and careers partially independent from family formation. The expansion of further education, in turn, as well as the increasing participation of women in the labour market, have been considered as explanations for the increasing prolongation and destandardisation of life course transitions. Another cause for more prolonged and complicated transitions into paid employment and adult independence were the major recessions experienced in Britain after the oil crisis in 1973, lasting from the late 1970s to the 1990s and bringing with them a sharp rise in unemployment, especially among young workers. In response to changing labour market opportunities and the introduction of new technologies in the modern knowledge economies, young people are now under increasing pressure to acquire further education and qualifications in order to secure a job at all (Blossfeld 2005; Bynner 2005; Shanahan 2000).

While some interpreted these changes as a widening of life chances and opportunities, others were more pessimistic. According to the theory of the second demographic transition there has been an 'ideational shift' characterised by changing social practices and the breakdown of many class- and gender-based constraints shaping demographic events (Lesthaeghe 1995). It has been argued that individual biographies have become more removed from traditional life scripts and more dependent on individual decision making and choice (Beck 1992; Giddens 1991). Others have questioned the importance of individual decision making and have interpreted the changes in life course transitions as difficult adaptations to external constraints (Buchmann 1989), or bounded agency (Evans 2002; Shanahan 2000). The assertion that individuals are now freed from class- and gender-based constraints in choosing their transition pathways into adult lives has been questioned, as there is persisting evidence of unequal access to educational and career opportunities (Bynner 2005; Furlong and Cartmel 1997; Schoon 2007).

STRUCTURE AND AGENCY

From the debates cited above, it appears that the processes shaping transition experiences in times of social change are not yet fully understood, and that the effects of the correlated structural and individual level variables are difficult to disentangle. In the following I draw on assumptions formulated within life course theory to gain a better understanding of the dynamic interactions between individuals and context. In life course theory it is argued that transition experiences and pathways through life have to be understood as developmental processes extending over time, that they are embedded within a larger socio-historical and cultural context, and are shaped by complex interdependent relationships, including links to one's family of origin, and individual agency processes (Elder 1985; 1998). The life course can be understood as a series of role transitions and trajectories that constitute individual biographies. Transitions denote changes in status or social roles, such as leaving school and entering full-time employment. Transitions are usually short in duration and indicate a change in a single state, moving from one social role or status to another. Transitions are embedded within trajectories that give them a distinctive form and meaning. Trajectories take place over an extended period of time and capture sequences of roles and experiences. The concept of 'career' is another way to describe the linking of role transitions across the life course.

Life course theory places great emphasis on the social construction and institutional embeddedness of individual biographies. Structural characteristics such as gender, socioeconomic status at birth and parental education have been linked to variations in academic attainment and motivation, to educational and occupational opportunities later in life, as well as to the timing of partnership and family formation (Duncan and Brooks-Gunn 1997; Schoon et al. 2007a). Individuals are, however, not passively exposed to these structural influences, and act upon their environment by making decisions and choices based on the alternatives and opportunities that they perceive are available to them (Schoon 2007).

Another key structural factor that shapes transitions and the pacing of work- and family-related transitions is gender. The female life course has been described as more complex than that of males, largely because of the greater interdependence of family- and work-related roles due to persisting gendered expectations ascribing women the main responsibilities for care and family tasks (Crompton 2006; Scott et al. 2008). Furthermore, women generally make the step into parenthood earlier than men, and their work and family transitions are more closely linked, rendering female participation in the labour market more interrupted and unstable than that of men (Martin et al. 2008). On the other hand, women are more ambitious than men regarding their educational and occupational aspirations (Mau and Bikos 2000), are more motivated at school, and are more likely than men to participate in further and higher education (Schoon 2006; 2009a; 2010).

It has been argued that the high aspirations and recent gains of women in the educational system are something of an anomaly, a trend that should not have happened given persistent disadvantages for women regarding subject choice and opportunities in higher education and the workplace (Arnot et al. 1999; Mickelson 1989). Women, for example, benefit less than men from a degree in terms of labour market participation and earnings (Purcell 2002). Some have argued that women might have different lifestyle preferences that cut across social class, education and ability differences, such as preferences for a 'home-centred', 'work-centred', or 'adaptive' lifestyle shifting in their emphasis for work versus family orientation over the life course (Hakim 2000). Others suggest that women may perceive and evaluate returns to education differently from men, placing more value on the potential of further education to enhance the quality of their personal, familial and community lives (Mickelson 2003), while others have questioned the importance of preferences or choice over structural constraints (Crompton and Lyonette 2005). In the following the associations between structure and agency in shaping aspirations of young people and their transition experiences will be assessed in more detail by taking a longitudinal life course perspective. Emphasising agency as well as social embeddedness of human development makes the life course perspective well suited as a gender-sensitive approach in the study of transition experiences.

AIMING HIGH

Comparing the educational and occupational aspirations of 16-year-olds in the two cohorts, that is the 1958 National Child Development Study (NCDS) and the 1970 British Cohort Study (BCS70) shows that the later born cohort has become more ambitious in their aspirations for the future, especially the young women (Schoon 2006; Schoon 2009a). More young people in the later born cohort want to continue in further education and aim for professional careers. While over two-thirds (63.4 per cent) of young people born in 1958 wanted to leave school at age 16, about three-fifths of young men and women born in 1970 wanted to continue with further education after compulsory schooling. In both cohorts girls show higher aspirations than boys, although the gender differences were greater in BCS70 than in NCDS, suggesting that girls have become increasingly more ambitious than boys in their educational aspirations.

Persisting Social Inequalities

In both cohorts there are systematic differences in aspirations by social background. Young men and women from relative disadvantaged backgrounds have generally lower aspirations than their more privileged peers. In NCDS about a fifth of young men and women from the most disadvantaged family background (that is parents in semi- or unskilled occupations) want to continue in further education beyond compulsory school-leaving age, compared to about two-thirds of the most privileged (that is parents in professional or managerial occupations). In BCS70 the aspiration gap ranges from about a third of young men and two-fifths of young women from the most disadvantaged backgrounds with high educational aspirations to over 70 per cent of the most privileged young people. In both cohorts, but especially so in BCS70, young women from relatively disadvantaged background have higher aspirations than young men growing up in similar circumstances. Similar observations apply to differences in occupational aspirations. Increasing numbers of young men and especially women aim for professional jobs requiring degree-level qualifications, yet men and women from relatively disadvantaged families have generally lower aspirations than their more privileged peers (Schoon 2006). Young women are generally more ambitious than men in their career aspirations, especially young women from less privileged backgrounds.

According to theories of social reproduction, aspirations are circumscribed by social background characteristics, and young people's consideration of which careers are possible for them are guided by their social class reference groups (McClelland 1990; Sewell and Shah 1968). One explanation for rising aspirations among young people refers to changing social backgrounds of young people in general (Goyette 2008). As parents are themselves more educated, the educational aspirations of their offspring are assumed to have changed as well. Furthermore, since the 1970s mothers' advances in the workplace and expanding opportunities for highly qualified women would suggest that parental aspirations as well as those of their children have increased, and have become less gender-typical.

There is no evidence that the aspiration gradient, that is differences in aspirations between relatively privileged and relatively disadvantaged young people, has reduced for the 1970 cohort (Schoon and Parsons 2002). In more contemporary cohorts, however, as for example in the Longitudinal Study of Young People in England (LSYPE) comprising students born in 1989/90, it appears that social inequalities in aspirations and expectations are decreasing (Schoon 2009b) – possibly due to generally higher education of parents and changing labour market opportunities requiring a better skilled work force. There are, however, persisting social differences in aspirations and expectations for the future, even after controlling for academic ability (Schoon 2006; 2009a). The findings rather suggest that young people in more contemporary cohorts, who are growing up in less privileged families, are relatively more disadvantaged compared to those born earlier, given the generally raised educational and occupational profile of parents in later born cohorts.

Linked Lives

The development and maintenance of motivation and aspirations is bound up with family circumstances. Being born into less privileged social backgrounds is associated with reduced access to the necessary financial resources and encouragement as well as the knowledge about how to navigate institutional practices in further and higher education (Reay et al. 2005). A number of studies have confirmed that parents play an important role in providing support and encouragement to their children. Parental aspirations are significantly linked to their children's academic motivation, their job aspirations and exam performance (Catsambis 1995; Eccles et al. 1990; Reynolds and Woodham-Burge 2007; Schoon and Parsons 2002; Scott 2004; Zellman and Waterman 1998), as well as the timing of parenthood (Schoon et al., 2007a).

The direct link between parental social class and teenage aspirations is mediated via socialisation experiences in the family, in particular through the experience of material hardship (Schoon and Parsons 2002). Although parental educational aspirations for their children have generally increased in the later born cohorts, parents employed in semi- or unskilled occupations and those with fewer economic resources are less likely to support further education for their children when compared to more privileged parents, suggesting persisting differences in aspirations by family social background (Schoon et al. 2007a). Nonetheless, young men and women from relative disadvantaged backgrounds who are supported by their parents in their future strivings for higher education or professional careers are more likely to achieve these goals than their peers in similar socioeconomic circumstances but without support from their parents (Schoon 2006). These findings confirm the importance of parent–child relations in supporting the educational and occupational development of their children.

Parental aspirations have also been identified as one factor underlying gender differences in educational aspirations. Surveys of students in the 1950s and 1960s show that although girls attained on average higher grades than boys, they received less encouragement from their parents and had lower educational aspirations (Alexander and Eckland 1974; Marini and Greenberger 1978; Sewell et al. 1980). More recent research, however, indicates a move towards less gender-biased attitudes and aspirations both among parents and their children (Schoon 2006; Tinklin 2003; Francis 2002). Support for further education is generally higher for daughters than for sons, especially among relatively less privileged families (Schoon 2009b). This finding might suggest persisting templates for male careers in traditional manual occupations among working-class parents, or perceptions of boys as being less suited than girls for participation in further or higher education, especially among parents in less privileged families. These findings also suggest complex interactions between social background and gender in shaping the formation of teenage aspirations.

Persisting Gender Inequalities

An explanation for rising educational and occupational aspirations among young women is that increasing aspirations and expectations reflect increasing gender equality in school and the workplace (Fan and Marini 2000; Mickelson 1989). The success and achievements of girls in the school system in the United Kingdom has been hailed as a story of extraordinary success of post-war egalitarian movements. In the early 1970s young women tended to gain fewer formal qualifications and were generally underrepresented in the universities. By the early 1980s the situation started to change. It has been argued that prior to the 1970s boys and girls were educated for very different occupational and domestic roles (Riddell 2000), while the 1975 Sex Discrimination Act made it unlawful to treat girls differently from boys regarding access to courses and educational and occupational opportunities.

The shift in the gender balance, however, with girls catching up or overtaking boys in their academic motivation and academic attainments, has to some extent brought about something of a moral panic, with appeals to the government to act in the name of underachieving boys (Epstein et al. 1998; Younger and Warrington 2006). The threat of boys' disengagement with the educational system has been of particular concern in the current era of growing knowledge economies requiring a highly skilled labour force. On the other hand, continuing inequalities and persistent disadvantages for women regarding subject choice and opportunities in higher education and the workplace have received less attention. Despite the fact that girls are more motivated to achieve and more likely to receive crucial support from their parents, in the long run they are less likely than men to enter the most prestigious occupations (Schoon et al. 2007a). Although women make up more than half of higher education students and almost half of the labour force, proportionately fewer women than men rise to the top of their professions (Crompton 2006; Farmer 1997). There continue to be barriers and obstacles to female career development, as reflected in gender role stereotypes, gender discrimination, and occupational sex-segregation (Scott et al. 2008).

Furthermore, despite the increase in educational and occupational ambitions among women and increasing participation of girls in further and higher education, subject and job choices are still largely gender-typical (Arnot, 2002; Francis 2000a; 2000b; 2002). In both cohorts, fewer young women than men showed interest in a career in science, technology or engineering (Schoon et al. 2007b). There is also evidence to suggest that girls report lower levels of self-confidence in their academic abilities than boys, especially in maths, despite good achievements. These findings confirm previous studies suggesting that girls tend to underestimate their abilities, especially in maths and science (Correll 2004; Eccles et al. 1998; Entwistle and Baker 1983), and indicate that gender differences in occupational choice can be understood as an example of social reproduction processes due to gendered perceptions of own capabilities.

The findings suggest that individual agency, the formulation of ambitions and plans for the future, is intrinsically intertwined with socially structured and gendered processes shaping the formation of individual preferences and values. Processes of individualisation have to be understood against the background of socially and gender-produced perceptions of capabilities and opportunities, and are embedded within socio-cultural constraints and persisting social inequalities.

LIFE PLANNING

The aspirations and expectations of young people are a vital expression of their hopes for the future and reflect their subjective assessment of how far in the education system and the occupational hierarchy they would like or expect to go. They can help to chart a life course, provide direction for spending time and energy during the school years, and are one of the strongest predictors of future educational and occupational attainments (Nurmi 1991; Schoon 2007; Sewell and Hauser 1975). The decisions made by individuals, within the particular constraints of their lives, can have important consequences for their future life course transitions across multiple domains. Findings from the cohort studies suggest that career development takes place in a life planning framework, where plans regarding education and employment are linked with outcomes such as educational and occupational attainment (Schoon 2006; Schoon and Parsons, 2002), but also with other life roles such as becoming a parent (Schoon et al. 2007a).

Linking Teenage Aspirations to Adult Outcomes

Linking early career orientations to adult outcomes, suggests that teenage aspirations are significantly linked to later educational and occupational attainment. In both the 1958 and 1970 cohorts, young people with high ambitions, including those from less privileged backgrounds, are more likely to participate in further education and to enter more prestigious occupations than their less ambitious peers (Schoon et al. 2007a; Schoon and Parsons 2002). However, young people from less privileged backgrounds with high ability and motivation on average achieve less than their more privileged peers (Schoon 2006). Furthermore, compared to cohort members born in 1958, those born in 1970 or later are finding that the stakes have been raised against them, as more young people continue with further education, gaining degree-level qualifications. Degree-level qualifications are increasingly becoming a requirement for high status employment (Bynner 2005; Bynner and Parsons 2002; Schoon et al. 2007a), and time spent in full-time education is by far the most important determinant of social status attainment, independent of motivation, cognitive ability and family social status (Schoon 2008). The findings suggest that those born in later cohorts have to invest more in their education in order to succeed, and that early school leaving might limit one's opportunities in the labour market, especially in the light of changing employment opportunities and increasing demand for a highly skilled labour force.

Participation in further education, in turn, is more strongly influenced by social background than ability, suggesting persistent inequalities in educational opportunities (Breen and Goldthorpe 2002; Bynner and Joshi 2002; Schoon 2008). Young men and women from relatively disadvantaged backgrounds are more likely to leave school early than their more privileged peers, even those with good abilities and high motivation. Early school leaving, in turn, is associated with lower social status in adulthood. There is also evidence to suggest that parental income has become a more important determinant of whether a young person continues into higher education or not (Blanden and Machin 2003; Machin and Vignoles 2004), and that the not-so-able individuals from privileged backgrounds have benefited most from the educational expansion (Galindo-Rueda and Vignoles 2005; Machin 2003; Schoon et al. 2001). The findings thus do not support the claim that the UK has become a meritocratic society (Bond and Saunders 1999; Saunders 1997; 2002), or that individuals have gained greater control and independence over their lives. The evidence rather points to an increasing polarisation of life chances, based on social origin and gender.

Polarisation of Transitions

Although social change has affected all young people, it has not affected all in the same way. There is a differentiation of transition pathways across different social groups in the population, and the preparation for adulthood has been elongated especially for those who can afford to invest in their education. A distinction has opened between those who take a slower route to adulthood involving longer education and delayed assumption of adult roles, and those who follow the traditional fast track transition, leaving school at minimum age, followed by early entry to the labour market and family formation (Berrington 2001; Bynner 2005; Jones 2002; Ross et al. 2009).

Cohort members with high aspirations who performed well in their examinations are more likely to delay the step into parenthood and pursue their occupational careers than their less ambitious peers. Yet life chances and opportunities remain circumscribed by gender and social origin, and the social and economic resources inherent in the connections young people have to their families are central to navigating the transitions into adult roles. For example, the influence of economic hardship has increased as a predictor of teenagers' school motivation and academic performance for the later born cohort. Economic hardship also has a slightly stronger effect on the timing of parenting transitions in the later born cohort, especially among women (Schoon et al. 2007a). The findings might suggest that access to economic resources has become more important in shaping transitions for the later born cohort, and that choices become increasingly constrained by financial considerations.

The negative consequences of early school leaving have already been mentioned, yet similar adverse consequences are associated with early family formation. Men and women making a relatively early transition to parenthood – this does not just refer to teen parenthood but also to becoming a parent in the early or mid-twenties – are at risk of experiencing adverse outcomes regarding education and employment (Bynner and Parsons 2002; Hobcraft 2002; Schoon et al. 2007a). Generally, the later someone becomes a parent, the greater the likelihood of rising on the occupational status ladder by the early thirties, while early parenthood is associated with a lack of career opportunities. Although this applies to both men and women, for women the effects of early childbearing are more adverse than for men. As more women have entered the work force and have taken on new roles, they have retained their position as the person responsible for childcare (Blossfeld and Drobnic 2001; Crompton 2006). For women the roles as mother and labour force participant appear to be interdependent and in conflict, while for men their roles as father and worker are more independent and easier to combine.

VARIATIONS IN TRANSITIONING

Current policy thinking is still dominated by the assumption of a linear career path moving from full-time education to full-time employment.

What is lacking is the attention to the timing and sequencing of work and family trajectories across the life course. Transitions such as leaving school, entry into the labour market, and timing of first birth are not discrete, clearly bounded events – but are interdependent, often requiring compromises regarding the coordination of work- and family-related roles (Elder and Shanahan 2007). While most previous research has focused on only one type of transition at a time, such as the transition from education to employment, or the transition to parenthood (Rindfuss 1991; Shanahan 2000), we need new models that assess and recognise multiple simultaneous role transitions (Macmillan 2005). The interdependence of transition states suggests the need for a more holistic, or person-centred approach, enabling the examination of how multiple transition experiences combine within individuals.

Multiple Interlinked Transitions

Drawing on economic activity data recording time spent in education, training and employment, and out of the labour force for cohort members between ages 16 to 29, it was possible to capture the dynamics of multiple interlocking pathways and the sequencing of different transitions over time (Martin et al. 2008). The greatest variability in transition experiences was observed among women, while most men followed a more or less standardised pattern of continuous employment after leaving school.

In both cohorts, men spent most of their late teens and twenties in full-time education or training followed by continuous full-time employment (about 90 per cent of men in each cohort, compared to 44 per cent of women in NCDS and 58 per cent of women in BCS70). In the later born cohort there has been an increase of cohort members engaged in postgraduate studies, although the majority of men and women had left school at minimum school-leaving age. A rising number of cohort members participated in government training, which was introduced in the 1980s to combat increasing youth unemployment (Furlong and Cartmel, 1997). In the later born cohort we find an increase in various minority pathways, suggesting problems in securing full-time employment. There has been an increase in interrupted and part-time careers among men, particularly among those who left school at age 16. Comparing the transition experiences of men who had left school at age 16 against those who stayed on in both cohorts, we find those who leave school at age 16 are more likely to experience long spells of unemployment, to work part-time, or to drop out of the labour market completely (Schoon 2010). The findings suggest that a small but increasing minority of men are encountering problems in establishing themselves in the labour market. These findings might thus suggest evidence of 'involuntary' individualisation, of being condemned to pursue and experience trajectories which are not collectively well-trodden pathways, and not necessarily the result of one's own choice (Buchmann 1989; Shanahan 2000).

Furthermore, the percentage of cohort members returning to full-time education after leaving early has increased in the later born cohort, especially among those who were motivated at school. This suggests that an increasing minority of men and women might be aiming to increase their educational credentials in order to succeed in a competitive labour market.

The Experience of Women

Women generally have more diverse transition experiences than men. Compared to men they are making the step into parenthood earlier, are less continuously attached to the labour market, and are more likely to drop out of paid employment completely, mostly to look after their children (Martin et al. 2008). In more recent birth cohorts, however, women appear to be more attached to the labour market. More women are experiencing continuous full-time employment after leaving education, and are less likely to drop out of the labour force even after childbirth. It could be argued that the life course of men and women has become more similar, in that women are becoming more attached to the labour market. However, despite increasing female labour force participation, women's work careers have remained discontinuous, and women are generally more likely than men to experience interrupted careers, to work in low-paid part-time jobs, or drop out of the labour market completely. Thus, gender differences in transition experiences persist. For women, work and family transitions are more closely linked and interdependent than they are for men.

Timing Matters

The findings suggest that timing of life course transitions is a crucial determinant of successful transitions. The timing of life course transitions is significantly influenced by social background, as young people from disadvantaged backgrounds are less likely to spend time in further and higher education. This is a particular issue for females, who are generally making the step into family formation and parenthood earlier than men. There are cultural norms about the timing of life course transitions: the right time to leave school, to get a job, to find a partner, and to start a family. Most government policies treat young people in transition to adulthood as a homogeneous group. In every society, age is used as a means of placing individuals in a template defining and regulating possible trajectories and transitions, thus creating a precise age stratification system (Riley et al. 1972). Most of these schemata and institutional practices are designed for a work force that could fit the typical male career templates of continuous, full-time schooling, followed by continuous, full-time employment. These templates should, however, be subject to continuous reassessment, in order to monitor demographic changes and gender and social variations in the timing and sequencing of economic and family-related transitions.

Transformations in male and female transition experiences over the last 30 years should lead to an appreciation of the complexity in transition pathways, especially in female careers, and the interdependency of multiple role transitions. There appears to be a mismatch between outdated occupational and public policy regimes focusing on occupational careers and the realities of men and women negotiating multiple roles in their transition to adulthood (Moen and Sweet 2004). Crucially, what is lacking is the recognition that careers extend beyond conceptions of full-time, uninterrupted education and paid work into other domains of people's lives, such as family careers. The life course is a holistic experience, involving not only educational and occupational transitions, but also the assumption of family-related roles. For a better understanding of how the life course unfolds over time, we have to learn more about how different transition experiences combine within individual lives.

CONCLUSION: REFRAMING CAREER TEMPLATES

Adopting a life course approach to the study of transition experiences provides a deeper understanding of the dynamic and interlinked nature of transitions, focusing on the multiple dimensions of the life course and variation in transition experiences within subgroups of the population. The life course perspective shifts our attention from the static to the dynamic, examining the antecedents, the timing, sequencing and duration of transitions. It highlights the role of cumulative disadvantages and the role of family disadvantage in shaping aspirations for the future as well as the timing of transition experiences. Social, economic, demographic, political and technological structures are the backdrop against which individual lives are lived, generating constraints, risks and uncertainties but also opportunities within which individuals make choices and experience the consequences of these choices. The life course is to a considerable degree a personal construction – but it entails selective processes and a sifting and sorting of persons into and out of various contexts, and one's position in society continues to be assigned to a considerable extent by one's family's social position and gender.

We have observed raised aspirations regarding education and employment, especially among girls and also among relatively disadvantaged young people, extended participation in further education and training, as well as women's increasing participation in, and attachment to the labour market even after childbirth. Focusing on the situation of women, the findings suggest that, despite the fact that girls are more motivated to achieve and more likely to receive crucial support from their parents, in the long run they are less likely than men to enter the most prestigious occupations (Schoon et al. 2007a; Farmer 1997; Crompton 2006). Although women are doing well in building up their academic credentials, there is no guarantee that these convert into economic and social privilege, and there continue to be barriers and obstacles to female career development, due to persisting gender role stereotypes, gender discrimination, and occupational sex-segregation (Scott et al. 2008). Women's transitions are generally more diverse than those of men. They are making the step into parenthood at an earlier age than men, and they are increasingly combining child-rearing with paid work (although often part-time). While some women are adopting a more 'male' pattern of career orientation without children, the majority of women have become mothers by the age of 30, and are facing the challenge of balancing multiple roles. The traditional breadwinner–homemaker template has to be revised to account for new forms of living arrangements and to enable the combination of work and family commitments. Furthermore, the disjuncture between gendered variations of educational success and gendered employment patterns is of great concern, and the equalisation of male and female chances in the labour market in times of social change has to become a critical issue for policy makers, especially in times of economic turmoil.

The findings suggest that current debates overstate the level of variability and choice. Transition experiences continue to be associated with structural factors, and there is evidence of increasing polarisation, where young people from more privileged backgrounds are more likely to participate in extended education and to delay the step into parenthood, while their less privileged peers follow the traditional fast-track transitions, characterised by early assumption of adult roles, in particular regarding family-related transitions.

Standardised life course patterns continue to exist (especially regarding school to work transitions), but they have changed (especially regarding patterns of family formation). Standardised models of the life course have never described the experiences of everyone in a particular age cohort, but have served both researchers and policy makers as a basis for understanding the ordering and sequencing of life events. Policy makers are guided in their decision making about adequate institutional structures and policies by their assumptions regarding life course patterns. The findings presented here suggest the need for the revision of currently dominant templates and the introduction of new, more flexible and diversified life course models, taking into account variation in transition experiences for different subgroups of the population, in particular women. We have to move away from static, age-defined snapshots and focus on the dynamics of conjoint trajectories in work and family transitions. Focusing on combinations of multiple role transitions gives us a better understanding of the experiences of young people, who at similar ages are nonetheless at different life stages.

The findings draw attention to the need for a more flexible, dynamic and multilevel conceptualisation of transition experiences. Recognising the interdependence of life course transitions, their dynamics, and the role of the wider socio-historical context in shaping individual aspirations and transitions, offers new avenues for future research on the changing structure of the life course and its implication for social and individual development. As long as the life course is conceptualised as a standard sequence from full-time education to continuous full-time work, it will not be possible to respond effectively to the experiences and needs of a sizable and increasing proportion of the work force, and there will be pronounced mismatches between existing regulations of transition experiences and today's realities of a changing work force (Moen and Sweet 2004). What is needed is support for opportunities for career path flexibility, which includes support for lifelong learning and second chances.

ACKNOWLEDGEMENTS

The analysis and writing of this article were supported by grants from the UK Economic and Social Research Council (ESRC): L326253061, RES-225-25-2001 and RES-594-28-0001, and the Jacobs Foundation. Data from the Cohort Studies were supplied by the ESRC Data Archive. Those who carried out the original collection of the data bear no responsibility for its further analysis and interpretation.

BIBLIOGRAPHY

Alexander, K.L. and B.K. Eckland (1974), 'Sex differences in the educational attainment process', *American Sociological Review*, **39**, 668–82.

Arnett, J.J. (2000), 'Emerging adulthood. A theory of development from the late teens to the late twenties', *American Psychologist*, **55**(5), 469–80.

Arnot, M. (2002), *Reproducing Gender. Essays on Educational Theory and Feminist Politics*, London: Routledge Falmer.

Arnot, M., M. David and G. Weiner (1999), *Closing the Gender Gap*, Cambridge: Polity Press.

Beck, U. (1992), *Risk Society. Towards a New Modernity*, London: Sage.

Berrington, A. (2001), 'Transition to adulthood in Britain', in M. Corjin and E. Klijzing (eds), *Transiton to Adulthood in Europe*, Dordrecht/Boston/London: Kluwer Academic Publishers, pp. 67–102.

Blanden, J. and S. Machin (2003), 'Educational inequality and the expansion of UK higher education', London: London School of Economics, Centre for Economic Performance, mimeo.

Blossfeld, H.P. (2005), *Globalization, Uncertainty and Youth in Society*, London: Routledge.

Blossfeld, H.P. and S. Drobnic (2001), *Careers of Couples in Contemporary Societies: from Male Breadwinner to Dual Earner Families*, Oxford and New York: Oxford University Press.

Bond, R. and P. Saunders (1999), 'Routes of success: influences on the occupational attainment of young British males', *British Journal of Sociology*, **50**(2), 217–49.

Breen, R. and J.H. Goldthorpe (2002), 'Merit, mobility, and method: another reply to Saunders', *British Journal of Sociology*, **53**, 575–82.

Brückner, H. and K.U. Mayer (2005), 'De-standardization of the life course: what does it mean? And if it means anything, whether it actually took place?', in R. Macmillan (ed.), *The Structure of the Life Course: Standardized? Individualized? Differentiated?* Amsterdam: Elsevier, pp. 27–54.

Buchmann, M. (1989), *The Script of Life in Modern Society: Entry Into Adulthood in a Changing World*, Chicago: Chicago University Press.

Bynner, J. (2001), 'British youth transitions in comparative perspective', *Journal of Youth Studies*, **4**(1), 5–23.

Bynner, J. (2005), 'Rethinking the youth phase of the life course: the case for emerging adulthood', *Youth and Society*, **8**(4), 367–84.

Bynner, J. and H. Joshi (2002), 'Equality and opportunity in education: evidence from the 1958 and 1970 birth cohort studies', *Oxford Review of Education*, **28**(4), 405–25.

Bynner, J. and S. Parsons (2002), 'Social exclusion and the transition from school to work: the case of young people not in education, employment, or training (NEET)', *Journal of Vocational Behavior*, **60**(2), 289–309.

Catsambis, S. (1995), 'Parents, their children, and schools', *Social Forces*, **74**(2), 751–2.

Correll, S.J. (2004), 'Constraints into preferences: gender, status, and emerging career aspirations', *American Sociological Review*, **69**(1), 93–113.

Crompton, R. (2006), *Employment and the Family: the Reconfiguration of Work and Family Life in Contemporary Societies*, Cambridge: Cambridge University Press.

Crompton, R. and C. Lyonette (2005), 'The new gender essentialism – domestic and family "choices" and their relation to attitudes', *The British Journal of Sociology*, **56**, 601–20.

Duncan, G.J. and J. Brooks-Gunn (1997), *Consequences of Growing up Poor*, New York: Russell Sage Foundation Press.

Eccles, J., J.E. Jacobs and R.D. Harold (1990), 'Gender role stereotypes, expectancy effects, and parents' socialization of gender differences', *Journal of Social Issues*, **46**, 183–202.

Eccles, J.S., A. Wigfield and U. Schiefele (1998), 'Motivation to succeed', in W. Damon and N. Eisenberg (eds), *Handbook of Child Psychology*, Vol. III, 5th edn, New York: Wiley, pp. 1017–95.

Elder, G.H. (ed.) (1985), *Life Course Dynamics: Trajectories and Transitions*, Ithaca, NY: Cornell University Press.

Elder, G.H. (1998), 'The life course as developmental theory', *Child Development*, **69**(1), 1–12.

Elder, G.H. and M.J. Shanahan (2007), 'The life course and human development', in R. Lerner (ed.), *The Handbook of Child Psychology*, Vol. I, 6th edn, New York: Wiley, pp. 665–715.

Entwistle, D.R. and D.P. Baker (1983), 'Gender and young children's expectations for performance in arithmetic', *Developmental Psychology*, **19**, 200–209.

Epstein, D., J. Elwood, V. Hey and J. Maw (1998), *Failing Boys?*, Buckingham: Open University Press.

Esping-Andersen, G. (2004), 'Social inheritance and equal opportunities policy', paper presented at the Social Mobility and Life Chances Forum, Oxford.

Evans, K. (2002), 'Taking control of their lives? Agency in young adult transitions in England and the New Germany', *Journal of Youth Studies*, **5**, 245–71.

Fan, P.L. and M.M. Marini (2000), 'Influences on gender-role attitudes during the transition to adulthood', *Social Science Research*, **29**, 265–83.

Farmer, H. (1997), *Diversity & Women's Career Development*, London: Sage.

Francis, B. (2000a), 'The gendered subject: students' subject preferences and discussions of gender and subject ability', *Oxford Review of Education*, **26**, 35–48.

Francis, B. (2000b), *Boys, Girls and Achievement: Addressing the Classroom Issues*, London: Routledge Falmer.

Francis, B. (2002), 'Is the future really female? The impact and implications of gender for 14–16 year olds' career choices', *Journal of Education and Work*, **15**(1), 75–88.

Furlong, A. and F. Cartmel (1997), *Young People and Social Change*, Buckingham: Open University Press.

Galindo-Rueda, F. and A. Vignoles (2005), 'The declining relative importance of ability in predicting educational attainment', *Journal of Human Resources*, **40**(2), 335–53.

Giddens, A. (1991), *Modernity and Self-identity: Self and Society in the Late Modern Age*, Cambridge: Polity Press.

Goodwin, J. and H. O'Connor (2005), 'Exploring complex transitions: looking back at the "Golden Age" of from school to work', *Sociology*, **39**(2), 201–20.

Goyette, K.A. (2008), 'College for some to college for all: social background, occupational expectations and educational expectations over time', *Social Science Research*, **37**, 461–84.

Hakim, C. (2000), *Work-lifestyle Choices in the 21st Century*, Oxford: Oxford University Press.

Hobcraft, J. (2002), 'Social exclusion and the generations', in J. Hills, J. LeGrand and D. Piachaud (eds), *Understanding Social Exclusion*, Oxford: Oxford University Press, pp. 62–83.

Inglehart, R. (1977), *The Silent Revolution*, Princeton, NJ: Princeton University Press.

Jones, G. (2002), *The Youth Divide: Diverging Paths to Adulthood*, York: Joseph Rowntree Foundation.
Jones, G. (2009), *Youth*, Cambridge: Polity Press.
Lesthaeghe, R. (1995), 'The second demographic transition in western countries: an interpretation', in K.O. Mason and A.-M. Jenson (eds), *Gender and Family Change in Industrialised Countries*, Oxford: Clarenden Press, pp. 17–62.
Machin, S. (2003), 'Unto them that hath. . .', *Centre Piece*, **8**, 4–9.
Machin, S. and A. Vignoles (2004), Education Inequality, *Fiscal Studies*, **25**, 107–28.
Macmillan, R. (ed.) (2005), *The Structure of the Life Course: Standardized? Individualized? Differentiated?*, Amsterdam: Elsevier.
Macmillan, R. and S. Eliason (2003), 'Characterizing the life course as role configurations and pathways: a latent structure approach', in J.T. Mortimer and M.J. Shanahan (eds), *Handbook of the Life Course*, New York: Plenum, pp. 529–54.
Marini, M.M. and E. Greenberger (1978), 'Sex differences in educational aspirations and expectations', *American Educational Research Journal*, **15**, 67–79.
Martin, P., I. Schoon and A. Ross (2008), 'Beyond transitions. Applying optimal matching analysis to life course research', *International Journal of Social Research Methodology*, **11**(3), 179–99.
Mau, W.C. and L.H. Bikos (2000), 'Educational and vocational aspirations of minority and female students: A longitudinal study', *Journal of Counseling and Development*, **78**, 186–94.
McClelland, K. (1990), 'Cumulative disadvantage among the highly ambitious', *Sociology of Education*, **63**, 102–21.
Mickelson, R.A. (1989), 'Why does Jane read and write so well? The anomaly of women's achievement', *Sociology of Education*, **62**, 47–63.
Mickelson, R.A. (2003), 'Gender, Bourdieu, and the anomaly of women's achievement redux', *Sociology of Education*, **76**, 373–5.
Moen, P. and S. Sweet (2004), 'From "work-family" to "flexible careers". A life course reframing', *Community, Work & Family*, **7**, 209–26.
Nurmi, J-E. (1991), 'How do adolescents see their future? A review of the development of future orientation and planning', *Developmental Review*, **11**, 1–59.
Purcell, K. (2002), 'Qualifications and careers: equal opportunities and earning among graduates', Manchester: EOC: Working Paper Series 1.
Reay, D., M.E. David and S.J. Ball (2005), *Degrees of Choice. Social Class, Race and Gender in Higher Education*, Stoke on Trent: Trentham Books.
Reynolds, J.R. and S. Woodham-Burge (2007), 'Educational expectations and the rise in women's post-secondary attainments', *Social Science Research*, **37**, 485–99.
Riddell, S. (2000), 'Equal opportunities and educational reform in Scotland: the limits of liberalism', in J.A.R. Salisbury (ed.), *Gender, Policy and Educational Change*, London: Routledge.
Riley, M.W., M. Johnson and A. Foner (1972), *Ageing and Society III: A Sociology of Age Stratification*, New York: Sage.
Rindfuss, R.R. (1991), 'The young adult years: diversity, structural change, and fertility', *Demography*, **28**, 493–512.
Roberts, K. (1980), 'Schools, parents and social class', in M. Craft, J. Raynor and L. Cohen (eds), *Linking Home and School*, 3rd edn, London: Harper & Row, pp. 41–55.

Ross, A., I. Schoon and P. Martin (2009), 'Family and nonfamily role configurations in two British cohorts', *Journal of Marriage and Family*, **71** (1), 1–14.

Saunders, P. (1997), 'Social mobility in Britain: an empirical evaluation of two competing theories', *Sociology*, **31**, 261–88.

Saunders, P. (2002), 'Reflections on the meritocracy debate in Britain: a response to Richard Breen and John Goldthorpe', *British Journal of Sociology*, **53**, 559–74.

Schoon, I. (2006), *Risk and resilience. Adaptations in changing times*, Cambridge: Cambridge University Press.

Schoon, I. (2007), 'Adaptations in changing times: agency in context', *International Journal of Psychology*, **42**, 94–101.

Schoon, I. (2008), 'A transgenerational model of status attainment: the potential mediating role of school motivation and education', *National Institute Economic Review*, **205**, 72–82.

Schoon, I. (2009a), 'Changing educational aspirations in three UK cohorts: the role of gender, parental education, and encouragement', *ISSBD Bulletin*, **1**, 14–18.

Schoon, I. (2009b), 'High hopes in a changing world: social disadvantage, educational aspirations, and occupational attainment in three British Cohort Studies', in C. Raffo, A. Dyson, H. Gunter, D. Hall, L. Jones and A. Kalambouka (ed.), *Education and Poverty in Affluent Countries*, London: Routledge, pp. 97–110.

Schoon, I. (2010), 'Social change and transition experiences among young adults in Britain', in R.K. Silbereisen and X. Chen (eds), *Social Change and Human Development: Concepts and Results*, London: Sage.

Schoon, I. and S. Parsons (2002), 'Teenage aspirations for future careers and occupational outcomes', *Journal of Vocational Behavior*, **60**(2), 262–88.

Schoon, I., P. Martin and A. Ross (2007a), 'Career transitions in times of social change. His and her story', *Journal of Vocational Behavior*, **70**(1), 78–96.

Schoon, I., A. Ross and P. Martin (2007b), 'Science related careers. Aspirations and outcomes in two British Cohort Studies', *Equal Opportunities International*, **26**(2), 129–48.

Schoon, I., A. Ross and P. Martin (2009), 'Sequences, patterns, and variations in the assumption of work and family related roles. Evidence from two British birth cohorts', in I. Schoon and R.K. Silbereisen (eds), *Transitions from School to Work: Globalisation, Individualisation, and Patterns of Diversity*, Cambridge: Cambridge University Press, pp. 219–42.

Schoon, I., A. McCulloch, H. Joshi, R. D. Wiggins & J. Bynner (2001), 'Transitions from school to work in a changing social context', *Young*, **9**, 4–22.

Scott, J. (2004), 'Family, gender, and educational attainment in Britain: a longitudinal study', *Journal of Comparative Family Studies*, **35**, 565–90.

Scott, J., S. Dex and H. Joshi (eds) (2008), *Women and Employment: Changing Lives and New Challenges*, Cheltenham, UK and Northampton, MA, USA: Edward Elgar.

Sewell, W.H. and R.M. Hauser (1975), *Education, Occupation, and Earnings: Achievement in the Early Career*, New York: Academic Press.

Sewell, W.H. and V.P. Shah (1968), 'Social class, parental encouragement, and educational aspirations', *American Journal of Sociology*, **73**, 559–72.

Sewell, W.H. and R.M. Hauser and W.C Wolf (1980), 'Sex, schooling, and occupational status', *The American Journal of Sociology*, **86**(3), 551–83.

Shanahan, M.J. (2000), 'Pathways to adulthood in changing societies: variability and mechanisms in life course perspective', *Annual Review of Sociology*, **26**, 667–92.

Tinklin, T. (2003), 'Gender differences and high attainment', *British Educational Research Journal*, **29**(3), 307–25.

Younger, M. and M. Warrington (2006), 'Raising boys' achievement', Norwich: Department for Education and Skills. Research Report RR636, available at http://www.dcsf.gov.uk/research/data/uploadfiles/RR636.pdf.

Zellman, G. and J. Waterman (1998), 'Understanding the impact of parent school involvement on children's educational outcomes', *Journal of Education Research*, **91**(6), 370–80.

2. Class reproduction, occupational inheritance and occupational choices

Fiona Devine

When class analysis was seriously challenged by its critics in the 1990s, it was robustly defended by its practitioners. Since then, sociologists within the sub-discipline have continued to debate the ways in which the study of class inequalities, and especially the persistence of those inequalities, should proceed. On the one hand, the American sociologist, David Grusky, has argued that class analysis should be refashioned to include different levels of analysis, focus on occupational inheritance and social closure and the socio-cultural dimensions of social reproduction. On the other hand, the British sociologist, John Goldthorpe, has insisted that class analysis should stick with its macro sociological concerns, concentrating on big classes and their shared economic characteristics, in explaining class reproduction. Both approaches have their strengths and weaknesses, of course, although Gruksy's ideas are pursued here. This chapter draws on a micro-level analysis of occupations and taps into the socio-cultural dimensions of occupations for what it reveals about processes of class reproduction.

Specifically, the chapter focuses on occupational inheritance and occupational choices. What occupational aspirations do parents have for their children? With issues of gender in mind, do fathers and mothers have similar or different hopes for their sons and daughters? The next section outlines the theoretical debate between Grusky and Goldthorpe more fully. The third section describes the research on which this chapter is based: namely, interviews with doctors, teachers and their husbands and wives. The fourth section concentrates on doctors, and reveals modest levels of occupational inheritance. As yet unrealised aspirations, however, indicate that medicine remains a highly desirable professional occupation for both sons and daughters. The fifth section focuses on teachers, and also reveals limited levels of occupational inheritance. Teaching, however, is regarded with ambivalence and not necessarily seen as a good professional career either for young women and, especially not for men. The conclusion considers these empirical findings in relation to the theoretical debate on different levels of analysis in the study of class and the importance of economic and cultural resources in class reproduction.

CLASS REPRODUCTION AND LEVELS OF ANALYSIS

Following the debate on the future of class analysis among American and British academics in the 1990s, there has been an ongoing discussion on how the study of class inequalities should proceed. David Grusky, for example, has sought to 'refashion' class analysis in order to develop new ways of describing and explaining how class inequalities are reproduced over time and space (Grusky and Sorensen 1998; Grusky and Weeden 2001; Grusky with Galescu 2005; Grusky and Weeden 2006). Theoretically, Grusky wants to shift class analysis out of the shadow of Marx and Marxism, with its strong emphasis on big classes as collective actors, to a more Durkheimian approach with a focus on occupations and collective action at the occupational level. From this theoretical position, methodological consequences flow. Grusky argues that the level of analysis should be 'ratcheted down' from that of aggregate classes to institutionalised occupational groupings that 'form around functional niches in the division of labour' (Grusky and Weeden 2001: 203).

Thus, disaggregation is required for a superior understanding of social stability and social mobility. The study of mobility at the level of occupation, for example, demands an exploration of social closure at the collective and individual levels. The '*gemeinschaftlich* character' of some occupational groups, for example, should not be ignored since local occupational social closure has the effect of restricting 'social interaction generating occupational subcultures that are correspondingly disaggregate' (Grusky with Galescu 2005: 71). By selecting employees who fit prevailing stereotypes, training new recruits in the world view of current job holders via graduate schools and the like, and restricting social interaction within occupational boundaries 'reinforces occupation specific attitudes values and lifestyles' (Grusky with Galescu 2005: 78). This approach underlines the view that occupations are 'socially constructed with various closure generating mechanisms . . . which make unit occupations relatively homogenous categories' (Grusky with Galescu 2005: 78–9).

Developing this argument further, Grusky and Weeden (2006) stress that the micro processes by which inequalities are transmitted across generations are not confined to the world of work and employment.

Reproduction theories have wrongly assumed that the spheres of work and home are completely separate. They argue that

> pockets of micro-class reproduction persist because many parents are deeply involved in their occupations, and thus bring home much in the way of specialised human, social and cultural capital. We are referring here to parents who work at home, who talk about their occupations at the dinner table and in other home settings, and who may even explicitly train their children in occupation-specific skills (Grusky and Weeden 2006: 102).

Other considerations here are the ways in which a 'taste' for occupations is developed within families while other occupations are considered 'distasteful'. Indeed, this kind of detailed analysis, embracing work and family, and looking at issues to do with networks, norms, lifestyles and other cultural practices suggests that a micro-level analysis could proffer a powerful account of the persistence of inequalities.

Grusky's proposed 're-tooling' of class analysis has been criticised by one of its principal proponents, John Goldthorpe. Many occupations, he argues, have common features in terms of pay, security and so on. This is why it is useful to aggregate occupations into big classes and a class structure (Goldthorpe 2007: 139; Goldthorpe and McKnight 2006). Goldthorpe argues:

> It is true that that some occupations tend, for various reasons, to have relatively high holding power in inter as well as intra-generational perspective: for instance, those of doctor or coal miner. But research into intergenerational mobility is concerned with not only or primarily with why doctors' children have a higher propensity to become doctors, or coal miners' sons a high propensity to become coal miners. More important are such questions as why those doctors' children (the majority) who do not become doctors are far more likely to move into other professional or managerial occupations than to become manual wage workers, or why those coal miners' sons who do not become miners (again the majority) are far more likely to move into some kind of wage work than to become professionals or managers (Goldthorpe 2007: 143).

Thus, for Goldthorpe, social closure is largely irrelevant to the study of class reproduction. After all, most occupations (and, indeed, most classes) are far from closed, and since closure practices vary over time and space, they are unlikely to explain class stability which has proved remarkably enduring. Grusky's proposed programme might rejuvenate the study of occupations but, at best, it would only be 'complementary to class analysis in some more conventional form and not as providing a substitute for it' (Goldthorpe 2007: 146). Overall, Goldthorpe (2007: 152) argues that Grusky's programme of research should not be considered as an 'adequate alternative to the class analysis as more usually practiced'. The class analysis as practised by Goldthorpe, of course, is one that considers the class structure and class mobility in terms of the economic sphere, in which classes are defined in terms of employment relations, and where socio-cultural norms and values are of no causal importance in the study of an 'economically grounded structure of inequality' (Goldthorpe 2007: 152).

In defending his own position, Goldthorpe makes some telling criticisms of Grusky's ideas. It is certainly correct to note that occupations share similarities (as well as peculiarities) and that these commonalities should not be lost in an analysis of structured inequalities. Some occupations and their members may exhibit high levels of social closure but many – indeed, the majority, do not. Even those occupations known for their closure practices – the long-established professions and professional associations – are far from closed. As Goldthorpe rightly points out, while the sons and daughters of doctors may have a higher propensity to enter medicine than those from other occupational backgrounds, most still do not do so. What is important is how and why sons and daughters enter other high-level professional and managerial occupations rather than routine non-manual or manual employment. Thus, Goldthorpe is right to highlight some of the limitations of an approach to class analysis that would focus exclusively on occupational inheritance.

Nonetheless, there are virtues to Grusky's ideas about how the study of occupational closure may help explain class – or social – reproduction. Class analysis does not have to be practised solely at the macroeconomic level. Much is revealed by 'drilling down' to different levels of analysis at the meso (occupations/occupational associations) and micro (individual/family) level for understanding how class reproduction takes place (Crompton 2008; Devine 1998; 2004). Describing how class reproduction occurs at different levels is crucial for explaining why it does so. Goldthorpe has argued that those in advantaged class positions look to hold onto those advantages and transfer them onto the next generation. This is how and why classes reproduce themselves. The same argument could apply to occupations: namely, those in desirable occupations want their children to have desirable occupations too. Goldthorpe acknowledges that some occupations have higher holding power than others. How and why there is such variation is worthy of further investigation in and of itself and in relation to class reproduction.

In other words, both Grusky's and Goldthorpe's theories have insights to offer on class and/or social reproduction. Occupational inheritance contributes to class reproduction, and to understand one facilitates an understanding of the other. Interestingly, there was a body of research in the 1970s and 1980s that looked at issues to do with the desirability of occupations, how they were perceived and evaluated by people in different social positions, the different criteria by which occupations are judged and the trade-offs between different dimensions of an occupation made when moving jobs (Coxon and Jones 1978; 1979; Coxon et al. 1986). Unfortunately, this research is now rather old and has not been updated. We know surprisingly little about the social standing of occupations today, why some are desirable while others are not, the criteria on which occupations are judged as good or bad, and whether members of different social classes judge the status of occupations in the same way or not.

A number of research questions come to mind. What kinds of occupations do parents aspire to for their children? Do parents want their children to follow in their footsteps and why? How do they shape the occupational choice of their children? Of crucial importance to all of these questions, of course, are issues around gender. Against the background of young women's substantial increase in levels of educational attainment, do fathers and mothers have the same level and type of occupational aspirations for their sons and daughters? Moreover, are different occupational choices considered as parents encourage their daughters (but not their sons) to make decisions that anticipate family responsibilities that may be combined with paid work in the future? Are occupations valued differently for young men and women in this light? This chapter answers these questions by drawing on research which involved in-depth interviews with doctors, teachers and their husbands and wives, investigating whether or not they wanted their sons and daughters to follow them into medicine and teaching.

RESEARCHING CLASS AND OCCUPATIONAL REPRODUCTION

This chapter draws on research into class reproduction in Manchester in the UK conducted in the late 1990s (Devine 2004; 2008).[1] Knowing middle-class stability is closely associated with occupations with particular mobility trajectories as noted above, a decision was made to focus on two 'case studies' of middle-class professions in contrasting 'class sub-groupings' – medicine and teaching – and to interview medics, teachers and their husbands or wives.

Doctors were chosen as an example of a high status, well remunerated profession in Class I (higher managerial and professional employees and large employers in the National Statistics Socio-economic Classification, NS-SEC). Historically, this male-dominated profession was known for its high level of occupational inheritance (Riska and Wegar 1993; Sinclair

1997; Witz 1992). Recently, the profession has been feminising, as young women now constitute over half (61 per cent) of students in medical school (Allen 2005). Women are unevenly distributed across generalist and specialist roles, however, and extensive 'internal segregation by sex' remains (Crompton et al. 1999). Women are more likely to be general practitioners (GPs), where there are opportunities to work fewer hours or part-time in combination with existing or anticipated family commitments. Women are less likely to be consultants (hospital specialists) and they are concentrated in some specialities (for example paediatrics, community medicine) while having a minimal presence in others (surgery). Male dominance continues. GPs earn between £52–79000 as employees in a practice and earn between £80–120000 as self-employed partners within the NHS. Consultants are highly paid. Their salaries can range from £73–173000, depending on additional performance-related rewards. Thus, men dominate the better paid positions.

Teachers were chosen as an example of a lower status, less well remunerated profession in NS-SEC Class II (lower managerial and professional employees). Historically, the profession has long been dominated by women (Dolton and Makepeace 1993, Machin and Vignoles 2005). It is increasingly feminised as the gender gap in new recruits into teaching has grown in recent years. Despite government attempts to increase the number of men going into teaching, the latest statistics (for 2006–07) from the Higher Education Statistics Agency (HESA) show that 76 per cent of new recruits were women while only 28 per cent were men. In that year, men were 16 per cent of primary school teachers and 46 per cent of secondary school teachers were men (*The Independent*, 2008). Young women embrace teaching as a caring profession which is compatible with family commitments, while young men seek out more financially lucrative careers in the city and elsewhere (Purcell and Elias 2008). Teaching is less well paid than medicine although there are opportunities to command a high salary in management. With degree-level qualifications, a teacher can earn between £21000–£30000 per annum while additional managerial activities can raise their salary from between £35000–£54000. The starting salary for Head Teachers is £40000 and the maximum salary is £100000 (TDA, 2009). It is men, however, who command the higher salaries in teaching.

Twelve doctors were approached by writing to GP practices and by mobilising contacts in a number of hospitals in Manchester to gain access to consultants. Ten male doctors and two female doctors agreed to be interviewed and an additional two doctors (one male, one female) were also interviewed as husbands and wives of the initial contacts. Thus, 14 doctors were interviewed in total (see Table 2.1). They were usually interviewed at work while their husbands and wives were interviewed at home. The

Table 2.1   Sample of British doctors and their families

Interviewees	Occupation	Names of children	Education or employment
Bruce Brown[1]	Consultant	Anne	Lawyer
Margaret Brown	Housewife	James	Accountant
Peter Smith	GP	Damian	**Consultant**
Diane Smith	Nurse	Danielle	Teacher
Ronald Watson	GP	Stuart	Accounting[2]
Celia Watson	Medical Secretary	Lois	Technician[3]
Barbara Coombes	GP	Sonia	Teacher
Donald Coombes	Teacher	Sally	Teacher
		Laurie	Teacher[4]
		Andrew	Computer programmer[4]
Edward Myers	Consultant	Catherine	**GP**
Sheila Myers	Teacher	Patricia	Lawyer
		Robert	Higher Education
Ian Lamb	Consultant	Ian	**SHO**[5]
Pamela Lamb	Counsellor	Geoff	**SHO**
		Molly	Further Education
Stephen Dodd	Consultant	Amy	Higher Education
Julia Dodd	Consultant	Michael	Higher Education
Gerald Jones	GP	Laura	Business Manager
Janet Jones	Radiographer	Sarah	Higher Education
		Fiona	Higher Education
Robert Ball	Consultant	Lydia	Higher Education
Eleanor Ball	Lecturer	John	Further Education
		David	Secondary
		Daniel	Primary
Roderick Hunt	Doctor	Teresa	Secondary
Mary Hunt	Teacher	Scott	Secondary
		Andrew	Primary
		Stephen	Primary
Lawrence Foster	Doctor	Christopher	Secondary
Heather Foster	Optician	Stephanie	Primary
Andrew Underwood	Doctor	Emily	Primary
Bridget Underwood	Doctor	Alison	Primary

Notes:
1. All of the doctors and their husbands and wives were interviewed in this case study so 24 interviews were completed in total.
2. Stuart Watson suffered from a range of health and learning disabilities which seriously interrupted his education, and his parents were grateful he had secured some qualifications to get a job in the firm of a family friend.
3. In a family life dominated by her older brother's disabilities, the Watsons' daughter was not especially academically inclined and had spent much of her twenties travelling the world rather than pursuing a career.
4. Lawrie and Andrew Coombes were brought up by their mother, a teacher like their father, rather than Donald Coombes and Barbara Coombes (their stepmother).
5. Senior house officer (medic in training).

doctors' wives were in a variety of typically female occupations including nursing, teaching, counselling, lecturing, a practice manager, an optician and a radiographer. Three of the male doctors were the sons of medics (Drs Underwood, Foster and Myers) while one doctor's wife, Mrs Jones (the radiographer), was a doctor's daughter. There was a small amount of occupational inheritance. Most of the male doctors were the sons of small businessmen, employees in the private sector (an industrial chemist) and teachers (of which there were two instances). The male medics, therefore, were mostly from lower middle-class backgrounds. The three women doctors were socially mobile from working-class backgrounds, being the daughter of a welder, labourer and mill worker. Of course, the class background of the medics is a reflection of the interviewees who constituted this study and does not reflect a wider class profile of medics from the population at large.

Twelve teachers were approached by writing to Head Teachers of primary and secondary schools across Manchester. Eight female and four male teachers agreed to be interviewed and an additional six teachers (four males and two females) were also interviewed as husbands and wives of the initial contacts. Thus, 18 teachers were interviewed in total (see Table 2.2). They were usually interviewed at work while their husbands and wives were interviewed at home. The other teachers' husbands were in a variety of occupations as an accountant, a journalist, a laboratory scientific officer, a computer system manager and a property businessman. One teacher, Mrs Hill – was the daughter of a teacher in that her mother taught while Mrs Bull's father spent his early working life as a glass technologist but moved into teaching after redundancy. Otherwise, the teachers' fathers were in a variety of middle-class (accountant, tax inspector) and working-class occupations (miner, weaver, taxi driver, labourer) and self-employment (art dealer, butcher, garage owner). Thus, the women teachers came from a mix of class backgrounds. None of the male teachers were from middle-class backgrounds. Indeed, all of their fathers had started in manual employment – mill work, mining, welding – although they moved into low-level non-manual positions later on. Thus, all of these men had been upwardly mobile into teaching.

The interviewees had 61 children between them ranging in age from 18 months to 30 years although at least one child in every family was in or had been through compulsory schooling. Accordingly, there were young people in primary and secondary school, further and higher education and those already established in the labour market. Depending on the age of their children, the interviewees spoke of early aspirations and expectations, their children's emerging hopes, dreams that had not been realised as well those that had been achieved. Drawing on Grusky's ideas, the rest

Gender inequalities in the 21st century

Table 2.2   Sample of British teachers and their families

Interviewees	Occupation	Names of children	Education or employment
Hilary Butler[1]	Teacher	Nigel	Accountant
Ken Butler	Head Teacher	Victoria	Doctor
Rosemary Hill	Head Teacher	Nicholas	Tax Officer
David Hill	Accountant	Mark	Youth and Community Worker
Yvonne Johns	Head Teacher	Samantha	**Teacher**[2]
Norman Johns	Teacher	Polly	Hotel Manager[2]
		Karl	Care Worker[2]
Sandra Booth	Teacher	Kirsten	Lawyer
Malik Booth	Businessman	Oliver	University
		Juliet	University
		Alex	Secondary
Jill Dowds	Teacher	Claire	Accountant
Graham Dowds	Computer Systems Manager	Rebecca	Further Education
Diane Willis	Teacher	Celia	Voluntary Worker[3]
John Willis	Head Teacher	Mark	Further Education[3]
Sheila Parker	Teacher	Melanie	**Teacher Training**
Dennis Parker	Teacher	Jonathon	University
Sylvia Harrison	Teacher	Jackie	Further Education
Roger Harrison	Teacher	Angela	Secondary
Muriel Crisp	Teacher	Alice	Further Education
Brian Crisp	Teacher	Bella	Secondary
		Julian	Secondary
Mary Bull	Teacher	Duncan	Further Education
Alan Bull	Laboratory Scientific Officer	Anthony	Secondary
Pauline Lomax	Teacher	Kathryn	Secondary
Martin Webb	Environmental Officer	Joseph	Secondary
Susan Parry	Teacher	Luke	Secondary[4]
Nick Parry	Journalist	Emma	Nursery

Notes:
1. Two of the husbands (Roger Harrison and Brian Crisp) did not agree to be interviewed in this case study. Thus, interviews were completed with 22 teachers and their partners.
2. Samantha and Polly were the daughters of Norman Johns and his first wife (also a teacher). They had brought the children up together and only divorced when their daughters were adults. Karl was the son of Yvonne's marriage to her first husband (also a teacher). Similarly, they had brought Karl up together, only divorcing when he was an adult.
3. The Willis' children were adopted. Their daughter, Celia, had health and learning disabilities and was only in the position to do a limited amount of voluntary work.
4. Luke was Susan Parry's son from her first marriage and she had brought him up with minimal involvement from his father.

of the chapter explores these occupational aspirations and the extent to which these children were following in their parents' footsteps.

MEDICINE AND OTHER CAREERS

The medics' children had a particular type of education. All but one of them (of the appropriate age) had gone to fee-paying private high schools. They included some of Greater Manchester's prestigious former grammar schools including Manchester Grammar School for Boys and Withington High School for Girls. These schools achieve top academic results in the country each year and the medics' children were invariably academically successful by securing the top grades at GCSE and A level. Clearly, the medical families mobilised their economic resources to increase the likelihood of educational success (Devine 2004). Also important was that most of these schools were single sex. This was sought out by the interviewees who were educated in private and state single-sex grammar schools in the 1950s and 1960s. Both fathers and mothers – especially the mothers who were medics – wanted their daughters to be as good at the arts and sciences. They strongly subscribed to the view that girls did better at the sciences in an all-female environment (Arnot et al. 1999).

There was some evidence of occupational inheritance. There were examples of sons who followed in their father's footsteps. They came from homogenous 'medical families' in that both fathers and mothers were employed in the medical field. As Grusky and Weeden (2006) imagined, this medical world dominated family life. The intrinsic rewards of medicine were discussed at home and amongst their networks of friends who were often medics. Dr Smith and his wife, Mrs Smith, a nurse, spoke of how their son, Damian, was training to be a hospital consultant in a specialism that his father pursued alongside his GP work. Dr Smith was the son of an industrial chemist who had directed him towards the sciences, as had his school. He had influenced his son in the same way, as had the very same school. Dr Smith noted the power of their network of friends, like a strong occupational community, alongside that of family. He noted, 'I didn't try but I think it was almost inevitable. Things like, you see, people would come here would be doctors. There'd be a lot of doctor talk'. He went on to say:

> There has always tended to be a bit of banter between the two of us you know. Certainly, we used to talk quite a bit and, of course, Diane having done nursing, there was the reinforcing of the medical ethos.

Indeed, as Mrs Smith indicated, Damian 'did not know any other life'.

There was one instance of occupational inheritance from father to daughter as Dr Myer's oldest daughter, Catherine, followed him into medicine (as a GP). Inheritance extended across generations as Dr Myers, a hospital consultant, was the son of a professor of medicine at a top medical school. One sister was a doctor while another was a physiotherapist. Dr Myers confessed, 'I was a bit Machiavellian. Whenever I was talking about what I was doing, I always said how interesting it was. Catherine was mostly neutral, and then she talked about it and then I tried to talk her out of it and then she headed that way'. She had attended the same medical school as her father and grandfather and he was tremendously proud of her. Mrs Myers reinforced these remarks. From a working-class background, she had met her future husband when he was a junior doctor and she worked as a laboratory technician (before retraining as a teacher). She wanted them to do well and 'better than herself'. The all-girls private school also promoted medicine amongst high-achieving women. Thus, occupational inheritance, as described by Grusky, included both fathers and sons and fathers and daughters.

Most of the other children of working age, however, pursued or were pursuing other professional and managerial careers including accountancy, law, HR and teaching, as Goldthorpe's argument suggests. That said, attempts had been made to persuade children into medicine which had failed. Three doctors (Dr Brown, Dr Dodd and Dr Coombes) spoke with considerable regret that their daughters had not specialised in the sciences and pursued medicine. It was especially painful for the two women doctors who had hoped their daughters would follow in their footsteps. There was only one example of parents who actively discouraged their children away from medicine. Dr Jones's oldest daughter had completed a science degree at Oxford before embarking on a graduate management traineeship with a major oil company. He explained,

> I think medicine is a very cruel profession, probably for men and women, but particularly for women. I think it makes enormous demands on your time and on your emotions at a stage when you're not necessarily very well equipped to cope with these things. Then, if you are a woman, you often want to make choices about your life, in your late twenties, and medicine imposes on you the career straightjacket so just at the time when you might be wanting to settle down and have some children is the very time when you've actually got to put your maximum career push in and I've seen that cause conflict in so many women.

Dr Jones' attitude that medicine was not a good career for women, especially if they were very likely to have children, was a minority view, however.

Among the younger sons and daughters still working their way through the education system, there was evidence of those who would follow in their parents' footsteps and others who would not. Dr and Mrs Ball, a doctor and a nurse turned academic, were pushing their two elder children into medicine. With regard to their eighteen-year-old daughter, Dr Ball acknowledged that 'I think she'd say we have brought both implicit and explicit pressure on her to do medicine'. Their daughter had secured an A grade in all four of her A levels and had accepted a place to do a law degree at a prestigious university. During her gap year, however, the ardour to do law had cooled. Now her parents were exploring options for a pre-med course, since her A levels were in the arts, which would facilitate their daughter's entry into medical school. Their son – who was just about to embark on his A levels – was good at the sciences and arts, especially Art. While he had expressed an interest in medicine periodically, his preference was to go to Art school. Revealingly, Mrs Ball spoke of how her husband (a consultant) had:

> sat down and rang around the colleges and asked what was essential if he wanted to do medicine. They said if he had A level Chemistry and two other A levels, that would be sufficient. He rang up the Arts colleges to see what was important and he would be able to do this. So, it's an option – only if he wanted to. We wouldn't force him. It's an option.

Dr and Mrs Ball, therefore, were doing everything they could to facilitate both their daughter's and their son's entry into medicine even though they had expressed different occupational aspirations. They did not treat them differently in this respect.

Interestingly, other parents spoke of their sons' medical aspirations for a medical career. These aspirations were being expressed at a remarkably young age. Dr and Mrs Foster's eleven-year-old son wanted to be a doctor, following in the footsteps of his father, his uncle and his grandfather. Mrs Foster (an optician) was happy with this aspiration. While the professions did not pay big salaries like those in the business world, they still paid well and they were high-status, stable careers. Dr Foster was somewhat ambivalent. He said, 'I suppose most doctors' sons would tend to look at medicine but I keep putting him off'. The relative income of doctors had declined so they could no longer afford big houses, big cars and private boarding school fees as his parents had done in the 1950s. Yet Dr Foster also wanted his son to have a stable career. Something of an entrepreneur, he had a successful business in the health field alongside his GP practice. He was very aware, however, that 'businesses can always fail so it's prudent to make sure the back door isn't shut behind you'. In this respect, a profession like medicine had these advantages.

There were no aspiring medics among the young daughters of the interviewees. A career in law was a popular choice for daughters who usually specialised in the arts rather than sciences (despite parental attempts to ensure they excelled at both). Parents stressed the importance of their young daughters doing well at school so they could go to university and get a degree. Revealingly, however, some of the parents of younger children spoke of how education was important for sons and daughters for different reasons. As Mrs Hunt, a teacher married to a GP and the mother of one daughter and three sons explained, education is important 'for a boy because he needs to support a family and support himself'. Education for women, however, was considered important for women to secure a high-level professional job (in itself) and one that could be combined with family commitments, including part-time employment or easy labour re-entry later on as children grew up or in the event of divorce and widowhood. Thus, parents had higher educational and occupational aspirations for their daughters than in the past. They expected daughters to do as well as sons. That said, they also imagined their daughters' careers (although not their sons' careers) would be interrupted by family commitments. A professional career, like medicine, was a good choice for sons and daughters in both similar and different ways. Occupational inheritance was highly desirable, thereby ensuring class reproduction.

TEACHING AND OTHER CAREERS

In comparison to the medics, the education of the teachers' children was more mixed. Some of the children went to private, single-sex grammar schools but most of them went to state schools which were usually mixed sex. Moreover, the teachers did not usually have the economic resources to pay for a private education for their children unless sacrifices were made. Many of the teachers, especially those from working-class backgrounds, were less culturally disposed to educating their children privately. Different economic and cultural resources were at play as compared to the doctors (Devine 2004). In contrast to the medics' children, some of the teachers were academically successful but others were not. There were academically high-flying daughters and sons who had entered or were planning to enter the 'top professions' in the higher echelons of the middle classes. There were others, however, who struggled in the education system and the move into careers – in the lower middle classes and in routine non-manual work – was, or was going to be, more complicated as a result. Thus, as will be seen, occupational inheritance was not desirable and class reproduction was not so easily secured.

There was some evidence of occupational inheritance among the teachers as daughters followed in their parents' footsteps. Again, examples were often found in homogenous families where mothers and fathers were teachers, as Grusky imagined. There was a degree of ambivalence about children becoming teachers, however. It was noted that salaries were low in comparison to other professions. Workloads were onerous, with marking often being carried out in the evenings and weekends. Mr Johns's eldest daughter chose teaching after doing a degree in French.

> I thought she could do better. I thought she could do . . . no, not better . . . no, that's not right. No. I don't mean that. I thought she could do better because I felt there were other jobs that would be more financially, and interest wise, more rewarding. It was not that it is not a prestigious job or any way that teaching wasn't good enough. That wasn't where I came from. I just felt she'd have a better quality of life if she chose other routes but that's what she's chosen and obviously, that's her choice.

He had imagined his daughter using her skills in business and working in France. His initial disappointment had given way to pride, however. He was still proud of her.

There were daughters who, as high academic achievers, had pursued other professions. The Dowds's oldest daughter, Claire, was training to be an accountant. Mrs Dowds was a teacher while Mr Dowds was a computing systems manager. Initially resistant to accountancy, their daughter secured a first-class degree in economics and then followed friends into one of the top four accountancy firms. Mr Dowds explained:

> You can't really tell them what to do but what we said to her was 'try to get into a profession or something where you have other options' . . . What we said was 'if you work for law or accountancy you could work for a partnership, you can go and work for a company, you can work for yourself, work part-time, travel all over'. So, we were keen, quite keen for her to go into a profession.

He added these options were important as he had witnessed many women facing the 'terrible decision' to have a career break to spend time with their children at the price of their careers. A professional rather than organisational career (Crompton and Harris 1998) opened up many more options for women. These aspirations explained why the interviewees' children went into other high-level professional careers as Goldthorpe suggests.

None of the teachers' sons pursued teaching. The academically successful went into careers like accountancy and other occupations in finance. The less able and less inclined went into youth and community work and social work. Teaching was considered very briefly as a career by Mr and Mrs Hill (an accountant and a teacher) for their second son, Mark, but he quickly dismissed the idea. At a private single-sex school, he had done moderately well in his O levels. Transferring to a mixed-sex sixth form college, he had failed his A levels twice. He eventually completed his A levels aged 23. As Mrs Hill explained, 'he didn't want to be a teacher. He said it was too much, too confining for him I think. He doesn't like the grind, and there is an element of grind, certainly with the national curriculum these days'. Through Mrs Hill's friend, Mark heard about a diploma course in Youth and Community studies which could be converted into a degree. The Hills were delighted that he achieved a degree even though he had secured only three temporary part-time jobs on qualifying. Thus, teaching was only considered for a young man, who had not been conventionally academically successful, very briefly indeed.

There were a number of young women still working their way through the education system. Again, careers in teaching were rarely considered among the high flyers. Law was frequently mentioned for young women pursuing the arts (which was more likely than specialising in the sciences). Mr and Mrs Harrison's two daughters were taking the science route at school. Sylvia Harrison, a primary school teacher, recalled that the single-sex private school she attended:

> was very academic, but to be perfectly honest, when we got the careers talk, all they told you was to go and be a teacher. We were told to be teachers unless you were very academic and you came from a medical family in which case you'd go and be a doctor.

Mrs Harrison was thrilled that her eldest daughter, Rebecca, had taken the same A level subjects as herself: chemistry, biology and maths. Rebecca was about to embark on a degree in genetics. Enthused by the topic as part of her A level biology, and inspired by a good biology teacher, she wanted to be a geneticist. It is interesting here to note the changing aspirations and influence of the school and schoolteachers on mothers and daughters over a 30-year period (Crompton and Sanderson 1990; Crompton 1992). Not all of the daughters were academic achievers or academically inclined, however. There were examples of young women facing other choices and decisions. Mrs and Mrs Crisp's oldest daughter, aged 18, was a straightforward academic success in pursuing A levels in the arts. In contrast, their second daughter, aged 16, was adamant that she wanted to leave school as soon as she could in order to work in hotel and catering. Both teachers, the Crisps were very nervous about their daughter's future. Mrs Crisp was insistent that she do some sort of training or studying to progress. Drawing on her cultural capital, she had explored all available opportunities for training and further study in her daughter's chosen career. She said,

I've looked into it a lot because my experience has been that you do your GCSEs and you do A levels and you go to college or university which is how it was with Alice. So, with Bella, I had to look. I mean, I didn't know what the difference was between a GNVQ and an NVQ and whatever. I've had to find out.

Vocational qualifications had to be achieved to ensure a career with opportunities for advancement.

Teachers' sons still taking the academic route through the education system appeared to be somewhat less assiduous than their sisters. Mr Parker and Mrs Parker, both teachers, had two children. Their daughter, the eldest of the two, had followed them into teaching by completing a degree and then a PGCE. Hard work rather than 'natural ability', they suggested, had secured her success. Their 'more able' son, however, had not been a diligent student during his A level studies. Obtaining moderate grades in the arts, he was in the first year of a degree in communication studies at a small, post-1992 university. The all-important issue for Mr and Mrs Parker was that their son got a degree. While nervous about career prospects in the media, Mr Parker hoped there would be options for his son to use his talent in English or exploit camera work skills or production work skills acquired on his course. Moderate academic success, therefore, was leading some young men into occupations in new industries and their parents hoped, albeit nervously, that career opportunities would be forthcoming.

For the less academically inclined sons, a preoccupation with finding careers with opportunities for advancement rather than dead-end jobs prevailed once more. Mrs Bull's eldest son was unhappy and struggling with his A levels and wanted to abandon his studies. Again, drawing on her cultural capital, she had brought home details of a Modern Apprenticeship in accountancy. Mrs Bull was categorical that he could not abandon his course for a job with no potential. She said:

> I would like him to find some sort of professional job in what area is entirely up to him. I would like it because I know he wouldn't be happy if he wasn't earning a certain amount. He himself would not be happy. I'd like him to have some sort of professional job that has some sort of possibility, potential to have a reasonable salary, but as to what it is, you know, that's up to him.

The advantage of a Modern Apprenticeship in accountancy was that NVQ credits could be put towards Chartered Accountancy examinations. If so inclined, her son could train to be a professionally qualified accountant. He might not be a high academic achiever but he still had the potential to make the best of opportunities for occupational success.

CONCLUSION

This chapter began by outlining the theoretical debate between Grusky and Goldthorpe on how class analysis should proceed. Although they appear to have contrasting positions, it has been argued here that class analysis can embrace the study of occupational social closure in its many forms. Occupational inheritance is one aspect of class reproduction. Drawing on qualitative interviews with doctors and their partners, only a modest amount of occupational inheritance was found so far. That said, if all of the plans were to come to fruition, occupational inheritance would be quite substantial among the small sample of doctors. Behind the scenes, so to speak, many of the doctors and their husbands and wives wanted their children to follow in their footsteps. Medicine was deemed a highly desirable professional occupation for both sons and daughters and, in the case of daughters, a good career that could be combined with children. The outcome was that both adult sons and daughters were following their parents' footsteps into high-level positions in the middle class and the younger sons and daughters were likely to do so too.

The in-depth interviews with teachers and their partners found only a few instances of occupational inheritance. In contrast to medicine, however, there was a degree of ambivalence as to whether teaching was a good professional career for daughters and sons. For high-achieving daughters and sons, there were more desirable careers on offer. For sons, highly-paid careers in finance and accountancy were sought after. For daughters, professional careers in medicine, law and accountancy were considered desirable, not least because they could be combined with childcare commitments. Teaching was considered as a good career for the less academically able or inclined daughters and, to a lesser degree, sons. Thus, in the small sample of teachers, there were examples of both adult daughters and sons being upwardly mobile within the middle class in the pursuit of more desirable high-level professional and managerial careers. Instances of occupational inheritance ensured some daughters retained their position within the lower middle class. Finally, among some of the younger children, parents were drawing on their cultural capital to circumvent the downward mobility of their less academically able sons so the pursuit of a career, rather than a job, was an option.

This research has highlighted that class analysis can take many forms. Indeed, to explain class reproduction, it is crucial to describe how it happens at different levels of analysis. This chapter has shown that 'ratcheting down' to the level of occupations, to explore issues such as the desirability of occupations, reveals the processes by which middle-class parents guide their children into middle-class professional and managerial careers and thereby ensure class reproduction. The interviews highlighted the importance of educational success in this process and, importantly, how parents intervene to circumvent downward mobility when academic success is not forthcoming. This chapter has also demonstrated the importance of looking at both economic and cultural explanations of class reproduction. That is to say, it is crucial to understand the ways in which parents – both fathers and mothers – mobilise their economic and cultural resources to ensure that their sons, and increasingly their daughters, retain the class position of the family over generations.

ACKNOWLEDGEMENTS

I would like to thank the editors, Rosemary Crompton and Jackie Scott, for invaluable advice on revisions to the paper, presented at the 2008 GeNet conference, which is the basis of this chapter. Thanks extend also to Susan McRae and Jane Elliott for helpful comments. The final draft was given at a seminar organised by the School of Social Sciences and Social Research Centre at the University of Queensland, Brisbane in early 2009. Special thanks go to John Western and Jenny Chesters for this opportunity and their insights on the subject at hand.

NOTE

1. The research reported here was part of a comparative project, involving interviews with doctors, teachers and their husbands and wives in Boston in the United States (see Devine 2004).

BIBLIOGRAPHY

Allen, I. (2005), 'Women doctors and their careers: what now?', *British Medical Journal*, **331**, 569–72.
Arnot, M. et al. (1999), *Closing the Gender Gap*, Cambridge: Polity Press.
Coxon, A.P.M. and P.M. Davies with C.L. Jones (1986), *Images of Social Stratification*, London: Sage.
Coxon, A.P.M. and C.L. Jones (1978), *The Images of Occupational Prestige*, London: MacMillan.
Coxon, A.P.M. and C.L. Jones (1979), *Class and Hierarchy*, London: MacMillan.
Crompton, R. (1992), 'Where did all the bright girls go?: Women's higher education and employment since 1964', in N. Abercrombie and A. Warde (eds), *Social Change in Contemporary Society*, Cambridge: Polity.
Crompton, R. (2008), *Class and Stratification*, 3rd edn, Cambridge: Polity Press.

Crompton, R. and F. Harris (1998), 'Gender relations and employment: the impact of occupation', *Work, Employment and Society*, **112**, 297–315.

Crompton, R. and K. Sanderson (1990), *Gendered Jobs and Social Change*, London: Unwin Hyman.

Crompton, R., N. Le Feuvre and G.E. Birkelund (1999), 'The restructuring of gender relations within the medical profession' in R. Crompton (ed.), *Restructuring Gender Relations and Employment*, Oxford: Oxford University Press.

Davies, C. (1996), 'The sociology of the professions and the profession of gender', *Sociology*, **30**, 661–78.

Devine, F. (1998), 'Class analysis and the stability of class relations', *Sociology*, **32**, 23–42.

Devine, F. (2004), *Class Practices: How Parents Help their Children get Good Jobs*, Cambridge: Cambridge University Press.

Devine, F. (2008), 'Class reproduction and social networks in the USA', in L.Weis (ed.), *The Way Class Works*, London: Routledge.

Dolton, P. and G. Makepeace (1993), 'Female labour market participation and the choice of occupation: the supply of teachers', *European Economic Review*, **37**, 1393–411.

Goldthorpe, J.H. (2007), *On Sociology, Volume Two: Illustration and Retrospect*, 2nd edn, Stanford, CA: Stanford University Press.

Goldthorpe, J.H. and A. McKnight (2006), 'The economic basis of social class' in S.L. Morgan, D.B. Grusky and G.S. Field (eds), *Mobility and Inequality*, Stanford, CA: Stanford University Press.

Grusky, D.B. with G. Galescu (2005), 'Foundations of a neo-Durkheimian class analysis', in E.O. Wright (ed.), *Approaches to Class Analysis*, Cambridge: Cambridge University Press.

Grusky, D.B. and J.B. Sorensen (1998), 'Can class analysis be salvaged', *American Journal of Sociology*, **103**, 1187–234.

Grusky, D.B. and K.A. Weeden (2001), 'Decomposition without death: a research agenda for a new class analysis', *Acta Sociologica*, **44**, 203–18.

Grusky, D.B. and K.A. Weeden (2006), 'Does the sociological approach to studying social mobility have a future?', in S.L. Morgan, D.B. Grusky and G.S. Field (eds), *Mobility and Inequality*, Stanford, CA: Stanford University Press.

The Independent (2008), 'Gender gap in teaching grows: only 24% of new recruits are men', 24 September.

Machin, A. and A. Vignoles (eds) (2005), *What's the Good of Education?*, Princeton, NJ: Princeton University Press.

Purcell, K. and P. Elias (2008), 'Wanting to "help people" exacerbates the pay gap for young professional women', *GeNeT Newsletter* 3, pp. 4–5.

Riska, E. and K. Wegar (eds) (1993), *Gender, Work and Medicine*, London: Sage.

Sinclair, S. (1997), *Making Doctors*, London: Berg.

Training and Development Agency for Schools (TDA) (2009), website www.tda.gov.uk, accessed 28 January 2009.

Witz, A. (1992), *Professions and Patriarchy*, London: Routledge.

3. Ethnic differences in women's economic activity: a focus on Pakistani and Bangladeshi women

Angela Dale and Sameera Ahmed

INTRODUCTION

The twentieth century saw dramatic rises in women's levels of labour market participation in the UK whilst those for men fell slightly. Official UK statistics (ONS 2008) showed that 79 per cent of men and 70 per cent of women of working age were in employment – although almost a half of employed women work part-time. Marriage and partnership no longer pose a barrier to women's employment and, whilst motherhood reduces women's levels of employment, this effect is much less for more highly educated women than for those less well qualified (Dex and Joshi 1996; Dex et al. 1998). These increased rates of employment and qualifications have led to arguments that women now expect to live an 'individualised' life, free to make their own choices (Beck and Beck-Gernsheim 2001; Esping-Andersen 2002), with marriage no longer a social or economic necessity, and childbearing a matter of individual choice dissociated from marriage.

In this chapter we explore the extent to which generalisations for women's employment for the UK as a whole are sustainable for different ethnic groups and, in particular, we focus on the very different employment patterns for Pakistani and Bangladeshi women. Headline figures[1] show that Pakistani and Bangladeshi women are much less likely to be working than white women and that family formation has a strong negative impact on their economic activity. By contrast, Black Caribbean women are more likely to maintain economic activity during family formation. However, there are also very major differences in patterns of family formation between ethnic groups. Thus Black Caribbean mothers are predominantly single (Lindley et al. 2004) whilst lone motherhood is relatively uncommon for Indian, Pakistani and Bangladeshi women and, where it occurs, is mainly due to separation, divorce or widowhood. Patterson (2005) points out that, amongst those of African origin, female-headed families are the norm across the Americas. He suggests that this may be traced to the disruption caused by slavery. Whatever the historical origin, increases in lone motherhood in the UK are particularly marked for women of Black Caribbean heritage (Lindley et al. 2004; Berthoud 2005), which may suggest a modern form of 'individualisation' where decisions about marriage are a lifestyle choice rather than a necessary prerequisite to childbearing (Berthoud 2005). By contrast, women from the Indian sub-continent are very unlikely to choose to have a child outside a formal marriage, and family patterns are much more traditional or 'old-fashioned' (Berthoud 2005). Earlier work (Duncan and Irwin 2004; Reynolds 2005) has suggested that, for Black Caribbean women, notions of 'good mother-hood' are associated with paid employment and economic independence, whilst for Pakistani and Bangladeshi women, 'good motherhood' means adopting traditional gendered roles within the family.

In this chapter we examine the role of partnership, children and level of qualification in explaining economic activity for White, Black Caribbean, Indian and Pakistani and Bangladeshi women, using data from the UK Labour Force Survey. We also introduce qualitative analysis of interviews with Pakistani and Bangladeshi women to explore some of the initial findings from the statistical analysis, and, finally, conduct some statistical modelling to test our explanatory framework. The interviews provide greater depth of understanding than can be gained with the survey data alone and also allow the generation of questions (or hypotheses) that can be tested on the survey data. We conclude by assessing whether there is evidence to support the thesis of 'individualisation' across different ethnic groups and, indeed, the extent to which generalisations can be made to specific ethnic groups.

EXPLANATORY FRAMEWORK

Analyses presented here are set within a life-course framework whereby we make comparisons between ethnic groups at specific life-course stages (Dale et al. 2008). We focus on three life stages: young women aged 19–34 who are single (no partner) and have no children; women of the same age who have a partner but no children;[2] and women with both a partner and a youngest child under 5.[3] For this latter category we make no restriction on mothers' age although most women are in their twenties or thirties. A focus on these three categories allows us to compare the impact of a partner and children on women's levels of economic activity for differ-ent ethnic groups. Previous work has shown that the effect of qualifica-tions becomes particularly marked where women have young children.

However, irrespective of life stage, better qualified women of all ethnic groups are more likely to be in paid work than women who are less well qualified (Dale et al. 2006).

In addition to the main drivers of life stage and qualifications, whether women were born and educated in the UK or settled in the UK as adults will influence factors related to employment, including fluency in English, the acquisition of UK-based qualifications and knowledge of the labour market. Ideally, we also need to take into account labour market factors including workplace discrimination. By using economic activity rather than employment as our outcome measure, we include unemployed women in our sample. However, labour market barriers for Pakistani and Bangladeshi women are only explored through our qualitative interviews.

DATA SOURCES AND METHODS

We use data from two sources: nationally representative survey data from the Quarterly Labour Force Survey and small-scale qualitative interviews with Pakistani and Bangladeshi women in the north-west of England.

The Quarterly Labour Force Survey (QLFS) is conducted by the Office for National Statistics. Interviews are achieved at about 59 000 addresses with about 138 000 respondents; respondents are interviewed on five successive occasions over a 12-month period. A response rate of about 77 per cent was achieved for the first wave of the survey in 2002. All first interviews (with the exception of a very small sample located north of the Caledonian Canal) are carried out by face-to-face interview. Subsequent interviews are carried out by telephone. We use data for England, Wales and Scotland for sweep 1 of each quarter, for all years from 1992–2005. Results from tables are weighted to produce population estimates in line with the latest census.[4]

The QLFS collects family and demographic information on each member of the household. This allows us to identify information about a woman's partner and her children. The survey asks extensive information on employment and qualifications that is consistent each year. In addition, questions on ethnicity, country of birth and year of arrival in the UK are asked. Whilst changes in question-wording have caused difficulty in comparisons over time for some ethnic groups, this has been minimal for the groups that are the focus of this analysis: Pakistani/Bangladeshi, White, Black Caribbean and Indian women. In most analyses we have had to combine Pakistani and Bangladeshi women because of small cell sizes. The UK Bangladeshi population has a rather younger age structure than the Pakistani population, with a smaller proportion of young people born in the UK (Lindley et al. 2004) and lower levels of educational attainment, all related to their more recent timing of arrival in the UK. These structural factors largely explain differences between Pakistani and Bangladeshi women in terms of economic activity (Table 3.1). However, in terms of crucial decisions over marriage, motherhood and employment – the focus of this chapter – all available evidence suggests that there is great similarity between Bangladeshi and Pakistani populations. Both populations in the UK came from traditional rural communities with few socioeconomic resources and, indeed, shared the same country of origin until 1971; both share Islam as their religion and as a central focus in their lives; early marriage and early childbearing is traditional in both populations and cultural assumptions about gender roles are also shared.

The statistical data is complemented by evidence from 18 in-depth interviews with Pakistani and Bangladeshi women in Rochdale and Manchester (14 Pakistanis, 3 Bangladeshis and 1 Kashmiri), conducted in 2006. Respondents were primarily recruited through voluntary organisations and were selected on the basis of either looking for work or being in work and were all born in the UK. They are not, therefore, representative of Pakistani/Bangladeshi women more generally. The interviews covered questions on educational attainment, decisions about careers, seeking employment, actual employment experiences, family and community, general attitudes towards work, employment aspirations and barriers to employment. The interviews do not allow us to make claims about the larger population of Pakistani/Bangladeshi women, but they provide insights into some of the issues brought out in the statistics and give a deeper understanding of the experiences of women represented in the statistical analysis. All interviews were taped and fully transcribed.

ETHNIC DIFFERENCES BY LIFE STAGE

We begin with some contextual information about the economic status of women in the major ethnic groups in Britain (Table 3.1) based on the LFS for 2001–05. For most groups, levels of economic activity[5] are about 70 per cent, with Black Caribbean and Black Other and White women rather higher than Indian, Chinese and Black African women. However, Pakistani and Bangladeshi women have much lower levels of economic activity than any other ethnic group. Table 3.1 also shows the high levels of unemployment of minority ethnic groups by comparison with white women. These figures are particularly startling for Pakistani and Bangladeshi women, given their very low levels of economic activity, and provide some indication of the labour market barriers faced by this group.

Table 3.1   Ethnic differences in labour market activity: women aged 19–60, 2001–05

Ethnic group	% econom- ically active Aged 19–60	Of those active: % unem- ployed	Total N in sample Aged 19–60	% FT student Aged 19–29	N 19–20
White	76.5	03.4	127 835	14.8	23 706
Black Caribbean	77.5	07.9	1 353	29.1	208
Black African	66.1	12.2	1 181	35.7	282
Black Other	77.1	13.3	482	24.0	167
Indian	69.9	05.7	2 465	24.5	545
Pakistani	31.1	14.8	1 549	18.7	513
Bangladeshi	20.8	15.6	560	09.7	236
Chinese	68.8	05.3	479	55.8	103
Other	76.5	08.7	2 272	28.4	557

Source: Quarterly Labour Force Survey, England, Wales and Scotland, weighted.

It is noticeable that, for all minority ethnic groups except Bangladeshis, the level of full-time students is much higher than for white women, rising to 56 per cent for Chinese women aged 19–29.[6] In subsequent analyses full-time students are omitted because their employment decisions are assumed to be primarily shaped by their status as students.

We now focus on specific ethnic groups and examine levels of economic activity within categories of life stage and qualification level. Figure 3.1 is based on the first life stage category – women aged 19–34 with no partner and no children. Although a five-point categorisation of qualifications has been used, just the highest and lowest categories (degree-level qualification and no qualifications) are shown here. Generally, there is a clear gradient across the levels of qualification, which will be apparent, later, in Table 3.4 which includes all qualifications levels. Ethnic groups are restricted to White, Black Caribbean, Indian and Pakistani/Bangladeshi. Because of small numbers the latter two are combined. Figure 3.1 provides an immediate contrast to the economic activity figures in Table 3.1. Across all ethnic groups, the women in the most highly educated category have levels of economic activity of over 90 per cent, with Pakistani/Bangladeshi women comparable to other ethnic groups. Women with no qualifica-tions have lower levels of economic activity but the key difference is for Pakistani/Bangladeshi women, where levels of economic activity are below

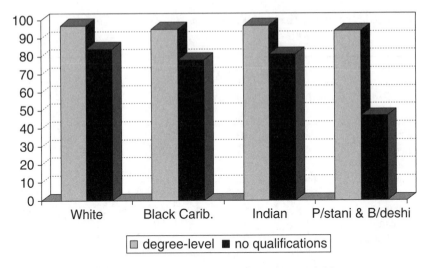

Figure 3.1   Economic activity, women aged 19–34, no child, no partner,
*   1992–2005*

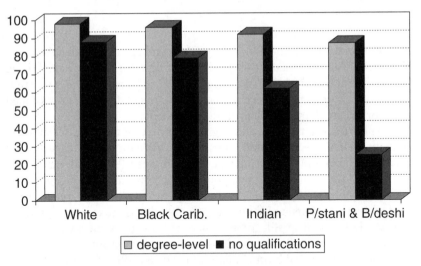

Figure 3.2   Economic activity, women aged 19–34, partner but no child,
*   1992–2005*

50 per cent. Our qualitative work, outlined later, explores why we find this large differential for women with no apparent domestic constraints.

Figure 3.2 shows levels of economic activity for young women (19–34) with a partner and no children. At both ends of the qualification spectrum

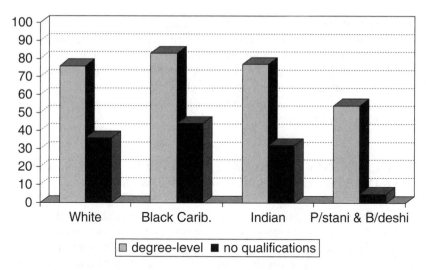

Figure 3.3   Economic activity, women with partner and youngest child under 5, 1992–2005

White and Black Caribbean women are slightly more likely to be economically active than their single counterparts (Figure 3.1) whilst Indian and Pakistani/Bangladeshi women are slightly less likely to be economically active. (The statistical significance of partnership for each ethnic group is formally tested in the model reported in Table 3.4.)

It is generally assumed that any cultural constraints associated with women working after marriage have disappeared and legal constraints such as the marriage bar finally ended in the 1960s. Indeed, the 'individualisation' thesis of Beck and Beck-Gernsheim (2001) assumes that partnership will not impact on women's economic independence. However, the very low levels of economic activity for partnered Pakistani/Bangladeshi women with no qualifications (25 per cent are economically active, by comparison with 47 per cent of single women with no children in Figure 3.1) call into question these assumptions. It would appear that for these women, the low levels of economic independence before marriage are amplified after marriage. However, we cannot tell from Figure 3.2 whether this is a causal relationship or whether it is explained by other factors.

Figure 3.3 focuses on women with a partner and a youngest child under 5. For all ethnic groups, levels of economic activity are much lower than for women with a partner but no children (Figure 3.2), but in this life stage there is a much larger differential by level of qualification (across all ethnic groups) than for women without children. Nonetheless, Black Caribbean women have higher levels of economic activity than any other group – at both extremes of qualification – whilst Pakistani/Bangladeshi women have much lower levels, with a very considerable differential between those with higher qualification and no qualifications. Although not shown here, Black Caribbean women who are single mothers also have considerably higher levels of economic activity than white mothers. For the Indian and Pakistani/Bangladeshi groups, there are too few single mothers to provide statistically robust figures.

EXPLAINING ECONOMIC ACTIVITY LEVELS FOR PAKISTANI AND BANGLADESHI WOMEN

The differences we have identified already take into account the major drivers of women's economic activity levels – life stage and qualifications. In the following sections we specifically focus on the Pakistani/Bangladeshi group and explore in more depth the reasons that may help to explain the marked differences with other ethnic groups.

Generally, the levels of economic activity for young single women (Figure 3.1) fit our normative view that women, like men, will be economically active unless there are reasons that prevent this (for example ill-health, family responsibilities, or, perhaps, a 'gap year'). Young women with no dependent children are, therefore, usually either working or looking for work (economically active) unless they are in full-time education. We need to understand why highly educated Pakistani/Bangladeshi women appear to behave in the same way as all other ethnic groups, but less than 50 per cent of young Pakistani/Bangladeshi women with no qualifications are economically active. Why do qualifications seem to have a much stronger influence on economic activity for Pakistani/Bangladeshi women than for other ethnic groups?

The Timing and Context of Settlement

An important factor in understanding ethnic differences is the timing of settlement in the UK and the reasons for migration. The Black Caribbean group came to the UK in the 1950s as a response to the post-war labour shortage, with a peak of migration between 1955–57 and, again, just before immigration controls in 1962 (Robinson and Valeny 2005). Both men and women came in roughly equal numbers, taking hard-to-fill, low-paid jobs in the London area, often to support the expanding health service and public transport (ibid.).

Migration from India was also driven by post-war labour needs and included a small but significant flow of doctors for the NHS and, in 1972, refugees from Uganda who, although bringing considerable skills and ability, had to leave behind all financial assets (Robinson and Valeny 2005). Pakistani men generally came to Britain in the early 1960s to take jobs that were not attractive to white men – often in the declining industrial areas of north-west England (Kalra 2000). A large proportion of the Bangladeshi men came somewhat later, in the late 1970s and early 1980s, settling in the South East and in East London in particular. Both Pakistani and Bangladeshi settlers arrived in difficult labour markets, many coming from the poor rural areas of Mirpur and Syllhet, respectively, with few economic or educational resources. Typically, men came first and established themselves in the labour market and then their wives and children joined them as dependents. Women from Pakistan or Bangladesh were therefore not entering Britain as economic migrants but coming from a culture where they expected to move to live with their husband's family on marriage (Shaw 2001) and where men were expected to be the breadwinners for the family.

These differences in the timing of migration are reflected in the LFS sample where, amongst respondents aged 19–50 in 2001–05, only 30 per cent of Black Caribbean women were born outside the UK by comparison with 61 per cent of Indian women, 63 per cent of Pakistani and 83 per cent of Bangladeshi women. Fluency in English – an important factor in obtaining employment (Leslie and Lindley 2001) – is also related to timing of settlement in the UK. Modood et al. (1997) found that only 40 per cent of Bangladeshi women and 54 per cent of Pakistani women spoke English fluently or fairly well, compared with 70 per cent of Indian women. (The question was not asked of Caribbean respondents as English is assumed to be their first language.) Levels of fluency were much lower for women who had come to live in the UK over the age of 25.

Table 3.2 focuses on Pakistani and Bangladeshi women aged 19–34 and shows the relationship between educational attainment and the timing of arrival in the UK. Rather than categorising women by whether or not they were born in the UK, we have classified them by whether they moved to the UK below the age of 16 or at 16 and above. We expect that those who moved to the UK before age 16 will have attended school in the UK and will thus be fluent in English and have UK qualifications.

We can see that almost all Pakistani/Bangladeshi women aged 19–34 with a formal UK-recognised qualification were either UK-born or arrived before 16. Conversely about 60 per cent of women with 'other' (which includes foreign qualifications) or no qualifications arrived in the UK at 16 or older.

Table 3.3 shows the level of economic activity by level of qualification and timing of arrival in the UK, for the same sample. Thus 84 per cent of

Table 3.2   Qualification level by time of arrival in the UK: Pakistani and Bangladeshi women aged 19–34, 2001–05

	Degree-level	A-level	O-level	Other qualifi-cation	No qualifi-cations	Total
Born/arrived UK before 16	87	94	96	40	39	723
Arrived UK 16+	13	6	4	60	61	415
	100	100	100	100	100	
Total	161	121	238	164	454	1138

Source: QLFS 2001–05, weighted.

Table 3.3   Percentage of women who are economically active by education and time of arrival in the UK: Pakistani and Bangladeshi women aged 19–34, 2001–05

	Degree-level	A-level	O-level	Other qualifi-cation	No qualifi-cations	Total
Born/arrived UK before 16	84	60	47	41	15	
Arrived UK 16+	–	–	–	16	10	
Total	161	121	238	164	454	1138

Note: – indicates base numbers below 25.

Source: QLFS 2001–05, weighted.

women with a degree-level qualification who were born or arrived in the UK before 16 are economically active, compared with only 15 per cent with no qualifications. The small numbers of women who arrived in the UK at 16 and over *and* have formal qualifications prevent a comparison of levels of economic activity for these groups. However, we can make comparisons for women with 'other' and no qualifications. These show that 'other' qualifications are associated with much higher levels of economic activity for women educated in the UK than for women who came to the UK at 16 and over. This is consistent with other findings (Dale et al. 2002a) that show that overseas qualifications for Pakistani and Bangladeshi women have very little labour market value. However, women with no qualifications have very low levels of economic activity (10–15 per cent), irrespective of the timing of their arrival in the UK. Thus the low levels of economic activity for women with no qualifications (Figures 3.1–3.3) is not readily explained by age of arrival in the UK.

Qualitative Analyses: Background

Whilst we have shown that there are important structural factors that underpin the differences observed between ethnic groups and, in particular, Pakistani and Bangladeshi women, qualitative research can provide more insight into some of the processes by which these operate.

Earlier qualitative work in Oldham (Dale et al. 2002a; 2002b) showed that it was the norm amongst young Pakistani and Bangladeshi women in this mill town in north-west England to live at home with parents until marriage and, although some young women moved away to go to university, this was seen as unusual. Parents still played an important role in decisions about young women's lives – in terms of education, employment and marriage. Although the influence of parents was often contested – and mothers and fathers sometimes held differing views – there was a prevailing assumption that a young woman did not act as an independent agent. Her family provided the context in which decisions were made and several young women explained that, for them, taking paid work was not the norm, but something to be negotiated with your family, where you had to 'prove yourself' able to work outside the home. On marriage, the parental family context was replaced by the husband and, if they lived locally, his family.

Whilst a commitment to family was expressed by women at all educational levels, a desire for independence and the confidence to face the labour market were both more apparent for women with higher qualifications. These women had often had to struggle to be allowed to attend university and, having achieved this, were determined to use their qualifications in the labour market (Dale et al. 2002a). Graduate-level women demonstrated a level of confidence, both in negotiating their domestic lives and in confronting the labour market, that provides some explanation for the differences in levels of economic activity between the most highly qualified and least highly qualified women in Figures 3.1–3.3. This commitment from women with higher qualifications was also borne out in our current interviews, discussed below.

Earlier work has also highlighted some of the problems experienced in the labour market. These included perceived stereotypes held by employers, particularly with respect to questions about whether women would be willing to work with men or to work evenings, and relating to dress. Women felt that going to an interview wearing a hijab (headscarf) was a major barrier. Some wore Western dress for interviews while others who wore a hijab used social interaction skills, for example maintaining eye-contact, to overcome this barrier. Once in the workplace, Western cultural assumptions often presented further difficulties, for example in terms of socialising in the pub, taking holidays around Eid and observing Ramadan.

Our recent interviews focused on barriers to paid work and give some insights into cultural assumptions about Pakistani and Bangladeshi women's employment and its relationship with marriage and childbearing and how these may be influenced by qualifications. Respondents were either born in the UK or had moved here at a very young age. In most cases their father had come to the UK as an economic migrant, followed by their mother and sometimes other family members.

Barriers to Work

When asked about barriers to paid work the two most frequent reasons given by respondents were their family and the labour market. We discuss both in turn.

Family

One interviewee made a very eloquent statement about how she saw her life by comparison with women from other cultures:

> [Referring to Pakistani women] I think their family is the biggest problem personally, they always have to put their families first and their husbands first and they don't put themselves first.
>   I mean in other cultures if women have dreams they go for them, our dreams – if the family back it then OK, if they don't then they will break. If you want to go ahead and do a job or career, you want to do law, they say 'oh what do you want to do that for, its not as if you are going to work, you are just going to get married and have kids'. With other women in other cultures they don't think that, they go for it. (11) (Pakistani, married, 32, 4 children, no qualifications)

Other women also emphasised the centrality of family life but in much more positive terms. For example a single, graduate Pakistani (no children or husband) said in response to a question about the role of work:

> I think my life revolves around my family, first and foremost. Then work and I think that's how I define myself. (1) (Pakistani, single, 26, graduate)

A much more negative view was expressed by a young woman who described the constraints faced by her best friend:

I've got – my best friend's at home – her brothers won't let her work – nothing. Since she left school, she's just been at home. And they've said to her 'We'll give you money, if you want £100 – we'll give you money . . .' (8) (Pakistani, single, 17, GCSEs)

In other interviews, women explained that parents were often keen for them to stay at home, sometimes to help in caring activities. Levels of long-term illness are high amongst older members of the Pakistani and Bangladeshi community and there is an assumption that care will be provided by daughters (or daughters-in-law) rather than formal care services. One respondent, whose mother was not in good health, felt under considerable pressure from her parents to stay at home and provide care:

They said 'Don't go too far, stay close' and in a way, my mum – like, when I started the course and things are going good for me, I've got a placement here and everything, she says 'You know, you can pack it in, if you like, you can just stay at home, you know, help me out.' I was just thinking – I do help . . . I do help my mum out a lot but I want to get out the house, go explore the world, see stuff. (8) (Pakistani, single, 17, doing a Modern Apprenticeship)

A Pakistani respondent who was a social worker and ran a support service for carers provided further evidence of young Pakistani and Bangladeshi women who were struggling to combine either study or employment with a caring role – often because families were very unwilling to ask for outside help.

As in our earlier research, several women with degree-level qualifications expressed very strong commitment to paid work and to economic independence after marriage. The view that 'staying at home' was simply not possible was one which occurred frequently in interviews with graduates.

I suppose it's all to do with security, with me because when you get married – pay for your wedding, you have to build your life, get a house – basically all them things. That's what working is for, I guess. I suppose for your head as well, it'll be good – it's good to sort of work, socialise with others . . . Yeah – you'll go crazy if you're sat at home five days a week. (9) (Pakistani, 22, single, graduate)

Respondents clearly felt strong family commitment – sometimes in a very positive way and sometimes in a way that seemed to impinge on their own desire for independence.

Husbands[7]

Our respondents were all working or seeking work and therefore the fact that all nine married women reported their husbands being supportive towards them working may not be too surprising. However, six of the nine, all UK-born, had had an arranged marriage to a spouse from their country of origin. Marriage to a partner from overseas is not unusual. Although firm statistics are hard to obtain, the LFS shows that just over 50 per cent of UK-born married Pakistani and Bangladeshi women (aged 19–44) had a husband who had arrived in the UK at 18 or older (Ahmed and Dale 2008). Our respondents expressed strong views that husbands from overseas were more traditional than UK-born men and would, for example, want their wives to stay at home and care for family, rather than go out to work. Typical quotes include:

> Well, my younger sister, she . . . she actually doesn't work – her husband's like a bit strict – he doesn't really want her to work or . . . it depends on the husband – because they're from back home, they think differently (2) (Pakistani, married, 28, children, NVQ2)

> I think a lot of the girls that get married from back home, their husbands would like them to sit at home and have the family – the children . . . They want a wife that wears a hijab and not step foot out the house (7) (Pakistani, married, 23, children, GNVQ)

However, the women who had had an arranged marriage to a man from Pakistan reported very different views of their own husbands:

> My husband, he's alright – he's quite good. I mean, he's my best friend as well – I can talk to him about anything and I can tell him I want to work and he won't mind if I study (2) (Pakistani, married, 28, children, NVQ2)

> I've always had loads of encouragement from my family. My husband, too, he's been brilliant, he has never stopped me doing anything. (7) (Pakistani, married, 23, children, GNVQ)

Another respondent, who had got married at 17 in Pakistan and then returned to the UK with her husband, had continued her education after marriage and was now a fully qualified teacher working full-time. She had one child and she and her husband shared the domestic work and childcare:

> We decided to have equal gender roles, rather than saying; 'Ok you bring all the money home and I'll cook and clean and stuff.' We said, 'Ok, we'll both bring the money home and we'll both have an equal share in the house. We'll both have an equal role, we'll make decisions together (15) (Pakistani, 25, married, degree, one child)

In this example, the respondent's parents and her husband's parents all placed a high value on education. Her three siblings all had professional jobs and, although the marriage was arranged and took place at an early age, there was a shared expectation that she would continue her education and take paid employment.

From our interviews we cannot establish whether an overseas-born husband does, in fact, have a negative impact on his wife's labour market participation. However, this is an important question and one which we address later in this chapter using data from the Labour Force Survey.

Although the issue of husband's employment did not arise directly in our interviews, it is well established that, in the UK generally, women with working partners are more likely to be economically active than women with partners who are either unemployed or economically inactive. The highest levels of male unemployment are found in the Pakistani and Bangladeshi community and therefore, using data from the LFS, we can assess how far the woman's low levels of economic activity are explained by the husband's unemployment. Results from this analysis are also presented later in this chapter.

Children and childcare

A number of studies (Brah and Shaw 1992; Ahmad et al. 2003; Aston et al. 2007) have found that Asian women, and Muslims in particular, prefer to use informal networks for childcare, particularly family members, rather than formal provision such as registered playgroups or nurseries. This may be explained by the importance Pakistani and Bangladeshi women attach to being at home to provide care and support for their own children (Dale et al. 2002a; Aston et al. 2007) and thus ensuring children learn the cultural values important to their family. It may also relate to the cost of childcare.

Of the nine married women in our sample, eight had children and all were either working, attending courses or seeking work or study. Only one woman, who was studying English one day a week and had a place for her child in the college crèche, was not using family members for childcare. Other women relied on parents, parents-in-law or their husbands, although sometimes this meant constraints on working hours.

One respondent had worked full-time after her first child, as her mother had provided childcare but now, after a second child, was looking for part-time work to fit in with her husband's work hours:

> And then, I became pregnant again, and, I think the main thing was I didn't want to land my children with my mother again, coz it wasn't fair on her to look after the children. And, I don't know, I'm not comfortable with child care. (22) (Bangladeshi, 27, married, children, GNVQ)

For women with parents or parents-in-law who were not able to look after children – because of health or geographical location – childcare posed considerable problems and seemed to depend on fitting work hours around the availability of their husband.

Barriers to Obtaining Qualifications for UK-born Women

So far we have implied that UK-born women experience no ethnic-specific barriers to obtaining qualifications. However, there is a considerable literature on the barriers within the educational system to attainment of minority ethnic groups (Connor et al. 2004) and nearly a quarter of UK-born/brought up Pakistani/Bangladeshi women aged 19–34 have no qualifications (calculations from LFS 2001–05) – a level higher than for other ethnic groups. Our interviews help to provide some reasons for this.

Two respondents were taking English classes because, having spent several years in Pakistan, they felt the need to increase their confidence in English. One said:

> Yeah – because – when I told you that my parents took us to Pakistan, they took us to Pakistan and I lived there, like, three years. So I kind of . . . I was 11 and when I came back I was about 14, you see. So, obviously, when I came back, I went straight into GCSE and it, obviously, you know, with my basic English – I couldn't really do GCSE, could I? (2) (Pakistani, married, 28, children, NVQ2)

A second woman explained:

> In terms of school – I stopped at year 10, we went abroad and then we came back and I didn't continue because my parents didn't wish to – you know, they're very culturised. Then after that I was just at home. (3) (Pakistani, 21, married, children, GCSE)

However, this woman had continued to study after marriage and is now doing a teaching assistant course while her in-laws look after her young child.

A UK-born Pakistani woman (aged 32, married, with four children), who had left school at 14, explained some of the barriers to obtaining qualifications – and also demonstrated a very large degree of determination, as well as support, from her husband:

> What they (parents) did was take me out of school and I went to Pakistan, and I got married at 16 . . . I really wanted to study, go to college, have education, have a job, I've never had that. I've just been with kids all my life. Now I want to do something with my life. I've always wanted to be a teacher since I was small, so I'm hoping to go for it now. My husband's supporting me, he goes 'Go for it!'

This woman is now learning to drive and plans to study for GCSEs. However, she also explained that college was a very daunting prospect:

> I've never been to college so it's really scary just to step into a college. It's a really big thing for me. (11) (Pakistani, married, 32, 4 children, no qualifications)

These interviews illustrate some of the intangible barriers that cannot be included in our statistical analysis but which help to explain the lower level of qualifications and economic activity for UK-born Pakistani and Bangladeshi women by comparison with other ethnic groups.

Barriers to Work: The Labour Market

Almost all respondents reported that they had experienced difficulties in the labour market. Table 3.1 shows the very high levels of unemployment for Pakistani/Bangladeshi women – about 15 per cent of economically active women aged 19–60 were unemployed in 2001–05, much higher than for any other ethnic group. Research (Dale et al. 2002a; Tackey et al. 2006) has identified some of the ways in which women are excluded from employment. These include a strong perception that employers are hostile to women wearing Asian clothing and, in particular, a hijab.

> No I don't, [wear a hijab] but I wear Asian clothes all the time and as soon as I walk into an interview the first thing is that when they look at you, first of all it's the colour of your skin, then it's what you're dressed like. (5) (Kashmiri, married, 28, no children, GNVQ)

Other women explained how they felt they did not 'fit in' to the work environment, with some feeling intimidated by the other women.

> I just felt so out of place, coz they were all English and they were all posh, and they were all like, their hair – they had their hair done first thing in the morning. I mean, the interview was at like, nine o'clock in the morning, and they looked like they'd just walked out of the hairdressers! You know, I was just like . . . you know I just felt like really out of place, I knew that I didn't have that job! (13) (Bangladeshi, 30, married, 2 children, who wore a hijab with Western clothes)

Many respondents felt that they did not have enough knowledge of the labour market and three of the five graduates had struggled to find a graduate-level job. For a number of women, call centres provided stop-gap jobs. However, a few women wanted to work in women-only environments and thus recognised that they were restricting their opportunities by these requirements.

FURTHER ANALYSIS USING THE LABOUR FORCE SURVEY

The interview data has provided some valuable insights into why we might expect marriage and family to have particularly strong influences on economic activity for Pakistani and Bangladeshi women. In this final section we are able to use data from the LFS to identify the impact of partnership, children, qualifications and timing of arrival in the UK on economic activity, not just for Pakistani/Bangladeshi women but also for other ethnic groups. We can thus establish not only the independent effect of each factor but also whether there are differences between ethnic groups in the importance of these various factors on women's economic activity.

In Table 3.4, explanatory variables include age, qualifications, whether UK born/brought up, year (1992–2005), age of the youngest child (under 5; 5–15), and the presence of a partner (model 1). The outcome variable is binary – whether economically active or not. In model 2 we refine the partner variable by distinguishing those partners who arrived in the UK before age 18 from those who arrived at 18 or older. Model 3 replaces this distinction with whether or not the partner is in work. In all cases the reference category is 'no partner'. Results are reported as the percentage change in the level of economic activity from switching from the reference category to the included dummy variable (marginal effects). Thus we see that for White women in model 1, there is a 22 per cent increase in the likelihood of being economically active for women with a degree-level qualification by comparison with women with no qualifications. Effects that are statistically significant are shown in bold.

These analyses confirm the strength of qualifications in promoting economic activity for all women and, in particular, the very large effect for Pakistani/Bangladeshi women, where those with degree-level qualifications increase their likelihood of being economically active by 46 percentage points, by comparison with women with no qualifications. For all women, the presence of a child under 5 has a large negative effect which reduces when the youngest child is 5–15, becoming non-significant for Indian women.

The effect of settling in the UK at age 16 or older is only significant for Pakistani/ Bangladeshi women and, for them, there is a 10 per cent reduction in levels of economic activity by comparison with the reference category (born/brought up in the UK). It is important to remember that this negative effect is *additional* to the effect of qualifications. We have not been able to include fluency in English in this analysis, but previous work (Leslie and Lindley 2001; Dale et al. 2002a) has shown that this correlates

Table 3.4   Marginal effects (%) for economic activity from logit model: active: not active separate models have been run for each ethnic group

	White			Black Caribbean			Indian			Pakistani/ Bangladeshi		
	Model 1	Model 2	Model 3	Model 1	Model 2	Model 3	Model 1	Model 2	Model 3	Model 1	Model 2	Model 3
Age in years	1.2	1.2	0.9	1.7	1.7	1.5	0.4	0.56	-0.00	**3.0**	**3.0**	**2.8**
Age squared	-0.02	-0.02	-0.02	-0.02	-0.02	-0.02	-0.01	-0.01	-0.00	**-0.05**	**-0.05**	**-0.04**
Degree level	**22**	**22**	**21**	**25**	**25**	**24**	**26**	**26**	**25**	**46**	**46**	**45**
A level	**16**	**16**	**15**	**16**	**16**	**16**	**20**	**20**	**19**	**34**	**34**	**34**
O level	**15**	**15**	**14**	**14**	**14**	**14**	**18**	**18**	**17**	**25**	**25**	**24**
Other qual	**10**	**10**	**9**	**8**	**8**	**8**	**11**	**11**	**10**	**17**	**17**	**17**
Child <5	**-30**	**-30**	**-30**	**-23**	**-24**	**-23**	**-25**	**-25**	**-25**	**-29**	**-29**	**-29**
Child 5–15	**-13**	**-13**	**-12**	**-10**	**-10**	**-10**	-2.7	-2.4	-3.3	**-14**	**-14**	**-14**
Not UK born	-1.5	0.8	-1.5	-1.9	-2.0	-1.7	-3.0	-2.6	-3.3	**-9.7**	**-9.6**	**-9.9**
Partner	**8**			**10**			2.1			-0.5		
Partner UK 18+		0.5			**10**			-0.3			-0.4	
Partner UK <18		**8**			**10**			3.1			-0.6	
Partner working			**11**			**12.3**			**5.4**			1.8
Partner not working			**-5.6**			3.5			**-7.1**			**-4.6**
Year	0.06	0.07	0.05	-0.1	-0.14	-0.12	0.8	0.78	0.7	-0.4	-0.44	-0.5
N cases	161266			1847			3325			2936		
Pseudo R²	0.1600			0.149			0.1338			0.3134		

Notes: QLFS, 1998–2005, unweighted, women aged 19–50, excludes FT students.
Calculated at the mean for each ethnic group; significant effects (at 5% level) in bold.

strongly with being born overseas and is likely to explain much of the effect observed in our analysis.

The positive effect of partnership on economic activity is apparent for White and Black Caribbean women – as in Figures 3.2–3.3 – but is not significant for Indian and Pakistani/Bangladeshi women. Thus, despite earlier suggestions that marriage *per se* may lead to a reduction in economic activity for Pakistani/Bangladeshi women, this is not supported by this analysis. In addition, a partner from overseas has no negative effect for either Indian or Pakistani/Bangladeshi women – despite the suggestions from interviews that this might be the case. However, the expected positive effect of a working partner is present for White, Black Caribbean and Indian women but *not* for Pakistani/Bangladeshi women. The expected negative effect of a non-working partner is present for all groups except Black Caribbean women, where the effect is not significant.

CONCLUSIONS

From this analysis we can conclude that qualifications are, indeed, of overriding importance in Pakistani and Bangladeshi women's decisions to enter the labour market. The qualitative analysis has provided some pointers to explain the much lower levels of economic activity for women without qualifications – for whom family commitments, including caring for parents and children, are hard to refute and coincide with a lack of knowledge about the labour market, discriminatory appointment processes and an alien and sometimes hostile employment culture. For women who come to the UK as adults – often for marriage – there is an additional, negative impact which may, at least in part, be due to low proficiency in English. For these women, the notion of an 'individualised' lifestyle, with freedom to make choices and retain economic independence, seems remote. However, it is important to avoid any blanket assumptions as our interview evidence showed that some women clearly wanted to retain the economic and individual independence that came with paid work.

Our results suggest that any policy intervention designed to promote employment for Pakistani and Bangladeshi women should focus, first, on helping women attain qualifications and then, of equal importance, helping them overcome some of the barriers to the labour market. It is also important to stress the lack of any statistical evidence to suggest that marriage to a man from the country of origin has any negative effect of women's likelihood to join the labour market.

However, for White and Black Caribbean women, partnership has a positive effect on economic activity which, for Indian women, also becomes larger when the partner is working. For Black Caribbean women only, a non-working partner has no statistical effect on the likelihood of being economically active. This is consistent with arguments that Black Caribbean women, unlike white women, do not adjust their employment status to that of their partner. This, together with Black Caribbean women's high levels of lone motherhood and economic activity, provides support for the idea of individualisation. However, Reynolds (2005: 119) points out that Black Caribbean women may feel constrained by the need to balance full-time work and motherhood, and some would prefer more personal freedom and flexibility in their lives.

It is evident that the balance between paid work and family life varies considerably, not just across the life course but also by ethnic group. While historical and cultural factors play an important role in shaping family structures and gender roles, educational attainment also plays a central role in influencing women's response to these factors. However, this must also be seen in the wider labour market context where discriminatory barriers continue to challenge ethnic minority women's ability to find jobs which allow them to realise their potential as individuals.

ACKNOWLEDGEMENTS

We are grateful to the Office for National Statistics and the Economic and Social Data Service for making available the data from the Quarterly Labour Force Survey.

NOTES

1. For example, in September 2006 the Department of Communities and Local Government set out proposals to investigate the economic exclusion of minority ethnic women stating that: 'Ethnic minority communities overall have a lower employment rate than the rest of the population, and for Bangladeshi and Pakistani women it is particularly low – 24 per cent and 24.2 per cent respectively. The average employment rate for women of working age is 70 per cent.' (http://www.communities.gov.uk/news/corporate/governmentactionplan).
2. Children are defined as aged under 16 and living in the same household as their mother.
3. In Table 3.4, which models the predictors of economic activity, we include dummy variables to indicate whether children are under 5 or 5–15.
4. Table 3.4, using a logit model, does not use weighted data because we are interested in relative probabilities rather than population-level distributions.
5. Economic activity is based on ILO definitions and includes those who are either employed or unemployed.
6. There is an extensive body of literature which seeks to explain the differences in qualification levels between ethnic groups (for example Connor et al. 2004). These explanations include the fact that those with aspirations to better themselves are more likely to migrate

and the fact that qualifications provide an important way to overcome disadvantage in the labour market (for example, discrimination, lack of knowledge of the labour market and lack of networks).

7. The incidence of cohabitation amongst South Asian women is minimal and therefore we use the term 'husband' rather than 'partner' as it is a more accurate description of women's status.

REFERENCES

Ahmad, F., T. Modood and S. Lissenburgh (2003), *South Asian Women and Employment in Britain: The Interaction of Gender and Ethnicity*, London: PSI.

Ahmed, S. and A. Dale (2008), 'Pakistani and Bangladeshi women's labour market participation', CCSR Working Paper 2008-01.

Aston, J., H. Hooker, R. Page and R. Willison (2007), 'Pakistani and Bangladeshi women's attitudes to work and family', Research Report No 458, London: Department for Work and Pensions.

Beck, U. and E. Beck-Gernsheim (2001), *Individualization*. London: Sage.

Berthoud, R. (2005), 'Family formulation in multicultural Britain: diversity and change', in G. Loury, T. Modood and S. Teles (eds), *Ethnicity, Social Mobility, and Public Policy: Comparing the USA and UK*, Cambridge: Cambridge University Press, pp. 222–54.

Brah, A. and S. Shaw (1992), 'Working choices: South Asian women and the labour market', Department of Employment, Research Paper 91, London: HMSO.

Connor, H., C. Tyers, T. Modood and J. Hillage (2004), 'Why the difference? A closer look at higher education minority ethnic students and graduates', London: DfES Research Report RR552.

Dale, A., J. Lindley and S. Dex (2006), 'A life-course perspective on ethnic differences in women's economic activity in Britain', *European Sociological Review*, **22**(4) 459–76.

Dale, A., J. Lindley, S. Dex and A. Rafferty (2008), 'Ethnic differences in women's labour market activity', in J. Scott, S. Dex and H. Joshi (eds), *Women and Employment*, Cheltenham, UK and Northampton, MA, USA: Edward Elgar.

Dale, A., N. Shaheen, V. Kalra and E Fieldhouse (2002a), 'The labour market prospects for Pakistani and Bangladeshi women', *Work, Employment and Society*, **16**(1), 5–25.

Dale, A., N. Shaheen, V. Kalra and E. Fieldhouse (2002b), 'Routes into education and employment for young Pakistani and Bangladeshi women in the UK', *Ethnic and Racial Studies*, **25**(6), 942–68.

Dex, S. and H. Joshi (1996), 'A widening gulf among Britain's mothers', *Oxford Review of Economic Policy*, **12**(1), 65–75.

Dex, S., H. Joshi, S. Macran and A. McCulloch (1998), 'Women's employment transitions around childbearing', *Oxford Bulletin of Economics and Statistics*, **60**(1), 97–115.

Duncan, S. and S. Irwin (2004), 'The social patterning of values and rationalities: mothers' choices in combining caring and employment', *Social Policy and Society*, **3**(4), 391–9.

Esping-Andersen, G. (2002), 'A new gender contract', in G. Esping-Andersen, D.

Gallie, A. Hemerijck and J. Myles (eds), *Why We Need a New Welfare State*, Oxford: Oxford University Press.

Kalra, V. (2000), *From Textile Mills to Taxi Ranks: Experiences of Migration, Labour and Social Change*, Ashgate: Aldershot.

Leslie, D. and J. Lindley (2001), 'The impact of language ability on the employment and earnings of Britain's ethnic communities', *Economica*, **68**, pp. 587–606.

Lindley, J., A. Dale and S. Dex (2004), 'Ethnic differences in women's demographic, family characteristics and economic activity profiles, 1992–2002', *Labour Market Trends*, **112**(4), 153–65.

Modood, T., R. Berthoud and J. Lakey (1997), 'Ethnic minorities: diversity and disadvantage', Fourth PSI Study, London: PSI.

ONS (2008), website http://www.statistics.gov.uk/cci/nugget.asp?id=1654, accessed 2 January 2009.

Patterson, O. (2005), 'Four modes of ethno-somatic stratification: the experience of Blacks in Europe and the Americas', in G. Loury, T. Modood and S. Teles (eds), *Ethnicity, Social Mobility, and Public Policy: Comparing the USA and UK*, Cambridge: Cambridge University Press, pp. 67–122.

Reynolds, T. (2005), *Caribbean Mothers: Identity and Experience in the UK*, London: Tufnell Press.

Robinson, V. and R. Valeny (2005), 'Ethnic minorities, employment, self-employment, and social mobility in postwar Britain', in G. Loury, T. Modood and S. Teles (eds), *Ethnicity, Social Mobility, and Public Policy: Comparing the USA and UK*, Cambridge: Cambridge University Press, pp. 414–48.

Shaw, A. (2001), 'Kinship, cultural preferences and immigration: consanguineous marriage among British Pakistanis', *Journal Royal Anthropology Institute*, **7**, 315–34.

Tackey, N. D., J. Casebourne, J., Aston, H. Ritchie, A. Sinclair, C. Tyers, J. Hurstfield, R. Willison and R. Page (2006), 'Barriers to employment for Pakistanis and Bangladeshis in Britain', Research Report DWPRR 360, Department for Work and Pensions.

PART II

Occupational Structures and Welfare Regimes

4. Gender and the post-industrial shift

Janette Webb

INTRODUCTION

Economic restructuring in industries, work and occupations over the last century has transformed the lives of men and women, and the relationships between them, with rising standards of living, and greater economic independence for many women. During this period, the more affluent countries have typically undergone a considerable shift in the material basis of economic relations away from manufacturing towards services. The paid work available to men and women in such societies has changed considerably, with factory jobs becoming much less common, while office work, retail, leisure and welfare services have grown. On average, women are more likely to be active in the labour market for longer periods, and are becoming more significant figures, alongside men, in public life.

This chapter focuses on the relatively recent changes in women's and men's paid work and occupations in four different countries – the UK, USA, Sweden and Japan – each exemplifying a form of advanced capitalism. It considers whether the apparently universal 'post-industrial shift' in these countries is accompanied by growing commonality in gender relations in employment, or whether there are meaningful differences between countries which derive from distinctive societal and cultural formations. Each of the four countries typifies the 'post-industrial shift' described above: employment in extractive industries, manufacturing, utilities and construction is in decline, relative to employment in business, commercial and welfare services. Although this trend is shared, each country has a different trajectory of industrial, and post-industrial, development and employment relations, and each one has pursued distinct political-economic policies: the UK and USA are examples of neoliberalism, with the state enabling deregulated markets and less employment protection, while Sweden and Japan represent contrasting variants of coordinated market economies, with higher levels of employment protection. Sweden's history of social democracy is also associated with more egalitarian social relations and recognition of individual rights (Lyon and Glucksmann 2008), while Japan's historically paternalistic politics have been associated with greater continuity in traditional family life, with more limited autonomy for women (Kumamoto-Healey 2005).

Three main questions are addressed here: the first concerns whether there is a difference between the more liberal and the more coordinated market economies in their impact on inequality between the sexes; the second asks whether the effects of any differences in political-economy are overridden by a universalising neo-patriarchal logic embedded in post-industrialism, which reinforces sexual divisions by entrenching occupational segregation; the third asks whether cultural differences between societies mean that neither political-economy nor universal neo-patriarchal forces can account for the particular patterns of inequality in men's and women's employment. If this is the case, then research would need to give greater explanatory significance to historical trajectories of gendered social relations, and to the nuances of gender ideology embedded in political-economic policies. The frame of reference for these questions is derived from two contrasting feminist theories: varieties of capitalism (VOC) (Estevez-Abe 2005; Soskice 2005) and post-industrialism (Charles 2005). The VOC model treats the spheres of markets and gender relations as independent from one another, with markets regarded as driving change in interaction with the social relations of gender. In contrast, feminist post-industrialism asserts that the logic of neo-patriarchal relations governs the economic. A contingent sociological model of changes in material inequality would argue that neither the 'economic' nor the 'social' realms are predominant, but that the economic relations of markets are constituted, and operate, through cultural rules of gender relations and sexual divisions.

VARIETIES OF CAPITALISM: THE FEMINIST INTERPRETATION

In a feminist re-interpretation of theories about the relative competitiveness of different varieties of capitalism, Estevez-Abe (2005) argues that liberal market economies (LMEs) are more conducive to sex equality than coordinated market economies (CMEs). In particular, women and men are expected to be more equally represented across occupations in liberal economic systems than they are in coordinated systems. This prediction is derived from an argument about the differences in the kinds of skills valued by employers in each regime, and in the associated welfare policies. LMEs are described as giving priority to education and training for general skills in a deregulated, individualised, labour market, where corporations aim to maximise short-term profitability. CMEs in contrast are described as prioritising longer-term investment in specific skills, oriented to particular industries and employers. In the latter context, economic and employee relations give more emphasis to coordination between the interests of the state, labour, finance capital and employers.

Different underlying skills regimes, and their associated employment practices, are expected to produce differential outcomes for men and women, because 'specific skills discriminate against women, whereas general skills are more gender neutral' (Estevez-Abe 2005: 181). Employers in CMEs, with stronger apprenticeships and vocational training, are expected to discriminate against women when deciding who to train, because of underlying beliefs that women are more likely to take breaks in employment to raise children, and hence to prioritise their husband's careers. LMEs are expected to place greater value on general, portable skills, and less value on long-term embedded skills, knowledge and loyalty, stimulating greater occupational mobility in a more fluid labour market, which it is argued results in less sex segregation.

Differences in social and welfare policies between LMEs and CMEs may, however, work to mediate the effects of employer preferences and skills regimes, with varying results for inequality between men and women. Investment by governments in public services has been associated with the growth of health, education and welfare professions. The conventional association of women with an ideology of caring as feminine has contributed to women being seen as suited to such professions, while the expansion of higher education has enabled women to gain the required formal credentials. In social democratic states such as Sweden, the state is the primary source of care provision and the primary employer of care workers (Lyon and Glucksmann 2008). The Swedish public welfare sector has a female-dominated work force, with considerable lower-paid, routine care work (Domeij and Ljungqvist 2006), as well as a relatively large number of higher paid professional and associated roles. The result is a pattern of horizontal occupational segregation, with women dominating the public, and men the private, sector. The implications for equality are disputed: Blackburn and Jarman's (2005) study of gender and social democratic states concludes that horizontal segregation produces differential, but equal, career opportunities for men and women, in a relatively egalitarian pay structure. Other work, however, reports that there is a 'career penalty' associated with women's concentration in public services. The high volume of more routinised care work, with limited career prospects, is seen as a barrier to women moving into higher-paid occupations (Bihagen and Ohls 2006). Nevertheless, income inequality between the sexes is lower in countries with stronger social democratic policies and better welfare and family provision. Mandel and Semyonov's (2005) analysis of labour market data for 22 countries concludes that women's labour market participation is facilitated by a developed welfare state, but that it is those same provisions for family and income support which result in greater sex equality, rather than women's improved access to higher-paid occupations. This suggests that the more individualised opportunity structures expected in LMEs may offer the potential for higher achievement for some women, but at the cost of higher levels of overall inequality. If the number of women gaining access to high-paid occupations is relatively small, then overall inequality between men and women is likely to be higher as well.

FEMINIST POST-INDUSTRIALISM

This alternative model of occupational segregation and sex equality suggests that different varieties of capitalism are less important as determinants of gender relations than the process of post-industrialism itself. In this model, a universal process is seen as working to marginalise women and to confine them to subordinate service roles. In her analysis of occupational segregation in ten market economies, Maria Charles (2005) concludes that the force of an institutionalised, dualistic and 'naturalised' ideology of gender difference, combined with highly rationalised service sector expansion, overrides any distinctions between varieties of capitalism. The result of post-industrial economic restructuring is to entrench, and even intensify, segregation and inequality. Her analysis highlights the remarkable continuity across services-dominated countries in the work done by women in routinised caring, clerical, sales and service roles. In these terms post-industrialism is a process imbued with an ideology of gender which allocates women to secondary economic roles:

> Among other things, this occurs through the symbolic association of women with tasks central to many rapidly growing service sector occupations and through workplace adaptations (e.g., provisions for part-time work) aimed at attracting women with extensive domestic obligations into the expanding lower non-manual sector of the economy' (p. 370).

Both of these accounts of the workings of markets and post-industrial restructuring offer valuable insights into the differential work experiences of men and women in contemporary capitalism. In proposing an explanation which relies largely on political-economic processes in the case of VOC, and a universalising gender ideology in the case of feminist post-industrialism, both are however reliant on macro-level concepts to explain complex patterns of social, cultural and political change. The distinction between liberal and coordinated market economies may be too simple to capture significant differences in gendered economic relations in different social and political contexts: the UK and the USA have both pursued neo-liberal economic models, while Sweden and Japan are both characterised as coordinated market economies, but each remain distinct societies by virtue of their histories of industrialisation, labour organisation, sexual divisions, state welfare provision and political structures.

Such societal differences also suggest that apparently similar post-industrial developments may have different precursors and different implications for divisions of class and gender. In their comparative study of North American and Nordic post-industrial societies, Clement and Myles (1994) conclude that the effects of post-industrial services development are powerfully mediated by politics. The quality of post-industrial jobs, and the distribution of occupational skills, autonomy and authority between the sexes, and between social classes, are the result of political differences between states, with different outcomes in different circumstances. In the 1980s, post-industrialism in neoliberal states, such as the USA, with weaker trade union organisation, stimulated the growth of a significant 'new' middle class of service managers and administrators, as well as a smaller poorly paid working class with few employment protections. The social democratic politics of the Nordic countries, however, resulted in a post-industrialism associated with a smaller 'new' middle class of business service managers, and a larger group of skilled workers in public services, as well as a larger working class with a significant public sector component. The latter group had higher levels of employment protection than working-class service employees in North American countries. On both sides of the Atlantic the resulting working classes were segmented by gender: women predominantly made up the service workers, while men continued to dominate the remaining manual production jobs. Variations in post-industrial employment patterns between countries were in fact 'experienced mainly by women' (Clement and Myles p. 35). Women benefited from the provisions for family and welfare in Nordic countries, but their opportunities for occupational mobility were curtailed in comparison with North America, particularly for those working part-time. There may be significant limits therefore to the explanatory power of any model predicting universal outcomes from labour market trajectories which appear similar at a macro level.

INDUSTRIES AND OCCUPATIONS IN THE LABOUR MARKETS OF THE UK, USA, SWEDEN AND JAPAN, 1985–2005

Both VOC and feminist post-industrialism derive their conclusions from labour market data from the 1990s. They use data sets specially designed to provide a detailed breakdown of occupational classifications by sex, but the significance of industrial sector is not considered. Given the pace of restructuring, 1990s data cannot offer a picture of recent evolution and change in the service sector. Neither can occupational data which are not disaggregated by industrial sector provide a strong evaluation of the thesis that post-industrial restructuring drives processes of segregation. Charles (2005) equates non-manual work with post-industrialism, but this conflates a manual/non-manual distinction with industrial sector, and may exaggerate the extent of post-industrial shift, or the extent of sex segregation.

The publicly available labour market data used here are derived from ILO statistics[1] compiled by each country. They are not sufficiently robust to provide a conclusive empirical evaluation of the two frameworks, but they do enable some critical questions to be explored. The data must be interpreted cautiously for a number of reasons. First they provide only a very broad occupational breakdown, which means that occupational segregation cannot be measured in a precise way. Second occupations are social constructs, and standard classification schemes are periodically revised, in line with shifts in the underlying industrial structure. Institutional logics of education and training interact with work organisation to produce particular societal patterns of work and employment (Maurice et al. 1980). Over time, occupations with the same title may vary in skill level, responsibility, exercise of discretion and so on. The skill composition and status of the 'same' occupation is also likely to vary from one country to another. Each of these factors causes problems of validity and reliability of cross-country comparisons over time. There are particular caveats to be made in relation to comparisons of managerial occupations. Tasks classified as specialist managerial jobs in one country may be regarded as integral to all skilled and semi-skilled work in another: the history of industrialisation in the USA demonstrates the emphasis given to direct control and supervision of labour by specialist managers, while Japan's work organisation relied historically on developing a technically skilled work force, with fewer management specialists. Nevertheless, and while recognising the need for caution in interpretation, such data enable more recent comparison of employment in different countries, and allow some mapping of change over time. The problem of aggregate occupational categories, such as the use of one broad category combining all higher-level public officials with all senior private sector managers, is compensated for to some extent by the ability to disaggregate occupation by industrial sector. The exploration of changes in occupational structure by industry should also cast light on the extent to which growth in services is universal, and enable some evaluation of the interrelations between service

Table 4.1   *Economic activity: relative proportions of men and women in the four countries*

	Sweden		USA		UK		Japan	
	1984	2004	1985	2005	1985	2005	1985	2005
% men	53	52	56	54	58	53	60	59
% women	47	48	44	46	42	47	40	41
Total N (000s)	4391	4459	117167	149320	24539	28166	59630	66500

Source: Reproduced from Webb (2009).

sector expansion, occupational change and relative occupational concentrations of men and women. Consistent patterns within the data over time also mean that a degree of confidence in the validity of observed changes is reasonable. Given the limitations of the data, the focus here is on descriptive statistics which show the relative proportions, and concentrations, of men and women in particular occupational groups and industries. These are used to explore the interactions of gender and labour markets, and to comment on the relationships between post-industrial restructuring and the occupational positioning of women and men in different societies, with distinctive political economies.

Women's and Men's Employment in the UK, USA, Sweden and Japan

The proportion of women in the working populations of the UK, USA, Sweden and Japan has increased since the 1980s, in conjunction with a growing work force in each case. This is most marked in the UK, where women have increased from 42 per cent to 47 per cent of employees. The UK, USA and Sweden now have similar proportions of men and women employees, while Japan continues to have the most male-dominated work force (59 per cent male/41 per cent female) (Table 4.1).

Post-industrial Shift in the UK, USA, Sweden and Japan?

In each country, there is evidence of an ongoing shift in the basis of economic activity away from material production to services. Over the last two decades, there is a marked growth in the proportion of all employment in service industries, relative to work directly concerned with production. In the UK, USA and Sweden, less than a quarter of the employed population now work in industries concerned with mining, utilities, manufacturing

Table 4.2   Change in the relative proportions of employment in extractive and transformative industries[a] and in services[b]

% by col.	Sweden		USA		UK		Japan	
Industry[c]	1984	2004	1985	2005	1985	2005	1985	2005
Extractive & transformative	34%	23%	31%	21%	34%	23%	42%	31%
Services	63	71	66	74	65	76	54	64
Other[d]	3	6	3	5	1	1	4	5

Notes:
a. Extractive and transformative industries are defined as agriculture, forestry and fishing, mining and quarrying, manufacturing, electricity, gas and water and construction.
b. Services are defined as wholesale, retail and repairs, hotels and restaurants, transport, communications and storage, finance, real estate and business services, community, social and personal services and employees in private households.
c. 1984/5 data is based on ISIC Revision 2. 2004/5 is based on ISIC Revision 3.
d. Different conventions of classification result in differences between the composition of the 'Other' category, as follows. Sweden: 1984 – unemployed; 2004 – not classified plus unemployed. USA: 1985 – not classified plus armed forces plus those unemployed looking for first job; 2005 – unemployed. UK: 1985 – unclassified; 2005 – unclassified plus extra-territorial. Japan: 1985 – unclassified plus unemployed; 2005 – unclassified plus unemployed.

Source: Reproduced from Webb (2009).

and construction. Even in Japan, where 42 per cent of employees worked in production in 1985, less than a third of employees now work in such industries. For a growing majority therefore, the normative experience of work is of services provision, whether in the public or the private sector, or in routinised, low-paid leisure, retail and personal care, or in higher-paid professions and management (Table 4.2).

At the same time that the balance of employment has shifted to services, male dominance of remaining work in production has increased. This is most evident in Japan, where women's employment appears to be converging with the pattern in the UK, USA and Sweden (Figure 4.1), such that women are now only 28 per cent of production employees.

Since employment in service industries is the norm for both sexes, it is instructive to look at change in the relative proportion of men and women in all services (Figure 4.2). This suggests again a degree of convergence between Japan and the other three countries in the pattern of women's concentration in service sector employment. In every case except Japan, women were already more than half of service industry employees in the 1980s. Only in Japan were men in the majority, with 65 per cent of jobs. Even in 2005, men remained in the majority (52 per cent), although the

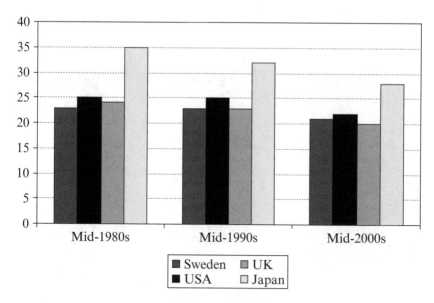

Source: Reproduced from Webb (2009).

Figure 4.1 *Women as a proportion of all employees in extractive and transformative industries*

proportion of women had increased considerably. In contrast in Sweden, with the most female-dominated service sector (60 per cent) in the mid-1980s, the opposite pattern is discernible: between then and 2004, men increased as a proportion of service sector workers from 40 per cent to 43 per cent.

It is difficult to be sure about the factors responsible for these opposing patterns of change without more detailed research. Part of the overall growth of service industry employment, relative to employment in production, may be accounted for by jobs being reclassified from production to services, even though their content remains much the same. This happens for example as the result of increased sub-contracting by large manufacturers, such that services previously provided in-house are now contracted out (Lynn 2005), and the associated jobs correspondingly reclassified as services. This may affect the relative proportions of men and women classified as services employees. For example, to the extent that men are the dominant group in IT, or related technical and business, services, these areas of work may be more likely to appear now as service sector jobs, because of sub-contracting in manufacturing. This should, however, also affect the classification of jobs more likely to be done by women, such as

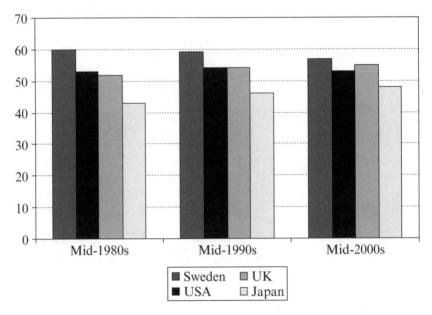

Source: Reproduced from Webb (2009).

Figure 4.2   Women as a proportion of all employees in service sector employment

those in catering and cleaning, or PR and marketing. Hence the global picture may disguise the particular forms of economic restructuring, but it seems unlikely that change in relative proportion of men and women in services is simply an artefact of the reclassification of certain jobs.

Charles's argument that post-industrialism universally reinforces the concentration of women in services thus receives some support, in that women's employment is indeed becoming more services-dominated, but this overall pattern is mediated by cultural and political processes. Given the increase in men as a proportion of services' employees in Sweden, it seems that post-industrial developments do not inevitably reinforce existing sex-segregation.

Do Liberal Market Economies give Women Greater Access to Career Occupations?

Regardless of post-industrial change, the feminist VOC model suggests that women are more likely to reach higher levels of occupations in LMEs, because of their more flexible, individualised employment and career opportunities, which are deemed to rely less on continuous service and organisation-specific skills. This expectation can be examined to some degree by a comparison between women's and men's presence in higher-level managerial, professional and associated occupations in the four countries. If the VOC model is correct, women should be better represented overall in these occupational groups in the UK and USA than in Sweden and Japan.

Figure 4.3a–d illustrates the differential representation of women and men in professional, technical and associated occupations, in comparison with managerial and administrative roles. In all cases, women are better represented in professional, associate professional and technical occupations, while men are always the dominant group in managerial and administrative occupations. Even in the most male-dominated work force in Japan (Figure Fig 4.3d), women are now 46 per cent of professional and related employees. This is in striking contrast to the 90 per cent of managerial occupations done by men. It is important to note, however, that both Japan and Sweden categorise only a small proportion of the work force as managers (3 per cent in Japan in 2005; 5 per cent in Sweden in 2004). In contrast, the UK classified 15 per cent of occupations as managerial in 2005, and the USA 14 per cent. This distinction in underlying occupational structures reflects the divergent histories of work organisation, which affect not only the creation of specialist management occupations, but also who is deemed suitable and acceptable in managerial roles. The USA is unique among the four countries in the significantly higher proportion (42 per cent) of women managers in 2005, in comparison with a 64/36 per cent split in 1985 (Figure 4.3b). The larger proportion of jobs classified as managerial in the USA and UK is likely to include a larger number of lower-level positions. Hence a more disaggregated analysis of this category would probably reveal considerable internal segregation, with women concentrated in less prestigious jobs.

Nevertheless for the two LME countries, the USA and the UK, with similar proportions of managerial occupations, the considerable difference in women's representation suggests that women have gained wider access to management jobs in the USA. Women comprised 34 per cent of managers and administrators in the UK in 2005, with little change since 1995. This is similar to the proportion of managerial occupations done by women in Sweden, whose presence has increased from 21 per cent in 1984 to 32 per cent in 2004. Given that Sweden has a very low proportion of specialised managerial occupations, this implies that women's access to higher-level managerial roles is at least as good as that in the UK. In professional, technical and associated occupations, women are the majority group in both the USA (56 per cent in 2005) and Sweden (52 per cent in

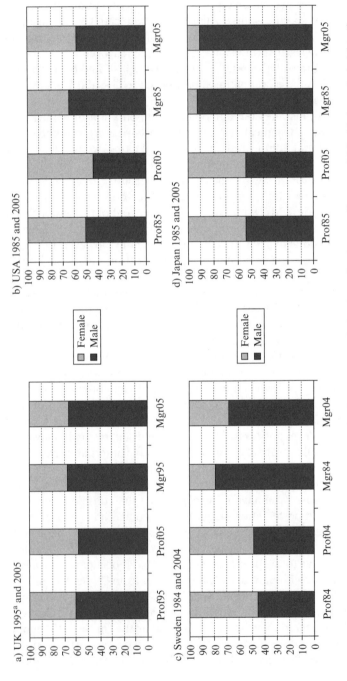

Notes: * Occupations grouped as follows: prof – all professional, technical and associated; mgr – all managerial, legislative and administrative.
ᵃ UK data compare 1995 with 2005, because no occupational breakdown by sex is available for 1985.

*Figure 4.3   Proportion of women and men in professional and managerial occupations**

2004). In the UK and Japan, men continue to be the majority group, with 58 per cent and 54 per cent of these jobs respectively.

This summary data suggests that there is no simple causal relationship between LME policies and greater access to higher-level occupations for women. The USA appears as the best fit to the model, with women increasing their presence in managerial, professional and related roles between 1985 and 2005. Counter to the feminist VOC model, however, women in the UK have experienced little change in access to higher-level professional or managerial occupations over the last decade. In Sweden women's share of managerial roles is similar to that in the UK, albeit Sweden classifies very few occupations as managerial. On the basis of this evidence, countries where liberal market policies are in place do not uniformly provide greater opportunities for women to gain access to higher-level occupations than countries where coordinated market policies are the norm. The pattern of men's and women's distribution among these occupations in the four countries suggests that, even if the relationship between labour market policies and skill regime is as predicted by feminist VOC, this does not necessarily translate into similar opportunity structures. It does, however, raise questions about the kinds of skills which are valued in different countries, and in different sectors, and the extent to which men and women have similar access to the full range of skilled occupations. Even these summary data suggest that skill regimes are more complex than envisaged by a feminist VOC model, and are likely to be shaped by cultural beliefs and practices concerned, among other things, with a gendered construct of skill and an associated hierarchy of value placed on different kinds of skill.

Are Women Increasingly Concentrated in Service Occupations?

If the feminist post-industrial model is accurate, then women should be increasingly concentrated in occupations associated with an ideology of femininity as equipping women for service and caring, notably in clerical and secretarial, as well as retail sales and welfare occupations. This pattern should hold regardless of differential market policies. Moreover this concentration should have increased over time. Comparison here is between the USA, Sweden and Japan only, with the UK excluded because of the change in UK occupational classifications for service and sales in the period 1995–2005.[2] In the USA, Sweden and Japan, the greater consistency in proportions of men and women in clerical and sales and service jobs over time suggests more consistent use of occupational categories (see Figure 4.4a–c).

The observed pattern does not provide straightforward support for a

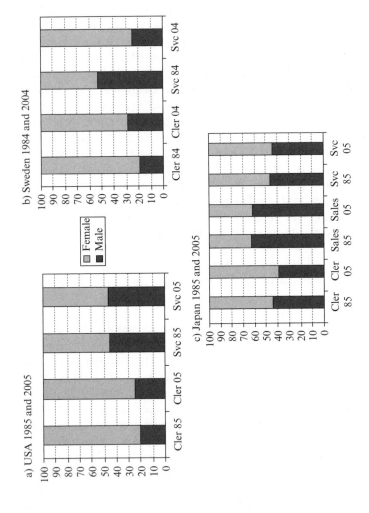

Note: ^a Occupations grouped as Cler – all clerical and secretarial; Svc – all routine service and sales occupations, except for Japan where sales and service are shown separately.

Figure 4.4   Women and men in clerical, secretarial and sales and services occupations^a

feminist post-industrialism model. Clerical and secretarial jobs are not universally more feminised. In both Sweden and the USA the proportion of men has increased slightly over 20 years. In services and sales, men retain the majority of sales occupations in Japan, perhaps stemming from the greater presence of production industries where sales jobs may be defined as technical and identified as masculine. In other cases, there is little change in the relative concentration of women in routine service occupations, although they are always the dominant group. Only in Sweden has the proportion of women noticeably increased (from 47 per cent in 1984 to 75 per cent in 2004), although again this may be partly the result of the reclassification of certain occupations. It is, however, Sweden which has the largest concentration of routinised, relatively low-paid service work related to state provision of welfare, and these jobs are dominated by women (Domeij and Ljungqvist 2006).

Men's and Women's Representation in Managerial and Clerical/Secretarial Occupations

The aim of this section is to take the above analysis a step further by examining what happens when relative occupational concentrations of men and women in managerial, or clerical/secretarial, work are examined separately for three industrial groups: (1) production, (2) business and financial services, and (3) personal and social services. If the feminist VOC model is broadly accurate, then in the two LMEs, the USA and UK, where similar percentages of occupations are classified as managerial, women should be similarly represented in managerial occupations across the different sectors. This is because they are assumed to be individually competing for jobs in a general skills framework with higher labour market mobility than in CMEs, and with less expected skills barriers between production and service sectors, or between social and commercial services. It follows that a feminist VOC model would also predict that, because women should have more equal access to higher-level occupations in LMEs, then they should also be less concentrated in clerical and secretarial roles. In CMEs, the reverse pattern should be observed, with women having less access to the small proportion of managerial work, and being more concentrated in clerical jobs. A feminist post-industrial model on the other hand would predict increasing concentration of women in clerical and secretarial occupations in all countries and sectors over time. The conclusions drawn from this comparison are tentative, given the limitations of the ILO data and the problem that work classified as 'managerial' differs in different societies.

Figure 4.5 shows the differential access of women to management

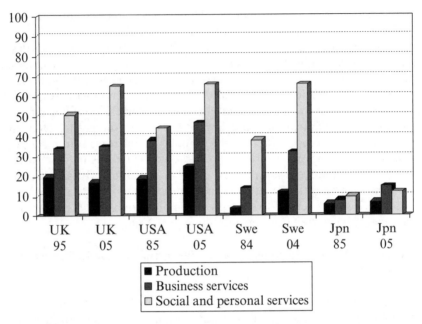

Figure 4.5 *Percentage of managerial occupations held by women in three industrial sectors (production, business services, and social and personal services)*

and related jobs in different sectors, as well as highlighting the divergent changes between countries over time. Women's presence in production management is higher in the LME, than in the CME, countries, but women are differentially represented in managerial roles in different sectors in every country. In all cases, women are far more likely to be in management and administrative roles in social and personal services than in production. In the former sector their presence has increased over time, to the extent that they comprise around two-thirds of such managers in the UK, USA and Sweden. In Japan, very few women are represented in any management jobs, although their presence has increased since 1985, and they are slightly better represented in business services than in personal and social services. In the UK the proportion of women in production management has declined slightly since 1995. There is no strong support in these data for a feminist VOC model of better opportunities for women to access any managerial role in LMEs in comparison with CMEs. There may, however, be qualified support in the sense that women in the USA have the highest level of representation in production, and the UK is next. This is true also for business and commercial services. In Sweden,

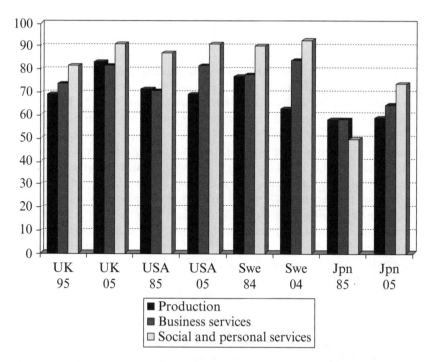

Figure 4.6   *Percentage of clerical occupations held by women in three industrial sectors (production, business services and social and personal services)*

however, women's access to management in each of these sectors, as well as in social services, increased rapidly between 1984 and 2004, to the extent that women in Sweden and in the UK have a similar proportion of managerial jobs in commercial, and in social, services. Since both Japan and Sweden have a small percentage of jobs categorised as managerial, it is necessary to be cautious about the broader significance of these differences for equality of access to senior occupations. The similar proportions of women managers in Sweden and the UK, however, imply that women are gaining relatively good access to senior roles in Sweden, where the small numbers of management occupations seem less likely to include lower-level jobs. In Japan, with the most traditional sexual divisions of labour and the most male-dominated work force, women remain largely excluded from managerial occupations, especially in production.

The picture for clerical occupations is in striking contrast (see Figure 4.6). Counter to a feminist VOC model, women's concentration in clerical and secretarial roles in the UK has increased over time in all sectors, while in the USA they are less dominant in production than they were in 1985, but more dominant in both commercial and social services. For the CME countries, women are not uniformly more concentrated in clerical support roles. Data for Sweden shows a more marked decline in women in clerical roles in production, from 77 per cent to 63 per cent, but a growing concentration of women among clerical workers in services. In Japan, men remain more significant as clerical workers than in any other country, but the pattern is differentiated by sector, and the increase in women's concentration is ubiquitous, although most marked in social and personal services (50 per cent to 74 per cent). It is certainly not the case that LME policies in the USA and UK have uniformly facilitated less concentration of women in clerical and secretarial support roles over time; Sweden and the USA appear more similar than the USA and the UK, while it is in Japan that men retain the greatest presence in such jobs. The feminist post-industrial model seems to be in this case a better predictor of the direction of change, particularly if it is assumed that the decline of women in clerical roles in production in the USA and Sweden is consistent with a dynamic of post-industrialism which locks women more firmly into service roles.

SOCIETAL DISTINCTIVENESS: VARIATION AND COMPLEXITY IN GENDER RELATIONS AND OCCUPATIONAL DIVISIONS

This brief exploration of gender and occupational change in different countries shows the complex interactions between political economy, labour market opportunity structures and occupations in different countries. Both VOC and feminist post-industrialism offer valuable insights into the significance of gender in occupational structures, but the different sexual divisions in the four countries cannot be accounted for solely by the macro-level variables of political economy or neo-patriarchal post-industrialism. Employment in each country is marked by some shared trends; notably there is growing concentration of work in services, and post-industrial work has been universally associated with increased concentration of men in production, while women continue to be concentrated in services. There is striking resilience and continuity in horizontal dimensions of occupational sex-segregation. In managerial, professional and clerical occupations, women are more likely to be found in social and personal services than in business services or in production. Each of these common trends lends weight to a feminist post-industrialism argument that there is a neo-patriarchal logic at work which reinforces women's disadvantage. Counter to predictions by feminist post-industrialism, however, pre-existing patterns of segregation have not been universally reinforced or deepened. Post-industrialism *per se* does not produce more entrenched sex-segregation, any more than it undermines it. It is not a unitary variable and the labour markets of the four countries examined have not converged around identical patterns of occupational segregation. Instead a more complex picture emerges of a post-industrial shift where political economy interacts with distinct societal patterns of gender relations and associated formal sex-equality measures to facilitate women's movement into a wider range of occupations. This is the case even in Japan, the country with the most traditional attitudes to the role of women.

These common trends are given different substantive expression in each country, according to historical relations between organised labour, employers and the state, and associated attitudes to social solidarity and sex equality. The composition of services and the types and quality of jobs available differ between countries, as does the likelihood of more or less egalitarian access to them. In particular, where men and women are more highly organised through trade unions, and social democratic values are more firmly embedded, then the difference in power relations means that employers are more constrained, and average quality of working life is higher (Gallie 2007). Among the four countries, Sweden is distinctive by virtue of the strength of egalitarian and solidaristic values, expressed through its history of democratic government and the highest density of trade union membership with a high proportion of women members (Gallie 2007). Sweden also continues to have the most universal social welfare provisions (Lyon and Glucksmann 2008), and the Swedish corporatism of the 1970s has adapted to changing global competition (Anxo and Niklasson 2006), with positive consequences for women's opportunities and access to careers. A limitation of both VOC and post-industrial theories is therefore the lack of recognition of societal differences in gendered power relations between organised labour and employers, their significance for political economy, and the consequences for sex equality.

Nor do the data suggest that liberal market economy policies inevitably result in less occupational sex-segregation. The LME policies pursued by the USA and UK, emphasising individualism and career mobility in deregulated labour markets, have not had the same outcomes. Again societal differences matter and women's role in the UK labour market remains different from that in the USA. In the UK, a high proportion of women work in low-paid part-time jobs, and are regarded as secondary income earners, in a labour market with considerable polarisation between women part-timers and men working long hours (Fagan and Burchell 2002; Warren 2008). While some women in the UK may have benefited from more individualised career routes, increasing inequality since the 1980s seems to have resulted in an opportunity structure which is less favourable to women than that in Sweden. In the UK in 2005, for example, barriers to women entering managerial occupations appear no lower than in Sweden, despite a larger proportion of jobs classified as managerial, and the Swedish social democratic model appears more effective in moving women into professional and associated occupations. In the USA, women are mostly in full-time employment, they are more likely to be continuously active in the labour market, and are better represented in managerial and professional and associated jobs, but long hours working in the USA imposes high costs on social life (Fuchs Epstein and Kalleberg 2004).

Further work would also be needed to demonstrate that the labour market experiences of women in the USA are the result of a skills regime which places a high value on general, rather than specific, skills, and that women and men have similar access to all grades of managerial work. There is no strong evidence that employers have been more inclined to treat women's and men's labour as interchangeable for the purposes of training and skills development. Women are unlikely to have the same authority as men in higher-level occupations, and 'when women and minorities hold positions of authority, they do so at lower levels of organizations. Furthermore, they receive lower returns for their positions than white men' (Di Tomaso et al. 2007: 477). From a feminist perspective, skill is not simply about technique, knowledge or formal credentials; instead skills are defined, and their particular value is negotiated, in the context of a pre-existing gendered hierarchy of occupations. The USA and UK classify a far higher proportion of occupations as managerial, raising the question of whether similar jobs might be classified as clerical or routine service occupations in Sweden and Japan. The social construction of managerial work, the definition of necessary skills, and the gendered assumptions about who is competent to fulfil such roles merit more scrutiny.

Different cultural norms also affect the particular forms of occupational segregation and their social reproduction. This is most evident in this case in Japan, which exemplifies a country where, despite formal sex equality, women continue to have a more marginal role in the labour market. The main reasons for this are the continuity of gendered forms of work organisation in a male-dominated corporate culture, with male-dominated enterprise unions, reinforcing patronising attitudes to women, their skills and their value (Benson et al. 2007). These practices result in the relative exclusion of women from tasks and experiences regarded as fitting people for responsible and demanding jobs. Organisations, for example, continue to operate differential rules for men and women seeking management training (Kumamoto-Healey 2005):

Japanese companies exclude women from the opportunity to accumulate company-specific human capital and expect them to leave the paid labour force after marrying male employees or bearing children and to dedicate themselves to household tasks (Fujimoto 2005: 653).

In recruitment to job vacancies, established connections between colleges and large firms result in women being routed into conventionally feminine support roles where they are seen as contributing to the role of the firm in upholding the marriage market and the male breadwinner model (Fujimoto 2005).

Historically the Japanese state has demonstrated a paternalistic attitude to women, such that measures concerned with 'protection' have dominated over those concerned with sex equality (Kumamoto-Healey 2005). Rapid economic growth after the 1950s led to rapid increase in women's labour market participation, particularly in part-time work, but this was also associated with a widening gap in incomes between men and women, and Japan continues to have one of the highest levels of sex inequality in any affluent country (Benson et al. 2007). Nevertheless, progressively stronger employment law has made discrimination in recruitment, training, promotion and pay illegal (Kumamoto-Healey 2005). A globalised economy and long-term recession in Japan, combined with more egalitarian attitudes among younger workers, have also eroded company commitment to lifetime employment and seniority reward systems. Together these processes suggest that there is likely to be some convergence with other market economies in attitudes to gender roles, with more opportunity for women to gain access to a wider range of occupations.

CONCLUSION

Continuing differences between societies in their articulation of economic policies through different social values means that any comparative typology will be limited in its ability to explain patterns of variation in occupational sex segregation. The feminist VOC theory draws attention to the potential significance of different political-economic policies for segregation, and the feminist post-industrial perspective highlights the continuing power of dualistic gender ideologies in all countries. Each provides valuable directions for feminist research. In order to account for the observed patterns of segregation in the UK, USA, Sweden and Japan, we need, however, to take more seriously the historical development of gendered employment relations in each country. From this sociological perspective, market economies are irreducibly cultural constructs, which are derived from distinct social relations and institutions (Haas et al. 2006; Fligstein and Dauter 2007). Different approaches to economic life, and different social values, are embedded via political decisions, as is most obvious here in the contrast between social democracies like Sweden, versus neoliberal societies like the USA. Cultural differences inflect the 'universalising' instrumental logics of labour markets and skills hierarchies with local and particular meanings, with material consequences for the class, gender and ethnic divisions manifest in occupations. What is seen as legitimate employment practice in relation to men and women in the UK is different from that in Sweden, Japan or the USA, by virtue of culturally framed assumptions and the history of organised labour and capital (Gallie 2007; Thelen 2004). The implications of this sociological model of gender and markets are for example that apparently similar political-economic frameworks will be understood and enacted differently in different societies, depending on the social relations which give them particular meaning and substance. Gender and markets are mutually constitutive; their particular trajectories are governed by different cultural and political values, and contest over the fairness and legitimacy of resulting social divisions.

NOTES

1. All labour market data derived from ILO Labour Statistics, available at www.laborsta. ilo.org, accessed 1 August 2007.
2. Examination of the classifications suggests that jobs mainly done by men in the manufacturing sector were classified as 'service and sales' in 1995, but reclassified as 'craft' occupations in 2005. Conversely for women, jobs in wholesale and retail sectors were classified as 'craft' occupations in 1995, but reclassified as 'services and sales' occupations in 2005.

BIBLIOGRAPHY

Anxo, D. and H. Niklasson (2006), 'The Swedish model in turbulent times: decline or renaissance?', *International Labour Review*, **145**, 339–71.
Benson, J., M. Yuasa and P. Debroux (2007), 'The prospect for gender diversity in Japanese employment', *International Journal of Human Resource Management*, **18**, 890–907.
Bihagen, E. and M. Ohls (2006), 'The glass ceiling – where is it? Women's and men's career prospects in the private vs. the public sector in Sweden 1979–2000', *Sociological Review*, **54**, 20–47.
Blackburn, R. and J. Jarman (2005), 'Gendered occupations: exploring the relationship between gender segregation and inequality', *GeNet Working Paper No. 5*.

Charles, M. (2005), 'National skill regimes, postindustrialism and sex segregation', *Social Politics*, **12**(2), 289–316.

Clement, W. and J. Myles (1994), *Relations of Ruling: Class and Gender in Post-Industrial Societies*, Montreal and Kingston: McGill-Queens University Press.

Crompton, R. (ed.) (1999), *Restructuring Gender Relations and Employment*, Oxford: Oxford University Press.

Di Tomaso, N., C. Post and R. Parks-Yancy (2007), 'Workforce diversity and inequality: power, status, and numbers', *Annual Review of Sociology*, **33**, 473–501.

Domeij, D. and L. Ljungqvist (2006), 'Wage structure and public sector employment: Sweden versus the United States 1970–2002', Stockholm School of Economics SSE/EFI Working Papers in Economics and Finance No. 638.

Estevez-Abe, M. (2005), 'Gender bias in skills and social policies: the varieties of capitalism perspective on sex segregation', *Social Politics*, **12**(2), 180–215.

Fagan, C. and B. Burchell (2002), *Gender, Jobs and Working Conditions in the European Union*, Dublin: European Foundation for the Improvement of Living and Working Conditions.

Fligstein, N. and L. Dauter (2007), 'The sociology of markets', *Annual Review of Sociology*, **33**, 105–28.

Fuchs Epstein, C. and A. Kalleberg (2004), *Fighting For Time: Shifting Boundaries of Work and Social Life*, New York: Russell Sage Foundation.

Fujimoto, K. (2005), 'From women's college to work: inter-organizational networks in the Japanese female labour market', *Social Science Research*, **34**, 651–81.

Gallie, D. (2007), 'Production regimes and the quality of employment in Europe', *Annual Review of Sociology*, **33**, 85–104.

Haas, B., N. Steiber, M. Hartel and C. Wallace (2006), 'Household employment patterns', *Work, Employment and Society*, **20**, 751–71.

Hall, P. and D. Soskice (2001), *Varieties of Capitalism: The Institutional Foundations of Comparative Advantage*, Oxford/New York: Oxford University Press.

Kumamoto-Healey, J. (2005), 'Women in the Japanese labour market, 1947–2003: a brief survey', *International Labour Review*, **144**, 451–71.

Lynn, B. (2005), *End of the Line: the Rise and Coming Fall of the Global Corporation*. New York: Doubleday.

Lyon, D. and M. Glucksmann (2008), 'Comparative configurations of care work across Europe', *Sociology*, **42**, 101–18.

Mandel, H. and M. Semyonov (2005), 'Family policies, wage structures and gender gaps: sources of earnings inequality in 20 countries', *American Sociological Review*, **70**(6), 949–67.

Maurice, M., A. Sorge and M. Warner (1980), 'Societal differences in organizing manufacturing units', *Organization Studies*, **1**(1), 59–86.

Moynagh, M. and R. Worsley (2005), *Working in the Twenty-First Century*, Leeds: ESRC Future of Work Programme.

Nolan, P. (2004), 'Shaping the future: the political economy of work and employment', *Industrial Relations Journal*, **35**, 378–87.

O'Reilly, J. (2006), 'Framing comparisons: gendering perspectives on cross-national comparative research on work and welfare', *Work Employment and Society*, **20**, 731–50.

Soskice, D. (2005), 'Varieties of capitalism and cross-national gender differences', *Social Politics*, **12**(2), 170–79.

Thelen, K. (2004), *How Institutions Evolve: the Political Economy of Skills in Germany, Britain, the United States and Japan*, New York: Cambridge University Press.

Warren, T. (2008), 'Universal disadvantage? The economic well-being of female part-timers in Europe', *European Societies*, **10**(5), 737–62.

Webb, J. (2009), 'Gender and occupation in market economies: change and restructuring since the 1980s', *Social Politics*, **16**, 82–110.

5. Penalties of part-time work across Europe

Tracey Warren

Clear gender differences persist in rates of employment in Europe. Despite women's increased entry to the labour force throughout the Western nations, men continue to dominate paid work while women continue to take major responsibility for unpaid caring work within the home. In addition to a female/male gap in work participation rates, women in the labour market typically spend far less time there than men, working fewer hours a week and over the life course (Anxo and Boulin 2006). Such short hours working has often been analysed as a way to help workers, particularly women, reconcile 'two roles' and balance demands from home and paid work, but working part-time disadvantages women in many ways (Fagan and Burchell 2002; Myrdal and Klein 1956; O'Reilly and Fagan 1998; Parent-Thirion et al. 2007).

In addition to the importance of gender in studying part-time jobs, a range of nine class-related themes can be identified in the literature that examines the advantages and downsides associated with women's part-time working (Box 5.1). A set of three influential themes concern women's entry into part-time jobs. First, to what extent is the part-time labour market largely for women with low levels of education and training (Büchtemann and Quack 1989; Devine 1994; Lind and Rasmussen 2008; Warren 2000)? Second, when compared with any previous employment, do women experience downward occupational mobility on entry to part-time jobs (Büchtemann and Quack 1989; Connolly and Gregory 2008; Dex 1992; Grant et al. 2005)? Third, does women's entry into lower-level occupations signal their search for less demanding employment and, hence perhaps, their weak commitment to the labour market? As part of this: to what extent is women's part-time working voluntary: do women choose or prefer to work in these jobs, and what shapes or constrains their choices and preferences (Bardasi and Gornick 2000; Devine 1994; Fagan 2001; Gash 2008; Ginn et al. 1996; Hakim 1991; 1998; Kauhanen 2008; Walsh 1999; Walters 2005; Warren 2000; Webber and Williams 2008a; 2008b)?

BOX 5.1   CLASS-RELATED THEMES IN THE STUDY OF FEMALE PART-TIME EMPLOYMENT

1   Are part-time jobs largely for women with few qualifications?
2   Do women experience downward mobility into part-time jobs?
3   Do less career-committed women choose or prefer part-time jobs?
4   What labour market disadvantages do women in part-time employment face?
5   Why do employers create low-quality part-time jobs?
6   Do part-time jobs represent a trap or bridge for women?
7   Do part-time jobs reinforce the gender division of labour in the home?
8   Does working part-time have longer-term economic ramifications for women?
9   What is the impact of low-level part-time jobs on the work force?

The next set of class-related themes concerns the ramifications of women's part-time employment. The fourth theme addresses job quality: to what extent do women meet wage and other forms of workplace disadvantage in their part-time jobs (Beechey and Perkins 1987; Burchell et al. 1997; Campbell and Chalmers 2008; Disney and Szyszczak 1984; Fagan et al. 1988; Manning and Petrongolo 2008; O'Reilly 1994a, 1994b; Plantenga 2002; Warren 2001)? Fifth, from an industrial relations perspective, why do employers offer part-time jobs and in the weak form that they do (Allaart and Bellmann 2007; Applebaum 1992; Beechey 1978; Beechey and Perkins 1987; Hallaire 1968)? Sixth, do women become trapped in a lower-level part-time sector of the labour market, unable to get back into full-time employment and/or higher-level occupations, thus damaging career prospects? Alternatively, do these part-time jobs act as a stepping stone or bridge for women (Büchtemann and Quack 1989; Elias 1990; Ginn and Arber 1998; Nätti 1993; 1995; O'Reilly and Bothfeld 2002; Smith 1987; Tam 1997; Whittock et al. 2002)? Seventh, does women's dominance of low-level part-time occupations reinforce the sexual division of labour in which men dominate breadwinning work whilst women take major responsibility for unpaid caring and domestic work (Smith 1987; Fagan et al. 1988)? Eighth, what are the longer-term economic implications for women of such low-waged occupations and the financial dependency on men and/or the state that invariably comes with them (Büchtemann and Quack 1989; Ginn and Arber 1998; Warren et al. 2001)? Ninth and finally, does the promotion and proliferation of poorly paying, low-level part-time occupations diminish standards for the workforce as a whole (Rubery 1998)?

These nine class-related themes have emerged from a range of national and cross-national examinations of part-time employment, with the research cited above taking place across Europe, the USA and Australia. The UK has featured strongly, however, because the problems that can result from working part-time appear extreme there. The majority of the UK part-time work force is female; female part-timers in the UK earn much lower wages than female full-timers, who themselves earn substantially less than male full-timers. In addition to persistent gender inequalities in work time and wages, however, there is also marked employment diversity amongst women in the UK according to their occupational class: women in part-time jobs have long been even more over-concentrated in lower-level occupations characterised by low hourly wages. Women who work part-time in the UK are commonly mothers who have returned to work after a period of child-rearing and, while a key question has been whether working short hours in a less demanding job has positive impacts for such women (see Warren 2004 for a review), a range of responses have at their centre the weak characteristics of part-time jobs in the UK.

In the context of the pivotal role played by occupational class in the nine dominant themes in the study of gender and part-time working, identified above, this chapter examines gender, class and work time inequalities in Europe. A female-dominated low-waged part-time work force is well documented in the UK but the ramifications of women's part-time hours working are moderated by specific national work time regimes (Bielenski et al. 2002; Rubery et al. 1998; see also Kalleberg 2000 and Thurman and Trah 1990 on cross-national heterogeneity in part-time working). Indeed, in the context of Europe, Britain has been described as having a particularly family-unfriendly, class-bound regime (Fagan 2001). It is not possible to explore each of the nine class themes within this chapter. What we do instead is to compare the occupations of female part-timers in different countries in Europe, since the women's occupational locations are so central to the classed debates, and then examine the impact on their economic positions.

DATA

The data analysed were from Wave 7 of the Users Database of the *European Community Household Panel Survey* (ECHP 2000 released in

June 2003. Eurostat 2003). The sample analysed was restricted to those aged 25–55 to minimise some of the cross-national differences that would arise in paid working because of variation between countries in patterns of early retirement and the typical durations of education. To explore gender inequalities by work time and occupational class, the sample was grouped into those employees working 1–29 hours (in the main job including any overtime) and those with 30 or more. Operationalising shorter, or 'part-time', hours like this is not without its problems. Indeed disaggregation within the part-time categories of the part-time/full-time dichotomy is known to be useful for differentiating between 'good' and 'bad' part-time jobs at the national level (Warren and Walters 1998), with cross-national variety in the typical weekly hours of 'part-timers' (that we will see below) creating more problems with using such a broad hours banding (Warren 2001). Unfortunately, due to sample size restrictions in many of the countries, it was not possible to disaggregate within the 'part-time' band whilst also examining variation according to occupational class. So, using a variable indicating occupation in current job, and taking into account the need to maintain sample sizes, a four cell matrix of work time (part-time and full-time) and occupation (higher and lower level) was created: PT Manager/professional/associate professional; FT Manager/professional/associate professions; PT clerical/manual; FT clerical/manual.

EMPLOYMENT AND WORK TIME IN EUROPE

There are clear gender differences in rates of paid work (that show the proportion of women and men who are self-employed or employees); of employment (showing employees only); and in paid work time for employees across the 13 countries for which full information was available. As Table 5.1 shows, in each and every country men had higher paid work and employment rates than women. The table also reaffirms that there was far greater cross-national variety amongst women across Europe than men. It is this heterogeneity amongst women that leads to diverse national gender gaps. Countries with the smallest gender gaps in paid work rates, for example, were Denmark (8 per cent) and Finland (11 per cent) where around 80 per cent or more of women were in paid work. Women were least likely to be in paid work, and the gender gaps were correspondingly wider, in the Mediterranean countries of Spain, Italy and Greece. Similar gender gaps resulted in the employment rates, which focus only on employees, though fewer women and men were classified as being 'in work' when the self-employed are excluded here.

A gender gap in work time was also universal across the countries

Table 5.1 Paid work; employed rates (for employees only); monthly wages; and weekly hours worked (aged 25–55)

| | Paid work rate | | Employed rate* | | Female/male gaps** | | | | Female employees' weekly hours in main job including overtime | | | | |
| | | | | | | | | | Hours distributions row % | | | Mean hours | |
	Women	Men	Women	Men	Paid work	Employ-ment	Wages*	Hours* (using means)	1–29	30–39	40+	Overall	'1–29' only
Austria	76	92	63	78	18	20	30	20	28	30	41	34	21
Denmark	85	92	76	81	8	5	15	12	12	77	11	36	24
Finland	79	89	71	73	11	3	16	9	5	71	23	38	19
France	66	89	62	76	25	19	19	12	19	61	20	35	22
Germany	74	89	58	76	17	23	35	17	24	30	46	36	21
Greece	53	88	35	53	40	34	20	11	15	21	64	38	21
Ireland	60	87	50	63	31	22	34	23	36	42	22	33	21
Italy	52	84	41	59	38	30	10	14	24	41	36	35	22
Luxembourg	63	94	57	85	34	33	35	14	27	10	63	34	21
Netherlands	71	92	54	84	23	35	39	27	46	35	19	30	21
Portugal	76	90	59	69	16	15	18	8	7	29	64	39	21
Spain	48	84	39	64	43	39	18	12	14	27	59	37	21
UK	74	89	62	74	17	17	35	22	29	38	33	36	21

Notes:
* Employees only.
** 100−((women's as % of men's)*100).

Source: European Community Household Panel data (2000).

in the sample. Focusing on employees, to avoid problems in establishing the weekly working hours of the self-employed (though see Warren 2007 for some problems with this), the table shows gender gaps in mean hours. With the widest gender hours gap at 27 per cent, the Netherlands stood out (Table 5.1). It was followed by Ireland, the UK, Austria and Germany. The narrowest gender gaps in work time were in Finland and Portugal, where most female employees worked full-time.

In Table 5.1, the hours worked by women employees are also arranged across hours bands. Short hours working for women was most widespread in the Netherlands and Ireland. The cluster of countries with the lowest prevalence of female short hours workers includes Finland, Portugal, Denmark, Spain and Greece, a set of countries represented by diverse national work time regimes. Average weekly hours for female employees overall and for women working 1–29 hours add to this picture of diversity. In this sample of women aged 25–55, the 'part-timers' worked the longest mean hours in Denmark (24) and the shortest in Finland (19). The chapter considers the economic implications of working part-time within these different contexts.

WOMEN, PART-TIME JOBS AND OCCUPATIONAL CLASS IN EUROPE

While gender gaps in paid work and work time are universal across Europe, there is diversity between nations in their size. There is also marked employment diversity within nations amongst women according to their occupational class. Using the UK as a starting point, the analysis confirmed that women's part-time jobs were over-concentrated in low-level employment. Yet Table 5.2 shows that this picture was not generalisable across Europe: instead a variety of typical occupational locations for female part-timers (aged 25–55) emerged. Examining the proportion of women within each occupational group who worked 1–29 hours, within each country, Austria was similar to the UK in that it was the women in low-level jobs who were more likely to work part-time. In Finland, France, Luxembourg and Spain, it was manual/elementary jobs (and not clerical) that were most associated with part-time working for women. In Denmark it was clerical/service work. The Netherlands and Ireland, the two countries with the most extensive female part-time working, saw part-time jobs impacting across occupational levels: they were prevalent for women in manual, clerical and in higher-level jobs. Finally, in Greece, Italy and Portugal, women in higher-level occupations were more likely to work shorter hours than the other groups of women. Given such cross-

Table 5.2   Hours worked by female employees (aged 25–55)

	Proportion of women working 1–29 hours within each occupational grouping			Average weekly hours in main job	
	Manager/ professional/ assoc. prof	Clerks/ service	Manual/ elementary	Median	Mean
Austria	17	32	35	20	21
Denmark	8	19	8	25	24
Finland	4	5	12	20	19
France	19	17	25	22	22
Germany	20	29	23	20	21
Greece	30	5	8	20	21
Ireland	30	41	36	20	21
Italy	39	16	16	21	22
Luxembourg	27	21	38	20	21
Netherlands	39	57	51	20	21
Portugal	14	1	8	22	21
Spain	12	9	24	20	21
UK	18	38	33	21	21

Source: European Community Household Panel data (2000).

national diversity in the occupational locations of female part-timers, the chapter looks next to the economic consequences for women.

WORK TIME AND CLASS: WOMEN'S WAGES IN EUROPE

Examining monthly earnings allows us to see how variations in actual hours worked combine with hourly wages to impact on living or breadwinning wages. This approach reveals deep and universal gender inequalities in earnings: in Table 5.1, men earned far more per month than women in each and every country. Nevertheless, there was substantial cross-national variety in the size of these wage gaps. Female/male monthly wage gaps were widest in the Netherlands, the UK, Luxembourg, Germany, Ireland and Austria, at 30 per cent and more, all countries where female part-time working was prevalent. They were narrowest, at 10 per cent, in Italy, where full-time working was most common for female employees.

Moving on to focus upon the impact of occupational class on the female

employees' wages, Table 5.3 confirms that, within each country, by far
the lowest relative monthly wages were earned by women in part-time
low-level jobs.[1] At the same time, there was diversity in the overall degree
of wage disadvantage associated with this class/work time grouping, with
the more wage-advantaged female part-time low-level workers found
in Denmark and the Netherlands and the most wage-disadvantaged in
Portugal and Finland. While the prevalence of part-time workers amongst
female employees in any one country has a sizeable impact on their relative wages, since they pull down the 'average' monthly wage for women,
in Denmark, even though few women were in part-time jobs (12 per
cent, Table 5.1), still the part-timers in low-level occupations were faring
relatively well. This is linked to their longer weekly hours (24, Table 5.1),
and to their higher hourly wages (Warren 2001). In Ireland and the UK,
in contrast, women in part-time low-level jobs were relatively poorly
waged (at 43 per cent) despite their prevalence in the labour force. In both
countries, female part-timers' mean weekly hours were 21. These findings
demonstrate a real diversity in the structure and economic ramifications of
low-level part-time jobs.

MOVING BEYOND WAGES: WOMEN'S ASSESSMENTS OF THEIR ECONOMIC POSITIONS IN EUROPE

To research the economic ramifications of inequalities of gender, occupational class and work time further it is beneficial to move beyond a sole
focus on wage gaps. In the UK, research has shown that not only are
female part-timers low waged, they also have lives that are marked by
financial worries (Warren 2004). Accordingly, women's subjective feelings about their economic lives in Europe were examined using data on
women's satisfaction with their earnings and their assessments of their
household economic positions.[2] Such subjective data raise a number of
methodological issues, not least because the processes that lie behind
expressions of satisfaction or dissatisfaction are complex, and we return to
their interpretation in the conclusion.

Beginning with wage satisfaction ('How satisfied are you with your
present job in terms of earnings?'), in Table 5.3 women in part-time jobs
in the UK, including those in lower-level occupations, were slightly more
likely to express wage satisfaction than those women working full-time.
The most satisfied women of all in the UK were the lowest waged part-
time manual workers (disaggregated data not shown). This incongruity
has fed into various debates, outlined earlier, over the types of women who

Table 5.3 Economic well-being of female employees (aged 25–55) by occupation and work time

	Austria	Denmark	Finland	France	Greece	Ireland	Italy	Lux.	Netherl.	Portugal	Spain	UK
a. Current gross monthly earnings as % median for all female employees												
PT. Clerical/manual	56	63	40	48	45	43	58	n.a	61	36	44	43
PT. Manag/prof/assoc prof	103	74	63	121	138	119	115	n.a	87	293	124	77
FT. Clerical/manual	102	92	87	91	92	102	98	n.a	108	88	87	94
FT. Manag/prof/assoc prof	153	116	110	143	121	166	119	n.a	139	257	155	156
b. Percentage who are satisfied with their earnings												
PT. Clerical/manual	79	86	49	64	15	75	31	n.a	76	n.a	35	74*
PT. Manag/prof/assoc prof	79	59	48	76	63	60	35	n.a	80	n.a	38	76*
FT. Clerical/manual	85	74	73	56	46	72	40	n.a	75	n.a	40	67*
FT. Manag/prof/assoc prof	81	73	68	72	66	75	49	n.a	85	n.a	61	70*
c. Percentage who report that their household has nothing/very little left to save												
PT. Clerical/manual	22	35	71	58	91	37	66	44	35	93	51	38
PT. Manag/prof/assoc prof	24	58	56	55	71	44	61	25	23	47	29	30
FT. Clerical/manual	23	35	52	58	84	46	64	46	28	84	45	28
FT. Manag/prof/assoc prof	21	31	47	46	70	26	52	30	20	58	31	24
d. Percentage who report that their household finds it difficult to make ends meet												
PT. Clerical/manual	58	25	26	43	85	52	54	29	26	93	62	35
PT. Manag/prof/assoc prof	35	27	54	14	57	30	48	3	12	47	12	33
FT. Clerical/manual	48	30	29	38	74	44	54	34	20	82	58	35
FT. Manag/prof/assoc prof	40	23	29	17	54	28	39	9	9	43	27	22

Notes: * British Household Panel Survey (BHPS) (1999).
n.a = Not available.

Source: European Community Household Panel data (2000).

take poorly paying part-time (and other) jobs and why; over how free the choice of low waged part-time employment is; as well as how we interpret an expression of satisfaction in quantitative surveys. Examining the other countries in the sample, it is clear that the wage-satisfied poorly-paid female part-timer is not a universal phenomenon.

Focusing on the extremes in the sample, the least wage-satisfied of the short hours low-level workers were found in Greece, and in Italy and Spain. In Greece, women in this work time/occupational grouping appear to be remarkably disadvantaged when compared with their national peers. In the other two countries, however, part-time managers were similarly wage-dissatisfied as their part-time manual/clerical peers. The most distinct part-time/full-time divide in expressions of wage satisfaction occurred in Finland, where there were far fewer satisfied part-timers than full-timers. Relative to their peers, the most wage-satisfied low-level short hours workers were in Denmark. Here they were earning only 63 per cent of the median wage, but were most satisfied. These assorted results clearly raise questions about the relationship between actual monthly wages and expressed feelings about wages, in different national contexts and under varying work time regimes, which we return to in the conclusion.

While diversity between countries marked the subjective individual economic positions of the women in low-level part-time jobs, a far more widespread class-related disadvantage emerged at the level of their house-hold economies. When women were asked whether their household had anything left to save (considering its income and expenses), a part-time low-level disadvantage was more common across the sample. Comparing occupational groups within each country, part-time low-level workers reported more financial problems (than women in the other three occu-pational groups in their countries) in Finland, Greece, the Netherlands, Portugal, Spain and the UK. The importance of class for savings behav-iour is demonstrated because these women were often similarly disadvan-taged as full-time low-level workers, or the full-time low-level workers were next most disadvantaged (France, Greece, Italy, Luxembourg, the Netherlands, Portugal, Spain and the UK).

Data on whether women felt that their households found it difficult to make ends meet added support to the picture of a disadvantaged house-hold economic position for low-level part-timers (in Austria, France, Greece, Ireland, Italy, the Netherlands, Portugal, and Spain, Table 5.3). The importance of class on this measure emerged because again close behind or similar were full-time clerical/manual workers (in the UK, it was only really full-time managers who stood apart, though part-time manual workers faced the most problems of all: details not shown). The main exceptions to this portrayal of class disadvantage at the household level were Nordic ones. The overall picture in Finland and Denmark was of less variation in women's overall assessments of their household economies, by hours worked or occupation. Nevertheless, the problems of 'making ends meet' expressed by the Finnish managers/professionals who worked part-time suggests that, under the Finnish full-time regime, these women (who are only a very small minority) do not fit into a privileged part-timer model (Tilly 1992).

CONCLUSION

This chapter has considered how gender and class shape employment in Europe. There are persistent gender differences in rates of employment and in paid work time across the countries examined, and these have created persistent gender gaps in wages. Using monthly wages as opposed to an hourly measure revealed a deep and universal gender inequality in living wages, with men faring much better than women. At the same time, there was cross-national variety in the size of these monthly wage gaps, and this was related to the proportion of women employees in part-time jobs. However, there was also marked diversity amongst women according to their occupational class. Stimulated by UK research into the economic ramifications for women of working in low-level jobs, which had shown part-timers in manual/clerical occupations to be in by far the weakest economic positions (Warren 2004), the chapter examined the penalties of part-time working in Europe.

The first main finding concerned the occupational location of female part-timers in Europe. The 'part-time equals low-level occupation' equation was not universally applicable. Whilst in the UK – and Austria – manual/elementary and clerical/service occupations were the ones more likely to include female part-timers, manual jobs featured more strongly for part-timers in Finland, France, Luxembourg and Spain; and it was clerical jobs for Danes. A more significant inconsistency emerges when we look to Greece, Italy and Portugal, however, where higher-level occupations contain more part-timers. This cross-national diversity in the typical occupational locations of female part-timers has important ramifications for how we understand their economic situations cross-nationally. Part-timers in low-level jobs did have the lowest relative monthly wages of all female employees, but, even then, the intensity of wage disadvantage they faced varied substantially between countries. It is clear that the wage penalties of part-time working vary for women in Europe (and see Bardasi and Gornick 2008). This chapter shows that this is true even for those in the lowest-level occupations.

This first finding has significant implications for theorising around gender and work time. The lower occupational class positions of most part-timers, and the associated disadvantages, have been fundamental in the development of the nine key class-related themes identified earlier. This chapter calls for ongoing research into exploring the applicability of the nine core themes in different national work time contexts. In the UK, all themes have been relevant, but how do other societies fare on these and indeed on further themes not identified here? Themes 3, 4, 5 and 6: women's preferences for part-time employment; the extent to which part-time working signals substantial work-place disadvantage; why employers offer part-time jobs; and whether a part-time job represents a trap or a bridge for women, have all received international attention, for example (Anxo et al. 2006; Blossfeld and Hakim 1997; Bardasi and Gornick 2008; Corral and Isusi 2004; O'Reilly and Fagan 1998; Rasmussen et al. 2004). But other themes, including number 8 on the longer-term economic consequences of part-time working for women, remain under-researched cross-nationally.

The second main finding of the chapter was that there was no correlation in each country examined between women's objective and subjective economic positions. The poorly paid female part-timer who expresses wage satisfaction, very familiar to researchers in the UK, was not a universal paradox. In some countries, women's monthly wages were low (and they reported that their households were in financial difficulties) yet still they expressed satisfaction with these wages, but in other countries they were dissatisfied.

This second finding calls for further research into workers' expressed satisfactions, with their wages, finances and other aspects of their working lives, by work time and occupational class in different national contexts. It also raises a number of methodological issues. On wage satisfaction in particular, a key question is how respondents interpret the question asked of them. The ECHP earnings data derives from the question: 'how satisfied are you with your present job in terms of earnings?'. Are the women reflecting on their hourly wage, perhaps, or on their total earnings? This difference has significant ramifications for the analyses carried out in this chapter, based as they are on grouping women expressly according to their monthly living or breadwinning wages. A low monthly wage could be the outcome of few hours of work at a high hourly rate or long hours of work at a poor hourly wage, with diverse consequences, of course, for how women might feel about their wages. The corresponding question in the British Household Panel Survey, the data set that feeds into the ECHP, asked about 'total pay' including any overtime or bonuses. It is thus vital that we make explicit what we are asking when analysing 'wage satisfaction'. More generally, it is widely accepted that the expression of dis/satisfaction in a survey is a simplified account of what are very complex processes of evaluations: a snapshot result from a combination of people's aspirations, expectations and the adaptations that they have made in their lives (Böhnke 2005; Rose 2003). Adding in a comparative dimension increases this complexity. The chapter thus highlights the need for further research into developing nuanced work attitude measures that can also be used in comparable cross-national data sets. Previous studies of low-waged women in Britain have shown, for example, that expressed satisfaction might be best interpreted as 'making do': in this regard satisfaction with low wages may well reflect women's assessments of what pay rates are available to them (Walters 2005). It is interesting to consider why poorly paid low-level part-timers are more likely to 'make do' in some countries, and further analysis that also explores state transfers that supplement wages is essential here.

The third main finding of the chapter was of a prevalent association between working part-time in a low-level occupation and expressing weak satisfaction with household economic positions. In the majority of countries, fewer low-level part-timers than other female workers reported their households being able to save, and more reported that their households had problems making ends meet. In most countries, however, it was the women's class positions rather than their work time that signalled these household problems since women in low-level jobs who were working full-time hours also reported difficulties. These findings on households' economies raise the key question of whether the economic impact of diverse work times and different levels of occupation is better viewed via an individual and/or household level analysis. Furthermore, they suggest that we should add a tenth household-level topic to the nine class-based themes in the study of gender and part-time working (Box 5.1), namely: to what extent do the poor wages associated with part-time working in low-level occupations contribute to severe financial problems for the women's households, in the short, medium and longer terms? A core part of this is whether women's low wages are contributing to an already precarious household income or whether they are being cushioned comfortably by other household incomes (such as wages from a higher-earning partner).

To conclude, the chapter has shown that a focus on wages – on levels and gaps – is fruitful for researching the economic penalties of part-time working and, more broadly, the economic implications of inequalities of gender, class and work-time. Nevertheless, a more expansive approach is now required that combines analysis of levels of economic resources with subjective indicators of economic positions. Research into objective and subjective indicators of 'economic well-being', at the individual and household level, offers a valuable way forward, providing a more comprehensive picture of the economic lives of workers and their families in Europe.

ACKNOWLEDGEMENTS

This research was co-funded by a grant from the European Commission under the Transnational Access to major Research Infrastructures contract HPRI-CT-2001-00128 hosted by IRISS-C/I at CEPS/INSTEAD Differdange (Luxembourg), and by the School of Sociology and Social Policy at the University of Nottingham.

NOTES

1. In Greece, clerical workers were lower waged than manual workers. In the other countries, the manual workers were the lowest waged.
2. Women report on their own 'financial situation' too but results were very similar to those on wage satisfaction and so are not discussed here.

REFERENCES

Allaart, P. and L. Bellmann (2007), 'Reasons for part-time work: an empirical analysis for Germany and The Netherlands', *International Journal of Manpower*, **28**(7), 557–70.
Anxo, D. and J-Y. Boulin (2006), 'The organisation of time over the life course: European trends', *European Societies*, **8**(2), 319–41.
Anxo, D., C. Fagan, M. Smith, M.T. Letablier and C. Perraudin (2006), *Part-time Work in European Companies. Establishment Survey on Working Time 2004–2005*, Luxembourg: Office for Official Publications of the European Communities.
Applebaum, E. (1992), 'Structural change and the growth of part-time and temporary employment', in V.L. duRivage (ed.) *New Policies for the Part-time and Contingent Workforce*, New York and London: ME Sharpe.
Bardasi, E. and J.C. Gornick (2000), 'Women and part-time employment: workers' choices and wage penalties in five industrialised countries', Luxembourg Income Study Working Paper 233.
Bardasi, E. and J.C. Gornick (2008), 'Working for less? Women's part-time wage penalties across countries', *Feminist Economics*, **14**(1), 37–72.
Beechey, V. (1978), 'Women and production: a critical analysis of some sociological theories of women's work', in A. Kuhn and A.M. Wolpe (eds), *Feminism and Materialism: Women and Modes of Production*, London: Routledge and Kegan Paul.
Beechey, V. and T. Perkins (1987), *A Matter of Hours: Women, Part-time Work and the Labour Market*, Cambridge: Polity Press.

Bielenski, H., G. Bosch and A. Wagner (2002), *Working Time Preferences in 16 European Countries*, Luxembourg: Office for Official Publications of the European Commission.

Blossfeld, H.P. and C. Hakim (eds) (1997), *Between Equalisation and Marginalisation: Women Working Part-time in Europe and the USA*, Oxford: Oxford University Press.

Böhnke, P. (2005), *First European Quality of Life Survey: Life Satisfaction, Happiness and Sense of Belonging*, Dublin: European Foundation for the Improvement of Living and Working Conditions.

Büchtemann, C.F. and S. Quack (1989), '"Bridges" or "traps"? Non-standard employment in the Federal Republic of Germany', in G. Rodgers and J. Rodgers (eds), *Precarious Jobs in Labour Market Regulation*, Geneva: ILO.

Burchell, B.J., A. Dale and H. Joshi (1997), 'Part-time work among British women' in H.P. Blossfeld and C. Hakim (eds), *Between Equalisation and Marginalisation: Women Working Part-time in Europe and the USA*, Oxford: Oxford University Press.

Campbell, I. and J. Chalmers (2008), 'Job quality and part-time work in the retail industry: an Australian case study', *International Journal of Human Resource Management*, **19**(3), 487–500.

Connolly, S. and M. Gregory (2008), 'Moving down: women's part-time work and occupational change in Britain 1991–2001', *The Economic Journal*, **118**(526), F52–76.

Corral, A. and I. Isusi (2004), *Part-time Work in Europe*, Dublin: European Foundation for the Improvement of Living and Working Conditions.

Devine, F. (1994), 'Segregation and supply: preferences and plans amongst "self-made" women', *Gender, Work and Organisation*, **1**(2), 94–109.

Dex, S. (1992), 'Labour force participation of women during the 1990s: occupational mobility and part-time employment', in R.M. Lindley (ed.), *Women's Employment: Britain in the Single European Market*, Equal Opportunities Commission, London: HMSO.

Disney, R. and E.M. Szyszczak (1984), 'Protective legislation and part-time employment in Britain', *British Journal of Industrial Relations*, **22**(1), 78–100.

Elias, P. (1990), 'Part-time work and part-time workers: keeping women in or out?', in S. McRae (ed.), *Keeping Women In*, London: Policy Studies Institute.

Eurostat (2003), 'European Community Household Panel UDB manual', *Waves 1 to 8*, DOC-PAN 168/2003–12, Luxembourg: Eurostat/European Commission.

Fagan, C. (2001), 'Time, money and the gender order: work orientations and working-time preferences in Britain', *Gender, Work and Organization*, **8**(3), 239–66.

Fagan, C. and B.J. Burchell (2002), *Gender, Jobs and Working Conditions in the European Union*, Dublin: European Foundation for the Improvement of Living and Working Conditions.

Fagan, C., J. O'Reilly and J. Rubery (1988), 'Challenging the "breadwinner" gender contract? Part-time work in the Netherlands, Germany and the UK', in M. Maurani and R. Silvera (eds), *Les Nouvelles Frontières de l'inégalité: Hommes et Femmes sur le Marché du Travail*, Paris: Éditions La Découverte et Syros.

Gash, V. (2008), 'Preference or constraint?: part-time workers' transitions in Denmark, France and the UK', *Work, Employment and Society*, **22**(4), 655–74.

Ginn, J. and S. Arber (1998), 'How does part-time work lead to low pension income?', in J. O'Reilly and C. Fagan (eds), *Part-time Prospects: an International Comparison of Part-time Work in Europe, North America and the Pacific Rim*, London: Routledge.

Ginn, J., S. Arber, J. Brannen, A. Dale, S. Dex, P. Elias, P. Moss, J. Pahl, C. Roberts and J. Rubery (1996), 'Feminist fallacies: a reply to Hakim on women's employment', *British Journal of Sociology*, **47**(1), 167–74.

Grant, L., S. Yeandle and L. Buckner (2005), *Working Below Potential: Women and Part-time Work*, Manchester: EOC.

Hakim, C. (1991), 'Grateful slaves and self-made women: fact and fantasy in women's work orientations', *European Sociological Review*, **7**(2), 101–21.

Hakim, C. (1998), 'Developing a sociology for the twenty-first century: preference theory', *British Journal of Sociology*, **49**(1), 137–43.

Hallaire, J. (1968), 'Part-time employment: its extent and its problems', paper No. 23219, Paris: OECD.

Kalleberg, A.L. (2000), 'Nonstandard employment relations: part-time, temporary and contract work, *Annual Review of Sociology*, **26**, 341–65.

Kauhanen, M. (2008), 'Part-time work and involuntary part-time work in the private service sector in Finland', *Economic and Industrial Democracy*, **29**(2), 217–48.

Lind, J. and E. Rasmussen (2008), 'Paradoxical patterns of part-time employment in Denmark?', *Economic and Industrial Democracy*, **29**(4), 521–40.

Manning, A. and B. Petrongolo (2008), 'The part-time pay penalty for women in Britain', *The Economic Journal*, **118**(526), F28–F51.

Myrdal, A. and V. Klein (1956), *Women's Two Roles. Home and Work*, London: Routledge and Kegan Paul.

Nätti, J. (1993), 'Atypical employment in the Nordic countries: towards marginalisation or normalisation?', in T.P. Boje and S.E. Olsson Hart (eds), *Scandinavia in a New Europe*, Oslo: Scandinavian University Press.

Nätti, J. (1995), 'Part-time work in the Nordic countries: a trap for women?', *Labour*, **9**(2), 343–57.

O'Reilly, J. (1994a), 'Part-time work and employment regulation: a comparison of Britain and France in the context of Europe', in M. White (ed.), *Unemployment and Public Policy in a Changing Labour Market*, London: Policy Studies Institute.

O'Reilly, J. (1994b), 'What flexibility do women offer? Comparing the use of, and attitudes to, part time work in Britain and France in retail banking', *Gender, Work and Organisation*, **1**(3), 138–50.

O'Reilly, J. and S. Bothfeld (2002), 'What happens after working part-time? Integration, maintenance or exclusionary transitions in Britain and Western Germany', *Cambridge Journal of Economics*, **26**(4), 409–39.

O'Reilly, J. and C. Fagan (eds) (1998), *Part-time Prospects: an International Comparison of Part-time Work in Europe, North America and the Pacific Rim*, London: Routledge.

Parent-Thirion, A., E. Fernández Macías, J. Hurley and G. Vermeylen (2007), *Fourth European Working Conditions Survey*, Luxembourg: Office for Official Publications of the European Communities.

Plantenga, J. (2002), 'Combining work and care in the polder model: an assessment of the Dutch part-time strategy', *Critical Social Policy*, **22**(1), 53–71.

Rasmussen, E., J. Lind and J. Visser (2004), 'Divergence in part-time work in New Zealand, the Netherlands and Denmark', *British Journal of Industrial Relations*, **42**(4), 637–58.

Rose, M. (2003), 'Good deal, bad deal? Job satisfaction in occupations', *Work, Employment, and Society*, **17**(3), 503–30.

Rubery, J. (1998), 'Part-time work: a threat to labour standards?', in J. O'Reilly and C. Fagan (eds), *Part-time Prospects: an International Comparison of Part-time Work in Europe, North America and the Pacific Rim*, London: Routledge.

Rubery, J., M. Smith and C. Fagan (1998), 'National working-time regimes and equal opportunities', *Feminist Economics*, **4**(1), 71–102.

Smith, V. (1987), 'The circular trap: women and part-time work', in A.S. Sassoon (ed.), *Women and the State: The Shifting Boundaries of Public and Private*, London: Hutchinson.

Tam, M. (1997), *Part-time Employment: a Bridge or a Trap?*, Aldershot: Avebury.

Thurman, J.E. and G. Trah (1990), 'Part-time work in international perspective', *International Labour Review*, **129**(1), 23–40.

Tilly, C. (1992), 'Short hours, short shift: the causes and consequences of part-time employment', in V.L. duRivage (ed.), *New Policies for the Part-time and Contingent Workforce*, New York and London: ME Sharpe.

Walsh, J. (1999), 'Myths and counter-myths: an analysis of part-time female employees and their orientations to work and working hours', *Work, Employment and Society*, **13**(2), 179–203.

Walters, S. (2005), 'Making the best of a bad job? Female part-timers' orientations and attitudes to work', *Gender Work and Organization*, **12**(3), 193–216.

Warren, T. (2000), 'Women in low status part-time jobs: a gender and class based analysis', *Sociological Research Online*, **4**(4), available at http://www.socres online.org.uk/socresonline/.

Warren, T. (2001), 'Divergent female part-time employment in Britain and Denmark and the implications for gender equity', *Sociological Review*, **49**(4), 548–67.

Warren, T. (2004), 'Working part-time: achieving the ideal work–life balance?', *British Journal of Sociology*, **55**(1), 99–121.

Warren, T. (2007), 'Conceptualising breadwinning work', *Work, Employment and Society*, **21**(2), 317–36.

Warren, T. and P. Walters (1998), 'Appraising a dichotomy: a review of the use of "part-time/full-time" in the study of women's employment in Britain', *Gender, Work and Organisation*, **5**(2), 102–18.

Warren, T., K. Rowlingson and C. Whyley (2001), 'Female finances: gender wage gaps, gender assets gaps', *Work, Employment and Society*, **15**(3), 465–88.

Webber, G. and C. Williams (2008a), 'Mothers in "good" and "bad" part-time jobs different problems, same results', *Gender and Society*, **22**(6), 752–77.

Webber, G. and C. Williams (2008b), 'Part-time work and the gender division of labor', *Qualitative Sociology*, **31**(1), 15–36.

Whittock, M., C. Edwards, S. McLaren and O. Robinson (2002), 'The tender trap: gender, part-time nursing and the effects of family-friendly policies on career advancement', *Sociology of Health & Illness*, **24**(3), 305–326.

6. Feminising professions in Britain and France: how countries differ[1]

Nicky Le Feuvre

INTRODUCTION

Most of the existing research on the feminisation of management and professional levels of the occupational hierarchy begin by recognising the significant inroads women have made into these occupations over the past twenty years, before going on to stress the ambivalent nature of such progress, notably in terms of internal occupational segregation, reduced promotion chances for women, and pay differences. Our own contributions to this field of study have attempted to unravel the precise significance of the progressive entry of women into such former 'male bastions', in a context characterised by the adoption of a series of equal opportunity (EO) measures, both at European (Commission européenne 2006) and national level (Crompton and Le Feuvre 2000; Le Feuvre 2006; Le Feuvre 2009). Most of the existing EO legislation is based on the implicit assumption that the level of women's access to managerial and professional occupations provides a reliable empirical measurement of the reduction in gender inequalities in the labour market. Thus, policy makers aim to increase the representation of women in those sectors of the labour market where they have been historically under-represented and tend to read any increase in the rate of feminisation as a sign of an advance in gender equality generally. The rationale behind such EO policy objectives is rarely questioned, despite increasing evidence that new forms of gender inequality rapidly emerge as women gain access to those professions or occupational groups from which they were previously excluded (Kantola 2008; Schultz and Shaw 2003; Siemienska and Zimmer 2007).

It is therefore interesting to analyse in more detail the precise mechanisms behind the increase in women's access to managerial and professional occupations and to frame this research with direct reference to the question of gender equality and equal opportunity policies (Le Feuvre 2009). Crompton has suggested that it is not too difficult to see the history of professional development as an important element in securing the masculine dominance of the modern occupational structure associated with the male-breadwinner model, in which women were, initially, systematically denied access to occupations which would have enabled them to live independently (Crompton 1999). If this argument is accepted, then to what extent can the changes observed in relation to women's access to higher-level occupations be seen as a sign of the transformation of the dominant 'gender contract' at the macro social level or of the dominant 'gender regime' at the meso occupational level (Connell 1987)?

Adopting a cross-national comparative perspective is particularly useful in unravelling the significance of the feminisation process, since it enables us to identify with greater clarity the diverse social mechanisms that underpin a given empirical phenomenon in different societal contexts (Crompton 1998; 2006; Pickvance 1986). France and Britain provide a particularly interesting frame of comparison, since they represent countries of a similar size and level of economic development, whilst providing examples of a very different historical legacy in terms of women's access to the labour market (Tilly and Scott 1987) and in terms of the dominant regime of social protection (O'Reilly 2006). Comparison across these two countries and across occupational groups may, therefore, lead to new insights as to the issues at stake around the feminisation process.

Based on the secondary analysis of statistical data on the rates and patterns of women's integration into medicine, law, pharmacy, accountancy, speech therapy, academia and banking and on a series of biographical interviews with men and women working in these professions between the early 1990s and the mid-2000s,[2] this chapter will address the following three questions.

First, to what extent does women's entry into these relatively prestigious occupations constitute a transgression of the dominant pattern of women's labour market participation in each country? Secondly, to what extent does the feminisation process represent a threat to the dominant 'gender regimes' historically present in these occupations? In other words, to what extent have women been admitted into these professions under the same conditions as their male counterparts (or as previous generations of men) or to what extent has the feminisation process been based on the creation of so-called 'family-friendly' (that is, usually female-specific) forms of employment? Finally, does the fact that women may enter these professions via 'bureaucratic' (salaried or equivalent) or 'practice' (self-employment) career paths have different consequences for the reproduction/reconfiguration of gender relations in each national context?

The distinctions between these two types of career pattern are usefully summarised as follows by Crompton:

The classic profession is characterized by a formal and extensive body of knowledge and expertise acquired through a long period of training. Professional standards are nationally (and usually internationally) recognized. Once the training and registration period has been completed, the professional is in possession of a 'licence to practice'. There has been a massive expansion of management training, but managers, unlike professionals, do not require a 'licence to practice'. Managerial careers are forged in an organizational context. In the classical bureaucratic model of organisations, the bureaucratic hierarchy provides a series of graded occupational slots to which managers can aspire. Trends, including 'delayering' and organizational 'downsizing', have had a considerable impact on the traditional bureaucratic career. However, this has not transformed the fundamental difference between classic professional and managerial occupations, which is that professional knowledge and expertise are regulated by an external standard, whereas managerial expertise is directly evaluated by the employing organization. (Crompton 1999: 123)

At the risk of over-simplifying the comparison, it could be said that 'bureaucratic careers' within large organisations are characterised by: access to varying levels of employment citizenship benefits (for example paid maternity leave); hierarchical internal organisational structures; individual performance-related recruitment and promotion criteria, where time commitment and geographical mobility often play an important role and, finally, 'up or out' management techniques (Anderson-Gough et al. 2001). In contrast, the standard 'practice career' offers almost no employment citizenship benefits, but is built on the basis of objective recruitment criteria (qualifications + mandate to practise), where the ability to mobilise personal contacts and construct networks act as the main criteria of professional success. They offer multiple forms of practice (individual self-employment, group practice, and so on) and relative 'time sovereignty' in the work–life interface, despite potentially long hours.

In practice, the distinction between these two types of career is becoming increasingly blurred, notably through the development of hybrid work relationships, on the border between employment and self-employment, referred to in the literature as 'dependant self-employment' (Muehlberger 2007; Muehlberger and Bertolini 2007). Furthermore, 'professional' qualifications may often act as recruitment or promotion criteria to 'managerial' salaried positions within firms (as in the case of accountancy in the UK). Whilst recognising the considerable overlap that may occur between these two types of career, as an ideal-type model, this distinction does enable us to adopt a useful framework for comparative analysis of the feminisation process, particularly given the national variations in the erosion of the frontiers between fully-externalised practice-based careers and the classical internalised 'management' careers (Muehlberger 2007; Muehlberger and Bertolini 2007).

A THEORETICAL FRAMEWORK FOR ANALYSING THE FEMINISATION PROCESS IN A COMPARATIVE PERSPECTIVE

In order to analyse the gender equality issues surrounding women's access to managerial and professional occupations, we propose to adopt a relatively simple definition of gender. Rather than using this term as a synonym for sex or as a relatively immutable social structure, it is more useful to think of the sex/gender system as the result of a two-fold process (Kergoat 2000), which can be historically located and which is open to change over time.

On the one hand, gender is based on the relatively systematic differentiation of two mutually exclusive categories (male/female; masculine/feminine), corresponding to what Rubin has called the 'similarity taboo' between the sexes (Rubin 1975). This implies that the social attributes of members of each of these categories have to be differentiated, although the outcomes of this process may be significantly different in varying national/historical contexts. Exactly what men and women should be or do thus varies over time and place, but the idea that they should be radically different and do radically different things is what constitutes the structural and symbolic basis of the differentiation process. Secondly, in order for gender to operate as a socially significant process, these binary differentiated groups or categories need to be organised hierarchically, with the specific attributes of the male/masculine placed above those of the female/feminine (Héritier 1996). When analysing women's exclusion from or limited entry to the centres of male/masculine power, it is therefore essential to consider both these aspects of the sex/gender system. This is a relatively straightforward task when accounting for women's historical exclusion from the male-dominated sectors of the labour market, and much of the existing literature has attempted to theorise gender on the basis of this exclusion. The task becomes somewhat more complex when the feminisation rates of these male bastions start to increase and when research no longer centres exclusively on the mechanisms through which women are excluded, but also attempts to comprehend the conditions under which they are potentially included.

We will demonstrate that, largely due to the varying levels of institutionalisation of equal opportunity policies in Britain and France (Crompton and Le Feuvre 2000), women in France who experience a relatively traditional gendered pattern of the work–life interface (based on what has been called a modified version of the 'male breadwinner/female carer' model) will tend to be drawn towards a practice-based type of career. On the contrary, French women whose biographical trajectories can be said, for a variety of reasons, to challenge the dominant societal gender norms are more likely to gravitate towards 'bureaucratic/managerial' career paths. In Britain, on the other hand, there is a clear generation effect, whereby women from the younger generations,[3] who have benefited from the relatively widespread adoption of EO policies and who aspire to a relatively traditional gendered pattern of the work–life interface, will tend to gravitate towards bureaucratic/management careers in large firms. On the contrary, British women in large organisations from the 'pioneer' generations could only make it up the career ladder by distancing themselves from the dominant national gender norms. In this sense, their experiences are closer to those of their similarly aged or younger French counterparts than to the younger generation of their compatriots. However, the older generations of well-qualified British women who experienced a relatively traditional pattern of gender relations were likely to adopt 'practice' careers, whereas this form of employment tends to be associated with lower levels of gender conformity amongst their younger counterparts. In conclusion, we discuss the implications of these cross-national differences from an equal opportunity policy perspective.

MACRO-LEVEL GENDERED WORKING PATTERNS IN BRITAIN AND FRANCE

In existing typologies of welfare state regimes, France often occupies a rather uneasy position, somewhere between the Nordic dual breadwinner and the Continental European male breadwinner model of social organisation. It is certainly the case that, in comparison to the UK, well-qualified French women have long tended to adopt full-time, continuous career patterns, whilst maintaining impressively high fertility rates (Fagnani 2007). The existence of comprehensive pre-school childcare facilities, long school hours and extensive after-school and holiday childcare services, limited opportunities for part-time employment until the beginning of the 1980s and various forms of state support for working parents, are often cited as determining factors in the relatively high levels of full-time female activity rates registered in France throughout the 1980s and 1990s. More recently, however, several factors have modified the dominant pattern of continuous, full-time employment for women – particularly mothers – in France. These include the gradual increase in levels of part-time work (Angeloff 2000), particularly amongst the least well-qualified women, and the introduction of a (poorly) paid, extended (three years) parental leave allowance (Afsa Essafi and Buffeteau 2006; Méda and Périvier 2007).

In contrast, women's activity rates in the UK have historically been characterised by discontinuous career paths and by high levels of part-time work, even among well-qualified women (Walters 2005; Yeandle 1999). The lack of comprehensive pre-school facilities and the high cost of private childcare arrangements, along with the above-average working hours of British men, are amongst the factors cited to explain the emergence of a 'modified male breadwinner' model of women's labour market participation patterns in this particular national context (Cousins and Tang 2004; Crompton et al. 2007). However, significant changes in legislation and practice have also taken place in the British context and, although female part-time employment rates are still high, there is some sign that mothers are returning more rapidly to employment after the birth of their children than was previously the case (Smeaton 2006). However, despite several recent government initiatives to encourage a better 'work–life balance' (Department of Trade and Industry 2005), there is some question as to the degree of 'choice' or 'constraint' that underpins the recent changes in women's employment patterns in Britain (Walters 2005; Warren 2004).

Thus, although women's employment rates are now systematically higher, on average, in the UK than in France (Figure 6.1), differences remain concerning women's working time. In Britain, the average working hours of men and women continue to differ significantly, with the majority of men working more than 40 hours a week and a significant proportion of women working less than 35 hours a week, whilst the average working week for men and women in France is between 35 and 39 hours (Figure 6.2).

ANALYSING THE OCCUPATIONAL FEMINISATION PROCESS IN CROSS-NATIONAL PERSPECTIVE

In so far as women's employment and working-time patterns have an impact on the organisation of childcare and other domestic activities and, perhaps more importantly, on the value systems that underpin these macro-level 'gender arrangements' (Pfau-Effinger 2004), aggregate cross-national differences are obviously important to consider when comparing the conditions under which women have gained access to managerial and professional occupations in different national contexts. However, there are also significant occupational differences within each national context and these are also important factors to include in any comparative analysis of the progressive entry of women into previously existing 'male bastions'.

As shown in Figure 6.3, a similar percentage of the labour force is employed in professional practice-based occupations (that is, those requiring a formal qualification and usually involving some form of

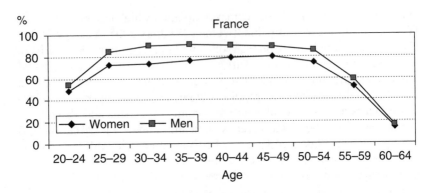

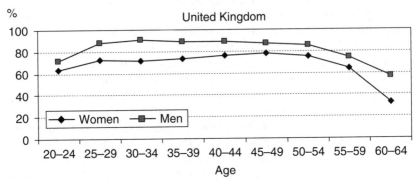

Source: OECD (2007a).

*Figure 6.1   Male and female economic activity rates by age in France and
             the UK, 2007*

self-employment, including 'dependant self-employment') in Britain and
France and the gender gap is relatively small in both countries. In contrast, there are huge differences in the proportion of male employees
classified as occupying a 'managerial' position in Britain and France and,
although the gender gap in the UK is one of the highest observed in all
OECD countries, significantly more women occupy managerial jobs in
this country than in France.

These differences obviously reflect macro-level variations in the structure of the labour market and in the occupational classification systems
used in different national contexts (Crompton 2008; Vallet 2001), but they
also raise questions as to the precise mechanisms behind the occupational
feminisation process within each country.

Our comparative studies of women in a series of highly qualified

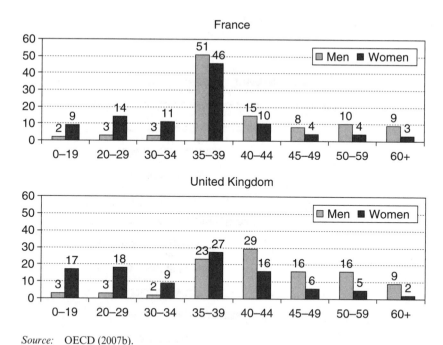

Source: OECD (2007b).

Figure 6.2 *Usual working hours per week by gender, France and UK, 2005*

occupations shed some light on the structural differences in the organisation of managerial and practice-based employment patterns in Britain and France (Crompton and Lyonette 2007). Preliminary analysis of this meso-level data revealed some interesting cross-national variations. Thus, despite huge expansion throughout the 1970s and 1980s, the total number of lawyers, accountants and bank managers was significantly lower in France than in Britain, whereas there were many more pharmacists and doctors in France than in the UK. To take just one example, in 2007, the national organisation of chartered accountants in France had 40 424 registered members (3433 women), including 5659 trainees (2530 women) and almost 1000 honorary members. Of all registered chartered accountants in France, only 2207 work in salaried positions within private companies, whilst 15 938 work as 'independent practitioners' and 14 742 in group practices. There is thus no equivalent to the so-called 'big 6' in the UK context, since the average number of accountants per employment structure (including trainees and honorary members) is just 2.6. The size and composition of the profession had barely changed since the early 1990s

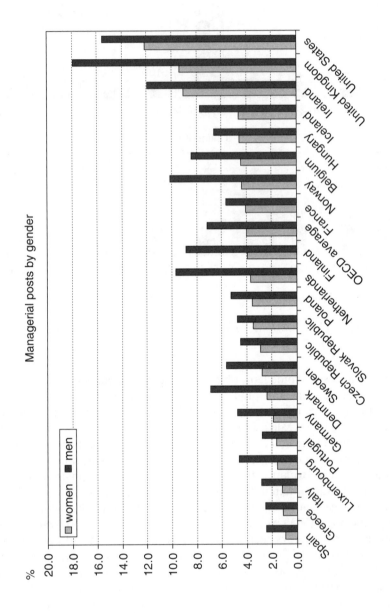

Managerial posts by gender

women ■ men

Spain
Greece
Italy
Luxembourg
Portugal
Germany
Denmark
Sweden
Czech Republic
Slovak Republic
Poland
Netherlands
Finland
OECD average
France
Norway
Belgium
Hungary
Iceland
Ireland
United Kingdom
United States

%
20.0
18.0
16.0
14.0
12.0
10.0
8.0
6.0
4.0
2.0
0.0

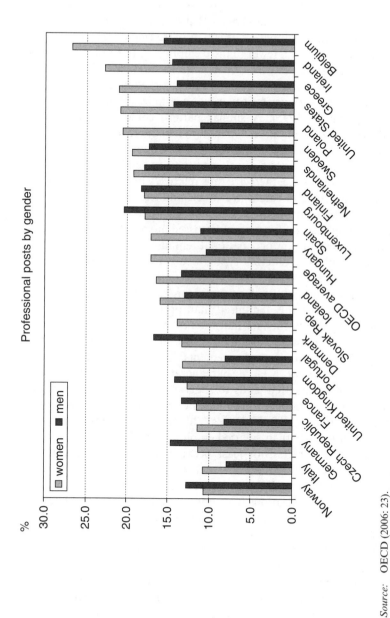

Professional posts by gender

%

Source: OECD (2006: 23).

Figure 6.3 Percentage of the labour force in managerial and professional occupations, OECD countries, 2004

(Hantrais 1995). In comparison, also in 2007, the largest professional accounting association in the UK (ICEAW) had over 130 000 members, half of whom where employed directly in private business, 41 per cent in private practice, and the remaining in public or non-commercial enterprises. Furthermore, in the mid-1990s, 41 per cent of the British accountants were employed in companies of 500 or more employees, as against 20 per cent in companies with fewer than 20 employees. In France, the spread was quite different: 78 per cent of accountancy firms had fewer than 10 employees and 30 per cent of all accountants worked in these small group practices, whilst only 19 per cent worked in companies of more than 100 employees (Hantrais 1995). A similar pattern could also be observed within the legal profession in each country (Le Feuvre and Walters 1993). It thus appears that the type of employment opportunities available to well-qualified women varies according to their societal context. Within a smaller occupational base, there are thus relatively more opportunities for a 'practice-based' type of career in France, and less chance of embarking on a 'bureaucratic/managerial' type of career than in Britain.

Two opposing theories have been discussed at some length in the existing academic literature on occupational feminisation (Hantrais 1995) as to the influence of these different types of career patterns on feminisation rates and gender equality generally. Some authors have suggested that managerial positions within large-scale organisations would progressively become more highly feminised than professional practice occupations, principally due to the fact that the best guarantees of 'employment citizenship' (Holmwood and Siltanen 1996), in the form of paid maternity leave, flexible working arrangements, training opportunities, and so on were to be found in large, bureaucratic structures. Somewhat to the contrary, other research tends to suggest that, despite the overruling tendency towards a rationalisation and bureaucratisation of many professional fields (Evetts 2002; Lane et al. 2002), women continue to prefer self-employment rather than salaried employment, that is practice rather than bureaucratic careers, not least because promotion to managerial positions within large bureaucratic structures continues to operate on the criteria that have historically underpinned the 'male breadwinner/female carer' model of gender relations (Crompton and Harris 1998) and because women still find it harder than men, on average, to conform to such criteria (Crompton and Birkelund 2000).

The Franco-British comparative perspective is particularly interesting for taking this analysis further. We are dealing with two societies where the employment patterns of highly qualified women are variable (medium levels of continuous employment and high part-time employment rates in Britain versus high levels of continuous employment and low rates of part-time work in France). Likewise, the structural characteristics of the professional and managerial labour markets are also different (widespread opportunities for employment within large bureaucratic organisational settings in Britain versus the relative availability of professional practice through various forms of self-employment in France). Thus, although France has historically offered better opportunities for women to compete on an equal footing with men in gaining access to higher-level occupational categories, on the basis of the 'qualifications lever' (Crompton and Sanderson 1986), Britain would seem to offer greater opportunities for access to a range of employment citizenship provisions, through the more widespread development of salaried positions within large firms. Furthermore, despite the existence of a comparable equal opportunities legislative framework in both countries, France has been notoriously slow in adopting any form of positive action measures in favour of women's careers (Laufer and Silvera 2008), whereas these are now relatively widespread in large British companies, despite some debate as to their effectiveness in practice (Commission européenne 2008).

Our biographical interviews with women in 'bureaucratic' and 'practice-based' careers in these different high-level occupations were able to shed some light on the social mechanisms behind the occupational feminisation process in each national context. Our objective was to understand the consequences of different rates and patterns of occupational feminisation with regard to the reproduction/transformation of existing gender arrangements in each national context. In order to do this, we needed to add a third level of analysis to the macro (societal level 'gender contract') and meso (occupational level) dimensions already mentioned. At the micro social level, we were interested in gauging women's subjective gender experiences, that is their perceptions of the existing gender arrangements within their own country as a whole, also within their chosen profession and their subjective relation to these perceived realities, in terms of conformity, contestation, transgression, and so on (Le Feuvre 1999).

This template enabled us to elaborate a series of ideal-type models of occupational feminisation, according to the degree to which the outcomes of this process represented a challenge to the two dimensions of the sex/gender system (gender differentiation and gender hierarchies) (Le Feuvre 2001).

From the Franco-British comparison, two dominant ideal-type models emerged.[4] On the one hand, it was clear that some women had entered high-level occupations with the intention of challenging the dominant work ethos or 'career scripts' (Le Feuvre and Lapeyre 2005; Rhode 2003) that presided over recruitment and promotion procedures. They argued (curiously echoing much of the academic literature on this theme) for the necessity to recognise the difficulties for women in general and mothers in particular to conform to the (male-centred) expectations about professional commitment and time-management, whilst insisting on the advantages of being able to carve out specific niches within their occupation that were compatible with a more 'balanced' work–life interface (Crompton and Lyonette 2007), either with regard to family and domestic responsibilities or, more rarely, to leisure activities (Warren 2004) or voluntary work. I have called this the 'feminitude' model of occupational feminisation (Le Feuvre 1999), since it is based on the idea (ideology) that men and women are fundamentally different and, therefore, will (should) 'normally' have radically different expectations and aspirations with regard to their professional and personal lives. According to this perspective, equal opportunity measures should aim to facilitate women's need to juggle with competing claims on their time and energy over the life course and to enable them to build their careers around their domestic calendars.

In stark contrast to this female specific model of occupational feminisation, another pattern of occupational feminisation, which I have called the 'virilitude' model (Le Feuvre 1999) was evident in some of our interviews. In this case, interviewees were particularly critical of the 'similarity taboo', arguing that women were just as capable as men of fulfilling the existing criteria for professional success. These criteria were thus generally seen in gender-neutral terms. It was the 'nature of the job' that determined the need for long hours, mobility, commitment and unlimited availability for the company/clients, rather than any hint of gender bias. The aim of equal opportunity measures (if required) should be to combat the stereotypical ideas about women's unreliability or lack of commitment and to give them the opportunity to show that they had 'got what it took' to excel in their chosen field. The women who developed this particular vision of gender inequalities were critical of any measures that could suggest that they had, as a group, any particular needs or aspirations that were not shared by the majority of their male counterparts. They were also critical of those women who made claims of 'special treatment' on the grounds of their sex.

CROSS-NATIONAL SIMILARITIES AND DIFFERENCES IN THE GENDERED EXPERIENCES OF OCCUPATIONAL FEMINISATION

The macro-level gender norms regarding women's employment patterns and the meso-level structural characteristics of the occupations studied combined to create very different opportunity structures for the gender experiences of our French and British respondents. Undoubtedly, adopting a full-time, continuous career appeared generally to be less problematic in France than in Britain, particularly amongst the older generations of qualified women interviewed. In itself, having a 'career' rather than a job presented more of a threat to the dominant macro gender arrangements in Britain than in France. However, once they had embarked on a career path, the subjective gender experiences of our respondents were strikingly similar from one national context to the other, and spontaneous accounts of blatant sexism and discrimination were offered in each country and in every occupation studied. However, the strategies adopted in the face of barriers to women's recruitment and promotion were not necessarily identical in each national context and they did not produce exactly the same patterns of occupational feminisation.

The women we interviewed from the 'pioneer' generations in salaried managerial positions in large (banking, accountancy, law, pharmaceutical) firms had very similar experiences in both countries. They could generally be said to conform to a 'virilitude' model of occupational feminisation, not least because they were acutely aware of the fact that any visible sign of 'difference' with regard to their male colleagues would have immediately disqualified them from any chance of promotion to management positions. For those women who had had children, there had been an explicit decision to exploit their employment citizenship rights with parsimony, in the full knowledge that the ability to symbolically 'neutralise' their femininity (Huppert-Laufer 1982) was a key factor in maintaining them on an upwardly mobile career path. Thus, although on paper French women from these generations had had better access to paid maternity leave than their British counterparts, our interviews abounded with heroic accounts of the use of these rights being kept to a strict minimum, with tales of waters breaking during strategic board meetings, clients' needs being catered for by phone from the maternity ward and young babies being breast-fed in offices and looked after by secretaries, in order for their mothers to keep up all appearances of continuity of service and commitment (Hantrais 1993; Hantrais and Walters 1994). It should nevertheless be noted that the symbolic and material cost of such strategies was not exactly comparable in each country. In the British case, older women we interviewed in managerial positions could definitely be seen as 'pioneers', whose experiences were far removed from those of the vast majority of women of their generation. This was far less the case in France, where combining work and motherhood had already become somewhat 'commonplace' (Marry 2002). Indeed, although we did not have a statistically representative sample to work from, we found that the older British women who had made it to managerial status within large organisations were more likely to be single and childless than their French counterparts.

The most interesting result of the comparison of women from the 'pioneer' generations concerns the fate of those who – through choice or constraint (Crompton and Le Feuvre 1997) – did not attempt to adapt their behaviour to the dominant work ethic or gendered career script within their particular occupation, that is those whose experiences came closer to the 'feminitude' model of occupational feminisation. We found examples of this type of career model amongst women who had adopted a practice-based profile at some point in their life course in both countries. However, the combination of macro- and meso-level structural forces made this a more frequent option for women in France than in Britain.

In the absence of widespread opportunities for part-time work or career breaks at management level within large firms, French women who aspired to a more traditional pattern of work–life 'balance', implying their availability for childcare and domestic management tasks, found fairly numerous opportunities to move into some form of self-employment. Although this did not necessarily imply a radical reduction in their working hours, it was presented as a way of gaining a higher level of 'time sovereignty', whilst maintaining a reasonable level of remuneration and professional competency throughout the critical periods of their life course (following childbirth, divorce, in the face of ageing parents or a sick relative). In the French case, the relative availability of practice-based employment opportunities within the occupations we studied was combined with a somewhat more porous boundary between bureaucratic and practice-based career paths, enabling some women to return to quite senior positions within large firms at a later stage in their careers.

In Britain, this kind of mobility between bureaucratic and practice-based forms of employment was rare. We found no examples of women who had adopted a period of practice-based employment before returning to a high-level managerial position in a large firm. In short, those older British women who sought to escape the pressures of an upwardly mobile bureaucratic career in a national context that was generally less conducive to women's full-time, continuous employment had fewer alternatives than their French counterparts. Although there were limited opportunities for self-employment in some of the occupations we studied (for example accountancy or law), this tended to take the form of sub-contracting to a larger organisation and was usually on a (short) part-time basis (an example of the 'dependant self-employment' model presented earlier). In the British case, this kind of 'alternative' employment status was rarely used as a short-cut back onto the bureaucratic career ladder or as a source of lasting economic autonomy. It necessarily implied the end of a 'career' and the shift to at least partial financial dependency on a spouse. The other alternative open to British women from this generation who aspired to a less demanding work life was simply to move off the career track and to adopt various forms of flexible employment within large firms, usually part-time work in a specialist/expert rather than managerial guise.

The profiles of the younger generations of women working in large bureaucratic organisations in each of these two countries were somewhat different. In Britain, we found a marked generational difference which can probably be explained by the widespread adoption of equal opportunity policies over the past twenty or so years. Unlike their predecessors, the younger qualified British women working in large firms now expect to be able to combine taking primary responsibility for their children and domestic life and to stay on a career track of some kind. This was not the case with the younger generation of French women we interviewed, who continue to envisage a period of practice-based self-employment as the most effective strategy for reaching the kind of work–life 'balance' that is characteristic of the 'feminitude' model of occupational feminisation. However, contrary to their British counterparts, several younger women working in large bureaucratic firms in France actively resisted the 'incentive to balance' that can perhaps be said to have become a new normative dimension of the 'similarity taboo' (Lapeyre and Le Feuvre 2004). Thus, whilst we identified few examples of adhesion to a 'virilitude' vision of occupational feminisation amongst the younger generation of British women in large bureaucratic organisations, the idea that building a career depends on adopting a 'surrogate male' (Crompton and Harris 1998) relationship to the employing organisation was still fairly widespread amongst the younger generations of women in this occupational context in France.

On the other hand, with the notable exception of female doctors working part-time in GP practices, the younger generations of British women working in a practice-based capacity were notably less likely than their predecessors to adhere to a 'feminitude' vision of work–life balance. Although they continued to stress the relative comfort of being able to organise their working time to a greater extent than women working in managerial positions in large organisations, they were nevertheless intent on pursuing a proper 'career' and were wary of the potential threat to their current or future financial autonomy by the claims made on their time by children and partners. In this sense, their subjective orientation to the work–life balance question was fairly close to that of their French counterparts engaged in the first stages of a bureaucratic career within a large organisation.

The differences observed in the type of 'practitioner' or 'managerial' careers developed in the two countries are confirmed by the results of a recent study of self-employment and childcare in Europe (Hildebrand and Williams 2003). In their secondary analysis of the European Community Household Panel survey data from the late 1990s, Hildebrand and Williams observed that, contrary to a widely-held belief, self-employed women did not spend more time on childcare than their salaried counterparts, the only exceptions to this rule being the Netherlands and the UK. The overall hours dedicated to childcare also vary significantly by country, with the highest levels observed in the UK (49.5 hours/week by salaried women and 61.0 hours/week by their self-employed compatriots) and the lowest figures in France (19.7 hours/week by salaried women and 21.6 hours/week by those in self-employment) (Hildebrand and Williams 2003). This reflects the societal-level differences in childcare arrangements mentioned above.

The differences observed between the two countries, including the 'generation effect', are summarised in Table 6.1.

DISCUSSION AND CONCLUSIONS

Results from our Franco-British comparison of the feminisation process in managerial and practice-based professional occupations indicate quite clearly that quantitative measures of the number of women entering these professions can only provide a partial understanding of the issues at stake. The precise mechanisms through which women gain access to the previous 'male bastions' at the top of the occupational ladder have important consequences when it comes to interpreting the meaning of recent and often quite radical changes to the gender composition of these occupations. Quite clearly, although macro-level differences in the prescriptive 'gender arrangements' do provide a necessary back-drop to grasping the cross-national similarities and differences observed, they do not enable a clear understanding of the different patterns of occupational feminisation that exist within a given national context. Attention also needs to be paid both to the meso-level opportunity structures offered in different occupations in different national contexts and to the micro-level aspirations and 'preferences' that are expressed by individual women at certain points in their life course. Contrary to Catherine Hakim's hypothesis, such 'preferences' are clearly not established once and for all (Hakim 2000), but evolve in interaction with the dominant societal-level 'gender arrangements' and the occupational-level 'gender regimes' that they also potentially influence in return.

Our empirical data would seem to suggest that women who enter

Table 6.1 *Cross-national similarities and differences in the gendered experience of occupational feminisation in Britain and France*

	Britain		France	
	Salaried/ managerial	Self-employed/ professional	Salaried/ managerial	Self-employed/ professional
'Pioneer' generation	'Virilitude' model dominant – single, no children. Acutely aware of discrimination and of their 'pioneer' status, both within the organisation and wider society	'Feminitude' model dominant – usually part-time, lack of financial autonomy, but career breaks accepted in the 'interests of spouse/ children'	'Virilitude' model dominant – divorced, with children. Less aware of discrimination/ barriers to promotion, more focused on 'choice'	'Feminitude' model dominant – usually flexible full-time, extensive use of paid external childcare + some informal support networks
'Post-EO' generation	'Feminitude' model dominant – periods of part-time, but aspirations for financial autonomy and promotion through 'EO/ fast track' company policies	'Virilitude' model dominant – time sovereignty, but long hours, requires strong informal support networks (partner, extended family)	'Virilitude' model dominant – tensions in work–life interface, lack of informal support networks. Aware of discrimination/ barriers to promotion	'Feminitude' model dominant – usually flexible full-time, extensive use of paid external childcare + few informal support networks

relatively prestigious and well-paid occupations find themselves constrained to choose between two opposing logics. On the one hand, they can attempt to side-track the gendered expectations of these 'time hungry' occupations, by carving out female-specific patterns of time management and by clustering in those occupational niches (Crompton and Lyonette 2007) that best enable them to continue to conform to the equally gendered encouragement to achieve some form of what is often abusively termed work–life 'balance'. In other words, they can continue to perform (or supervise the performance of) the multitude of tasks that are assigned to women under the 'male breadwinner/female carer' model of gender arrangements. Alternatively, they can adhere to the 'standard' male-typical career scripts and adopt personal life options that enable them to challenge or circumvent the idea that, as women, they should prioritise their family and partnership commitments in relation to their professional careers, thus achieving 'imbalance' of another kind.

The cross-national comparative analysis takes these issues further, by showing that the 'choice' between these two options leads to different outcomes in each of the national settings studied here. On the one hand, the occupational niches which provide the opportunity for female-specific (and, therefore, relatively unspectacular) career paths are unevenly distributed between bureaucratic and practice-based employment locations in the two countries. Practice-based careers are more closely associated with a 'feminitude' pattern of occupational feminisation amongst all generations of highly qualified women in France, but only with this pattern of occupational feminisation amongst the 'pioneer' generation of women in Britain. On the other hand, achieving a career within a bureaucratic employment structure tends to require the adoption of a 'virilitude' orientation to the work–life interface amongst all generations of highly qualified women in France, but only amongst the 'pioneer' generations of British women. The younger British women who have more recently embarked on a bureaucratic career in a large organisation are more likely to aspire to (and to achieve) various forms of institutional support, enabling them to shoulder the vast majority of what continue to be seen as 'their' domestic and family commitments. Their practices and preferences are thus closer to those found in the 'feminitude' ideal-type model of occupational feminisation.

It should perhaps come as no surprise to find that the career patterns that are the most attractive (partly because they are also the most accessible) to the vast majority of women in each national context are precisely those that pose the least threat to the existing 'gender arrangements', based on the assignment of the socially fundamental unpaid care activities as women's primary responsibility (Folbre 1994). What is perhaps more unexpected is the fact that the career patterns that best provide for this form of gender conformity are not located in exactly the same position on the bureaucratic/practice-based employment continuum in each national context.

These results obviously raise questions about the effectiveness of some of the so-called 'equal opportunity' measures that have been adopted to promote women's access to managerial status in some national contexts (Commission européenne 2008). In so far as these are based on what we have called a 'feminitude' model of occupational feminisation, they obviously provide valuable career opportunities for those women who, through choice or constraint, refuse to 'sacrifice' a certain degree of conformity to the dominant gender order. Their potential role in transforming the material and ideological foundations of the existing gender order is therefore somewhat debatable (Le Feuvre 2009).

Our findings also suggest that caution is needed when comparing levels of occupational feminisation across countries. We have shown that women's engagement in bureaucratic and practice-based careers does not necessarily have the same implications, in terms of conformity to or transgression of the dominant gender arrangements, in each national context. It is impossible to read and interpret these cross-national variations from the standard statistical indicators of rates of occupational feminisation. Gauging the country-specific meaning of a given rate of feminisation requires more qualitative methodological tools. In turn, this raises serious questions as to the significance of the now widespread adoption of 'benchmarking' indicators of the degree of gender (in)equality that can be measured comparatively across national contexts.

NOTES

1. A previous version of this chapter has been published in French: N. Le Feuvre 2008, 'La pluralité des modèles de féminisation des professions supérieures en France et en Grande-Bretagne' in H. Hirata, M.R. Lombardi and M. Maruani (eds), *Travail et Genre. Regards Croisés France – Europe – Amérique Latine,* Paris: La Découverte, Coll. 'Recherches': pp. 263–76.
2. During successive individual or collective research projects throughout the 1990s and 2000s, we have completed biographical interviews with over 200 men and women working in professional and managerial occupations in Britain and France: lawyers (45), doctors (45) academics (25 interviews and a questionnaire survey of 1500 French university professors and senior lecturers), speech therapists (80 interviews + a questionnaire survey of 345 practitioners), pharmacists (25) and bank managers (25). In each case, a similar biographical interview guide was used covering primary socialisation experiences, education and careers paths, family formation patterns and gender values, in order to analyse the work–life interface of individuals, usually with dependant children, at varying stages in their careers (see references for Le Feuvre's earlier publications based on these data).
3. Our observed 'generation effect' is not directly related to age, but more to a distinction between those women who entered these occupations as 'pioneers' (with very few female colleagues who could act as role models) and those who experienced women's presence within the occupations as relatively 'commonplace' (Marry 2004).
4. The two other ideal-type models of occupational feminisation identified were less frequently represented.

BIBLIOGRAPHY

Afsa Essafi, C. and S. Buffeteau (2006), 'L'activité féminine en France: quelles évolutions récentes, quelles tendances pour l'avenir?', *Economie & Statistique*, No. 398–9, pp. 85–97.

Anderson-Gough, F., C. Grey and K. Robson (2001), 'Tests of time: organizational time-reckoning and the making of accountants in two multi-national accounting firms', *Accounting, Organizations and Society*, **24**, 99–122.

Angeloff, T. (2000), *Le travail à temps partiel: un marché de dupes?*, Paris: Syros-La Découverte.

Commission européenne (2006), *Une feuille de route pour l'égalité entre les femmes et les hommes 2006–2010*, Bruxelles: Commission européenne – Direction générale de l'emploi, des affaires sociales et de l'égalité des chances, unité G1.

Commission européenne (2008), *Les femmes et les hommes dans la prise de décision en 2007. Analyse de la situation et tendances*, Bruxelles: Commission européenne, DG Emploi, affaires sociales et égalité des chances.

Connell, R.W. (1987), *Gender & Power: Society, the Person and Sexual Politics*, London: Polity.

Cousins, C.R. and N. Tang (2004), 'Working time and work and family conflict in the Netherlands, Sweden and the UK', *Work, Employment & Society*, **18**, 531–50.

Crompton, R. (1998), 'Women's employment and state policies', *Innovation*, **11**, 129–46.

Crompton, R. (1999), *Restructuring Gender Relations and Employment: The Decline of the Male Breadwinner*, Oxford: Oxford University Press.

Crompton, R. (2006), 'Some issues in cross-national comparative research methods: a comparison of attitudes to promotion and women's employment in Britain and Portugal', *Work, Employment & Society*, **20**, 403–14.

Crompton, R. (2008), *Class and Stratification*, Cambridge: Polity.

Crompton, R. and G. Birkelund (2000), 'Employment and caring in British and Norwegian banking: an exploration through individual careers', *Work, Employment & Society*, **14**, 331–52.

Crompton, R. and F. Harris (1998), 'Gender relations and employment: the impact of occupation', *Work, Employment & Society*, **12**, 297–315.

Crompton, R. and N. Le Feuvre (1997), 'Choisir une carrière, faire carrière: les femmes médecins en France et en Grande-Bretagne', *Cahiers du GEDISST*, **19**, 49–75.

Crompton, R. and N. Le Feuvre (2000), 'Gender, family and employment in comparative perspective: the realities and representations of equal opportunities in Britain and France', *Journal of European Social Policy*, **10**, 334–48.

Crompton, R. and C. Lyonette (2007), 'Women's career success and work–life "balance" in the accountancy and medical professions in Britain', Cambridge: *GENet Working Paper 26*.

Crompton, R. and K. Sanderson (1986), 'Credentials and careers: some implications of the increase in professional qualifications amongst women', *Sociology*, **20**, 25–42.

Crompton, R., S. Lewis and C. Lyonette (2007), *Women, Men, Work and Family in Europe*, London: Palgrave.

Crompton, R., L. Hantrais, N. Le Feuvre and P. Walters (1990), *Une comparaison franco-britannique des femmes cadres et membres des professions intellectuelles supérieures*, Bruxelles: Rapport à la Commission des Communautés européennes, Direction Générale V Emploi, relations industrielles et affaires sociales, September, V/342/91-FR.

Department of Trade and Industry (2005), *Work and Families. Choice and Flexibility. A Consultation Document*, London: Department of Trade and Industry.

Evetts, J. (2002), 'New directions in state and international professional occupations', *Work, Employment & Society*, **16**, 339–51.

Fagnani, J. (2007), 'Fertility rates and mother's employment behaviour in comparative perspective: similarities and differences in six European countries', in R. Crompton, S. Lewis and C. Lyonette (eds), *Women, Men, Work and Family in Europe*, London: Palgrave.

Folbre, N. (1994), *Who Pays for the Kids? Gender and the Structures of Constraint*, London: Routledge.

Hakim, C. (2000), *Work-Lifestyle Choices in the 21st Century. Preference Theory*, Oxford: Oxford University Press.

Hantrais, L. (1993), 'The gender of time in professional occupations', *Time & Society*, **2**, 139–57.

Hantrais, L. (1995), 'A comparative perspective on gender and accountancy', *The European Accounting Review*, **4**, 197–215.

Hantrais, L. and P. Walters (1994), 'Making it in and making it out: women in professional occupations in Britain and France', *Gender, Work and Organizations*, **1**, 23–32.

Héritier, F. (1996), *Masculin/féminin: la pensée de la différence*, Paris: Odile Jacob.

Hildebrand, V. and D.A. Williams (2003), 'Self-employment and caring for children: evidence from Europe', *Luxemburg: IRISS Working Paper Series* n°2003–06, Centre for European Policy Studies.

Holmwood, J. and J. Siltanen (1996), 'Gender, the professions and employment citizenship', in T.P. Boje (ed.), *A Changing Europe: Trends in Welfare State and Labour Markets*, New York: M.E. Sharpe.

Huppert-Laufer, J. (1982), *La féminité neutralisée? Les femmes cadres dans l'entreprise*, Paris: Flammarion.

Kantola, J. (2008), 'Why do all the women disappear? Gendering processes in a political science department', *Gender, Work and Organizations*, **15**, 202–25.

Kergoat, D. (2000), 'Division sexuelle du travail et rapports sociaux de sexe', in H. Hirata, F. Laborie, H. Le Doaré and D. Senotier (eds), *Dictionnaire Critique du Féminisme*, Paris: Presses Universitaires de France.

Lane, C., M. Potton and W. Littek (2002), 'The professions between state and market: a cross-national study of convergence and divergence', *European Societies*, **4**, 235–60.

Lapeyre, N. and N. Le Feuvre (2004), 'Concilier l'inconciliable? Le rapport des femmes à la notion de "conciliation travail-famille" dans les professions libérales en France', *Nouvelles Questions Féministes*, **23**, 42–58.

Latour, E. and N. Le Feuvre (2006), 'Les carrières universitaires françaises à l'épreuve du genre', in E. Ollagnier and C. Solar (eds), *Parcours de femmes à l'université: perspectives internationales*, Paris: l'Harmattan.

Laufer, J. and R. Silvera (2008), 'Accords sur l'égalité professionnelle suite à la loi du 9 mai 2001: premiers éléments d'analyse', Paris: Emergences, available at www.emergences.fr.

Le Feuvre, N. (1999), 'Gender, occupational feminisation and reflexivity', in R. Crompton (ed.), *Restructuring Gender Relations and Employment: The Decline of the Male Breadwinner*, Oxford: Oxford University Press.

Le Feuvre, N. (2001), 'La féminisation de la profession médicale en France et en Grande-Bretagne: voie de transformation ou de recomposition du "genre"?', in P. Aïach, D. Cebe, G. Cresson and C. Philippe (eds), *Femmes et hommes dans le champ de la santé: approches sociologiques*, Rennes: Editions de l'ENSP.

Le Feuvre, N. (2006), 'The enforcement of social policies: the case of the equality in employment laws in France', in A. Guichon, C. van den Anker and I. Novikova (eds), *Women's Social Rights and Entitlements*, London: Palgrave.

Le Feuvre, N. (2007), 'Les carrières sexuées des orthophonistes', in L. Tain (ed.), *Langage, genre et profession: le métier d'orthophoniste*, Rennes: Ecole Nationale de Santé Publique.

Le Feuvre, N. (2009), 'Exploring women's academic careers in cross-national perspective: lessons for equal opportunity policies', *Equal Opportunities International*, **28**(1), 9–23.

Le Feuvre, N. and N. Lapeyre (2005), 'Les "scripts sexués" de carrière dans les professions juridiques en France', *Knowledge, Work and Society/Travail, savoir et société*, **3**, 101–26.

Le Feuvre, N. and P.A.Walters (1993), 'Egales en droit? La féminisation des professions juridiques en France et en Grande-Bretagne', *Sociétés contemporaines*, **16**, 41–62.

Le Feuvre, N. N. Lapeyre, M. Cacouault and G. Picot (2003), *La féminisation des professions libérales: l'exemple des femmes médecins et avocats*, Toulouse: Rapport au Service des Droits des Femmes et de l'égalité.

Marry, C. (2002), 'Pour un mélange des genres dans les comparaisons internationales', in M. Lallemant and J. Spurk (eds), *Stratégies de la comparaison internationale*, Paris: Editions du CNRS.

Marry, C. (2004), *Les femmes ingénieurs. Une révolution respectueuse*, Paris: Belin.

Méda, D. and H. Périvier (2007), *Le deuxième âge de l'émancipation. La société, les femmes et l'emploi*, Paris: Seuil.

Muehlberger, U. (2007), *Dependent Self-Employment. Workers on the Border between Employment and Self-Employment*, Basingstoke and London: Palgrave Macmillan.

Muehlberger, U. and S. Bertolini (2007), 'The organizational governance of work relationships between employment and self-employment', *Socio-Economic Review Advance Access*, 21 December, 1–24.

OECD (2006), *Men and Women in OECD Countries*, Paris: OECD.

OECD (2007a), Family Database, Paris, OECD, available at: http://www.oecd. org/els/social/family/database, accessed 4 September 2009.

OECD (2007b), Database on Labour Force Statistics, Paris, OECD, available at http://stats.oecd.org/Index.aspx, accessed 4 September 2009.

O'Reilly, J. (2006), 'Framing comparisons: gendering perspectives on cross-national comparative research on work and welfare', *Work, Employment & Society*, **20**, 731–50.

Pfau-Effinger, B. (2004), 'Socio-historical paths of the male breadwinner model

– an explanation of cross-national differences', *British Journal of Sociology*, **55**, 377–99.

Pickvance, C. (1986), 'Comparative urban analysis and assumptions about causality', *International Journal of Urban and Regional Research*, **10**, 162–84.

Rhode, D.L. (2003), 'Gender and the profession: an American perspective', in U. Schultz and G. Shaw (eds), *Women in the World's Legal Professions*, Oxford: Hart Publishing.

Rubin, G. (1975), 'The traffic in women: notes on the political economy of sex', in R.R. Reiter (ed.), *Toward an Anthropology of Women*, London: Monthly Review Press.

Schultz, U. and G. Shaw (2003), *Women in the World's Legal Professions*, Oxford: Hart Publishing.

Siemienska, R. and A. Zimmer (2007), *Gendered Career Trajectories in Academia in Cross-National Perspective*, Warsaw: Scholar.

Smeaton, D. (2006), 'Work return rates after childbirth in the UK – trends, determinants and implications: a comparison of cohorts born in 1958 and 1970', *Work Employment & Society*, **20**, 5–25.

Tilly, C. and S.W. Scott (1987), *Women, Work and Family*, London: Methuen.

Vallet, L-A. (2001), 'Stratification et mobilité sociale: la place des femmes', in J. Laufer, C. Marry and M. Maruani (eds), *Masculin-féminin: questions pour les sciences de l'homme*, Paris: Presses Universitaires de France.

Walters, S. (2005), 'Making the best of a bad job? Female part-timers' orientations and attitudes to work', *Gender, Work and Organizations*, **12**, 192–216.

Warren, T. (2004), 'Working part-time: achieving a successful "work–life" balance?', *British Journal of Sociology*, **55**, 99–122.

Yeandle, S. (1999), 'Women, men and non-standard employment: breadwinner and caregiving in Germany, Italy and the UK', in R. Crompton (ed.), *Restructuring Gender Relations and Employment: The Decline of the Male Breadwinner*, Oxford: Oxford University Press.

PART III

The Challenge of Integrating Family and Work

7. Gender segregation and bargaining in domestic labour: evidence from longitudinal time-use data

Man Yee Kan and Jonathan Gershuny

It is well known that nowadays in the UK and other developed countries, women still undertake the bulk of housework (Gershuny 1992; Kan 2008; Layte 1999). Although some studies suggest that the gender gap in household labour participation has been gradually closing over the past three decades, the change appears to have been slow so that, for example, full-time employed women in the 1980s and 1990s were still responsible for more than 60 per cent of housework (Gershuny and Robinson 1988; Sullivan 2000).

Previous studies on the domestic division of labour were usually based on cross-sectional data and tended to focus on routine types of housework, such as cleaning, cooking and washing the dishes, rather than on care for family members and less gender-traditional types of household work, such as household repairs, gardening and grocery shopping. A major aim of this chapter is to identify whether gender segregation exists in these two broad types of domestic labour. We expect to find that the gender divide in the domestic division of labour is more rigid in the case of routine housework, and that the social mechanisms that explain the gender gap in these two major types of domestic work are not entirely the same. It is because routine housework (for example cooking and washing up) tends be carried out on a daily basis and can be less flexibly adjusted according to one's work schedule compared with non-routine types of housework (for example shopping and gardening), which can be scheduled to be undertaken during holidays and weekends. Furthermore, research has suggested that routine housework is associated with women's feminine identities (deVault 1990), while men are more likely to undertake childcare and less 'feminine' types of housework (for example household repairs) (Gershuny 2000; Robinson and Godbey 1997).

What explains the gendered division of domestic labour? First, neoclassical economic theory explains it by the comparative economic advantages of women and men in domestic work and market work respectively (Becker 1991 [1981]; 1985). Under this perspective, the gendered domestic division of labour is expected to be intensified after major lifecycle events, such as having a child, since both the demand for domestic labour and the relative advantages of women in the domestic sphere are supposed to increase in the wake of these events.

Another closely-related and commonly employed approach in recent studies is the resource bargaining theory. Although also stressing the role of rational actions, it postulates that husbands and wives attempt to maximise their individual interest rather than joint welfare (for example, Manser and Brown 1980; McElroy and Horney 1981). It hypothesises that both men and women dislike and try to avoid housework, and a higher level of their economic resources vis-à-vis their partners will predict a smaller share of their domestic labour. This approach has received support in recent studies based on national survey data (for example, Bianchi et al. 2000; Brines 1994; Presser 1994, using US data; Bittman et al. 2003, using Australian data; Kan 2008 using British data).

Nonetheless, some scholars argue that gender role expectations will interact with the resource bargaining process. West and Zimmerman (1987) and West and Fenstermaker (1993) put forward the view that both men and women may 'do gender' (that is, display and reproduce their gender identities) through the domestic division of labour. Because of the gendered nature of housework, it can be taken as a stage for the symbolic enactment of identities when gendered expectations are not fulfilled in the economic domain, for example, when the husband fails to perform the breadwinner role and when the wife earns a significantly higher income. In supporting the 'doing gender' hypothesis, Brines (1994) reported that there is a curvilinear relationship between housework hours and men's housework hours in the US, that is, economically dependent men tend to undertake less housework than predicted by the bargaining theory. Building on Brines's work, Greenstein (2000) reported similar findings for economically dependent men and breadwinner wives in the US. Bittman et al. (2003), analysing Australian data, found a U-shaped relationship between relative earnings and housework hours in the case of married women but not in the case of married men. In these and many other studies, the authors have identified, when the wife becomes the chief earner, a reversal of the expected relationship between bargaining power and the domestic division of labour, which they interpret as an attempt to compensate for the challenge to conventional gendered expectations.

This chapter contributes to research on the topic by employing longitudinal data on time use that covers both routine housework and non-routine domestic work (in which care is a major part and was often overlooked in past studies). It will chart changes in time use for men and women since their partnership and investigate how lifecycle events will trigger changes in the division of the two main kinds of household work between partners. We will also evaluate if the bargaining theory is useful for explaining the gender division of these two types of domestic work. Furthermore, we will test the bargaining theory and the 'doing gender' hypothesis more appropriately by employing a measure of potential labour market wage rather than actual labour market income. Past studies testing the theory unavoidably committed a selection bias in their samples by employing actual incomes of partners to calculate relative resource bargaining power. Many women leave the labour market or change to part-time employment during the life course, and especially just after childbirth, and therefore have a relatively low income. But their bargaining power relative to their partners should not only depend on their actual income but also their economic well-being should the relationship end, that is their potential income should matter more than their current income. The longitudinal data we deploy has advantages over previous studies in testing the bargaining theory, since it allows us to control for unobserved characteristics of individuals that may confound the relationship between their domestic work participation and relative resource levels in the models.

DATA AND METHODS

We have a unique data set which combines the strength of high-quality diary time-use data and household panel survey data. We calibrate a set of time-use variables for a long-running panel survey, the British Household Panel Survey (BHPS, 1994–2005) with evidence derived from a smaller-scale panel survey that collected time-use information by both survey questionnaires and diaries from the same respondents (the Home On-line Study, HoL, 1999–2001). The questionnaire part of the HoL shares a similar set of time-use predictor variables with the BHPS. These questions include respondents' usual hours of routine housework and paid work, the frequencies at which they participated in various forms of leisure activities, and whether or not they were responsible for common types of household work. We regress diary-based time-use estimates in HoL on its stylised time-use estimates,[1] and then multiply the resulting regression coefficients with the same stylised predictor variables in the BHPS. Thus we obtain a calibrated measure of time-use patterns. This covers all five major daily activities: (1) paid work/study; (2) routine housework; (3) care and other domestic work; (4) consumption and leisure; and (5) sleep, rest and personal care.[2] The BHPS does not contain direct measures of the time spent on activities (3), (4) and (5). Our data add to the strength of the original stylised measures of domestic work time in the BHPS, which include only routine types of housework (for example cleaning, cooking, and doing the laundry) but exclude important categories such as care and non-routine types of domestic work (for example gardening and shopping).

Time-use Changes over the Lifecycle

We have a strong panel of data from the BHPS with a calibrated index of time use for the respondents. In order to investigate the effect of changes in family stage, we adopt the frequently used panel analysis technique of pooling pairs of successive years of relevant cases to increase the number of observations in family transitions. The pooled sample, derived from the 1994–2005 data collection waves, contains eleven successive pairs of observations. We present cases from the pooled sample as a 'pseudo-panel' to illustrate the conventional form of the family lifecycle starting from partnership formation. We examine transitions and changes in time-use practices in the successive years.

Ordinary Least Squares (OLS) models will be employed to examine the relationship between relative potential earnings and time-use changes after partnership and after childbirth respectively. Then OLS and individual-level fixed-effect models will be applied to a pooled sample of married and cohabiting men and women who are within the first seven years of their partnership. The aim is to test whether bargaining power, as indicated by relative potential earnings, has formed different patterns of relationships with routine domestic work, and care and non-routine domestic work, and if so, whether the relationships are curvilinear or linear.

Relative Economic Independency

Following Brines (1994) (who herself followed Sorensen and McLanahan 1987), we measure the relative economic independency by an index of income transfer R, defined as the difference between the respondent's potential hourly wage and the partner's divided by their sum. $-1 < R < 1$. $R > 0$ if the respondent has a higher level of potential earnings than the partner; $R < 0$ otherwise. Potential hourly wage is estimated by the Essex Score, which is calculated based on respondents' educational qualifications, their most recent occupation, and labour market statuses in the 48 months prior to the interview. It has been shown to be a valid indicator of social position and a significant predictor of earnings from the labour market (Kan and Gershuny 2006b).

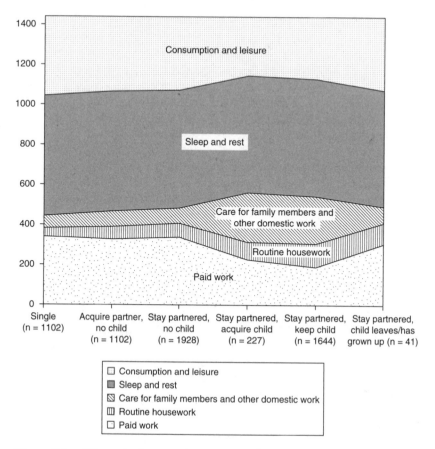

Figure 7.1   Women's time use (minutes per day) over the life course

FINDINGS

Changes in Time-use Practices since Partnership

Figures 7.1 and 7.2 illustrate changes in men and women's time spent on paid work, routine housework, care and other domestic work, sleep and rest, and consumption throughout the conventional family life course after partnership.

Only small changes in time use between the years are seen in the case of static family circumstances (in terms of partnership formation and the presence of children). For example, for men and women who had stayed

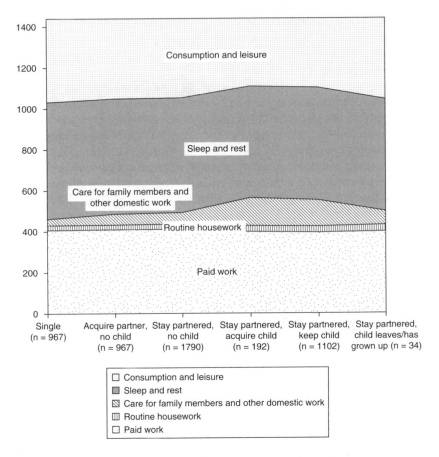

Figure 7.2   Men's time use (minutes per day) over the life course

partnered with no child in two successive years, there was only a small increase in paid work time. Moreover, neither men nor women changed their paid work time significantly in the year immediately after entering partnership (women's average paid work time was reduced from 340 to 327 minutes per day, while men's changed from 406 to 409 minutes per day). Major changes in paid work time occurred in the year after having a child: women and men reduced their paid work time from 361 to 227 minutes and from 435 to 398 minutes respectively. Women's reduction in paid work time was therefore significantly larger than men's (the proportions being 37 per cent and 9 per cent respectively). Moreover, women's paid work time continued to decrease until the child left home or reached 16 years old. But men's paid work time remained more or less stable after the birth of the child.

Turning to domestic work time, we see much greater gender differences than in the case of paid work time, especially in the year just after the beginning of partnership and that just after having a child. Here we are particularly interested in finding out whether there are differences between the changes in routine housework time, and those in care and non-routine domestic work in the wake of lifecycle events. In the case of routine housework, women already undertook more housework (42 minutes per day) than men (24 minutes per day) in the year just before partnership. Time on routine housework was relatively stable in the period where there was no observed change in family status. Significant increases in routine housework time were observed in the period where individuals had acquired partners, but the change was more substantial in the case of women: their housework time increased by 50 per cent (from 42 to 63 minutes). Having a child brought a substantial rise in routine housework time for women (from 58 to 87 minutes). On the contrary, men did not increase their routine housework time significantly after partnership or after childbirth. In Figure 7.2, we can see that their routine housework time hardly changed, and stayed under 30 minutes per day over the lifecycle. On the other hand, women's routine housework time continued to increase over the life course, peaked at 120 minutes per day when the young child was present, and did not drop much even after the child grew older or left home.

Time spent on care for family members and other non-routine types of domestic work revealed a somewhat different gendered pattern from that of routine housework. Women's time was still longer than men's in the year just before partnership (61 compared with 32 minutes). But both men and women increased their time on these activities significantly after forming a partnership, and after having a child. Women's time increased to 77 minutes and men's to 53 minutes in the year just after partnership. Their times peaked at 248 and 136 minutes respectively in the year just after the birth of the first child. These patterns form a contrast with men's relative stagnant routine housework time over the life course. As expected, women's and men's time spent on childcare and non-routine domestic tasks reduced gradually as the child grew up or left home.

Men's consumption and leisure time was longer than women's at all stages of the family lifecycle. Both women's and men's figures dropped to some extent after partnership formation and significantly after the birth of a child (from 357 to 294 minutes per day and from 380 to 332 minutes respectively). Their time on these activities did not recover when the child remained co-resident with them, but increased significantly when the child was old enough to leave home. Time on sleep and rest was reduced slightly over the lifecycle. Overall, women spent slightly longer time on sleep, rest and personal care than men.

There are several important initial observations on the gender segregation of domestic division of labour over the life course. First, women reduce their level of participation in paid work and spend more time on both routine and non-routine domestic work (which mainly consists of care) after partnership and childbirth. But men's paid work time is relatively stable over the life course. Second, men increase their domestic time significantly only on care and non-routine types of housework but not on routine types of housework. Contrary to findings of previous studies based on cross-sectional data, however, our longitudinal findings reveal that men do increase their participation in domestic work over the life course. Referring again to Figure 7.2, we can see that the ratio of men's total domestic work (including routine and non-routine domestic work) to paid work increased gradually since partnership and reached the maximum in the year after having a child. From Figure 7.1, we can also observe that this ratio increased even more dramatically in the case of women. Finally, women and men had similar total work time (including paid work and all unpaid domestic work) throughout the life course. The total work time for women and men was 467 and 486 minutes respectively in the year just after partnership, peaking at 562 and 562 minutes respectively in the year just after childbirth. Nonetheless, women had increasingly spent more time on unpaid domestic labour rather than on paid work.

Bargaining and Changes in Domestic Work Time

The earlier results have revealed a serious limitation in using conventional stylised measures of housework hours, which are usually based on routine housework rather than care and other non-routine types of domestic work, for the study of the domestic division of labour. Since there is gender segregation in domestic work, the social mechanisms that explain the division of routine and non-routine types of domestic work between men and women are likely to be different. Women share most of the routine and non-routine domestic work and increase their time on both significantly after partnership. In contrast, men's time on routine housework is stable but their time on non-routine types of housework is relatively malleable to lifecycle events. Accordingly, we should expect to find that one's relative potential income (as an indicator of bargaining power) should have different effects on these two main types of housework. It is likely that relative potential income will have greater effects on women's domestic work time than men's. It is also likely that men's time on care and non-routine domestic work is more subject to changes according to the relative potential income, since men on average increase their time on these activities significantly after partnership and childbirth. Of course, men may tend to undertake non-routine types of domestic work because of factors other than their resource level or bargaining power. For example, these tasks may simply fit better with their schedules than routine housework because they are relatively flexible and can be arranged to take place during holidays and weekends. In addition, people may find childcare more emotionally rewarding and may feel under more normative obligation to undertake it compared with routine housework. Therefore we might expect to find that one's resource bargaining power has little effect on the time spent on these activities. In the following, we test the associations between relative potential earnings and changes in the two main types of domestic work.

Models of Table 7.1 pool all cases involving partnership formation in the sample. The dependent variable is the difference in time spent on routine housework, care and non-routine domestic work, and total domestic work in the wake of partnership formation (year after − year before). Men and women are included in two separate sets of models, which control for age, and household income and presence of dependent children.

The models have a higher explanatory power for male partners' domestic work time (the R^2 is larger). However, relative earnings potential is a significant predictor only in the women's routine housework model, but not in the rest of the models. These findings demonstrate that relative earnings are a good predictor of *changes* in women's routine housework time after marriage. But for men, the other control variables such as total household earnings are much better predictors of changes in their domestic work time. A high relative earnings potential in the case of women is associated with a significant decrease in routine housework time after partnership (the coefficient being − 10.05). But relative earnings are not associated with changes in their non-routine domestic work time (the coefficient being small and insignificant) and the total domestic work (the coefficient is significant only at 10 per cent level but not at 95 per cent level). In the case of men, as we will see in later sections, relative earnings are associated significantly with their domestic work time in a single year, but are not significant predictors of *changes* in domestic work time after partnership.

In Table 7.2, the models include all cases where men and women had had a child within the first seven years of their partnership. The dependent variable is the change in domestic work time just after childbirth (year after − year before). On average, having a child is accompanied with an increase in total domestic work time for men and women. Accordingly, we see from the table that the increase in domestic work time is negatively associated with the level of household income for women (the coefficients being negative and significant), but relative potential earnings are not

Table 7.1   Changes in domestic work time and relative potential earnings after partnership

| | Women | | | | | | Men | | | | | |
| | Routine housework | | Care and non-routine housework | | Total domestic work | | Routine housework | | Care and non-routine housework | | Total domestic work | |
	B	SE	B	SE	B	SE	B	SE	B	SE	B	SE
Age	0.065	0.087	-1.238***	0.193	-1.172***	0.235	-0.708***	0.070	-0.893***	0.122	-1.601***	0.149
Log (Household income)	-8.060***	1.410	-1.746	3.142	-9.806*	3.833	4.012**	1.199	-0.819	2.086	3.194	2.559
Presence of child (Yes = 1, No = 0)	5.967**	1.976	21.89***	4.403	27.86***	5.371	8.504***	1.761	74.52***	3.064	83.02***	3.759
Relative potential earnings[a]	-10.05*	4.509	-0.954	10.05	-11.01	12.26	-0.023	3.984	2.953	6.932	2.930	8.504
Constant	82.86***	10.99	67.66**	24.48	150.5***	29.86	-9.726	9.269	54.33**	16.126	44.61*	19.78
R²	0.056		0.063		0.064		0.134		0.444		0.425	
F	14.84***		16.77***		17.17***		32.71***		166.0***		153.4***	
Df	4		4		4		4		4		4	

Notes: Data from a pooled sample of the British Household Panel Survey, 1994–2005. For women, $N = 1004$. For men, $N = 837$.
[a]Defined as the difference between one's own potential hour wage and spouse's potential hourly wage divided by the sum of the two.
$*p < .05. **p < .01. ***p < .001.$

Table 7.2 Changes in domestic work time and relative potential earnings after childbirth

	Women						Men					
	Routine housework		Care and non-routine housework		Total domestic work		Routine housework		Care and non-routine housework		Total domestic work	
	B	SE	B	SE	B	SE	B	SE	B	SE	B	SE
Age	1.372*	0.556	-6.990***	0.794	-5.618***	1.129	-0.127	0.336	-3.066***	0.647	-3.194***	0.693
Log (Household income)	-8.280*	4.159	-35.52***	5.941	-43.80***	8.445	-14.27***	3.129	13.64*	6.017	-0.629	6.445
Relative potential earnings[a]	-26.91	15.70	-16.84	22.44	-43.75	31.89	-28.23**	10.077	7.076	19.38	-21.15	20.76
Constant	56.78	31.32	623.00***	44.74	679.8***	63.59	127.3***	24.835	67.16	47.76	194.4***	51.16
R²	0.053		0.492		0.317		0.154		0.136		0.131	
F	3.15*		54.23***		25.95***		9.70***		8.37***		8.03***	
Df	3		3		3		3		3		3	

Notes: Data from a pooled sample of the British Household Panel Survey, 1994–2005. For women, N = 172. For men, N = 164.
[a]Defined as the difference between one's own potential hour wage and spouse's potential hourly wage divided by the sum of the two.
*p < .05. **p < .01. ***p < .001.

significantly associated with their change in domestic work time (although the coefficient is negative). In the male partners' models, the coefficients concerning household income and relative potential earnings have different signs in the routine housework model and the care and non-routine housework model, implying that the mechanisms explaining changes in the two types of domestic work are different. As can be seen, higher household income and high relative earnings are negatively associated with routine housework time for men. As for care and non-routine domestic work, these factors have a positive association.

In sum, it is unlikely that changes in care and non-routine domestic work time of men and women are the results of resource bargaining. Bargaining power, as measured by relative potential earnings, explain better changes in routine housework time of women after partnership, and of men after the birth of a child.

Bargaining and 'Doing Gender'?

Are domestic work hours mainly explained by relative economic advantages in the labour market? Do men and women 'do gender' by undertaking respectively less and more housework than predicted by their relative earnings? To investigate this, we will introduce the U-shaped relationship implied by the reversal in the relationship between potential relative earnings and domestic work time. In Tables 7.3a–b and 7.4a–b, women and men who are in the seven years after partnership are pooled in the sample. The dependent variables are routine housework, non-routine domestic work, and total domestic work time in a single year of the survey. The OLS models in Tables 7.3a and 7.4a take into account multiple observations of some individuals when calculating the standard errors. However, if there are unobserved and unchanged characteristics of the respondents that are correlated with the errors of models, the parameter estimates will be biased. We therefore introduce the individual-level fixed-effect models in Tables 7.3b and 7.4b, which control for the unobserved heterogeneity of individuals with repeated observations. The bargaining approach predicts that individuals' potential earnings relative to that of their partners will be negatively associated with the time spent on the two main types of domestic work. But under the 'doing gender' hypothesis, women with a very high level and men with a very low level of relative potential earnings will undertake respectively more and less domestic work, that is the squared term in the models will have an opposite sign to the linear term.

In Tables 7.3a and 7.4a, the OLS models show that for both women and men, domestic work times (including routine, non-routine and total) are strongly and negatively associated with their relative potential earnings

Table 7.3a OLS models of domestic work time and relative potential earnings: women

	Routine housework		Care and non-routine housework		Total domestic work		Routine housework		Care and non-routine housework		Total domestic work	
	B	Robust SE	B	Robust SE	B	Robust SE	B	Robust SE	B	Robust SE	B	Robust SE
Age	2.406***	0.091	-1.393***	0.166	1.013***	0.198	2.355***	0.090	-1.519***	0.170	0.835***	0.197
Log (Household income)	-16.73***	1.271	-26.64***	3.245	-43.37***	4.049	-16.91***	1.281	-27.08***	3.283	-43.98***	4.103
Number of adults	4.464**	1.412	2.303	2.371	6.768*	3.066	4.587**	1.416	2.606	2.392	7.192*	3.088
Number of children	21.20***	1.105	66.32***	2.383	87.52***	2.986	21.16***	1.103	66.24***	2.370	87.40***	2.968
Relative potential earnings[a]	-41.00***	4.560	-59.15***	8.988	-100.1***	11.46	-37.09***	4.135	-49.47***	8.041	-86.56***	10.38
Relative potential earnings[a] squared							36.46**	11.69	90.10**	27.26	126.56***	32.09
Constant	111.0***	9.958	340.7***	26.44	451.7***	32.47	112.3***	10.01	344.0***	26.73	456.31***	32.87
R²	0.598		0.598		0.619		0.568		0.601		0.623	
F	283.01***		260.68***		317.79***		241.73***		227.38***		275.73***	
Df	5		5		5		6		6		6	

Notes: Data from a pooled sample of the British Household Panel Survey, 1994–2005. For women, $N = 3655$.
[a]Defined as the difference between one's own potential hour wage and spouse's potential hourly wage divided by the sum of the two.
*$p < .05$. **$p < .01$. ***$p < .001$.

165

Table 7.3b Fixed-effect models of domestic work time and relative potential earnings: women

	Routine housework		Care and non-routine housework		Total domestic work		Routine housework		Care and non-routine housework		Total domestic work	
	B	Robust SE	B	Robust SE	B	Robust SE	B	Robust SE	B	Robust SE	B	Robust SE
Age	3.110***	0.273	0.031	0.518	3.141***	0.662	3.074***	0.273	-0.001	0.519	3.073***	0.663
Log (Household income)	-7.914***	1.106	-10.02***	2.098	-17.94***	2.680	-7.957***	1.105	-10.06***	2.098	-18.02***	2.679
Number of adults	2.778*	1.165	1.568	2.211	4.347	2.824	2.840*	1.164	1.621	2.211	4.461	2.823
Number of children	18.47***	1.110	70.80***	2.106	89.28***	2.690	18.55***	1.109	70.87***	2.107	89.42***	2.690
Relative potential earnings[a]	-22.14***	5.189	-26.15**	9.846	-48.29***	12.58	-16.32*	5.734	-21.15	10.89	-37.47**	13.90
Relative potential earnings[a] squared							34.97*	14.71	30.00	27.94	64.97	35.68
Constant	27.56**	10.43	167.5***	19.79	195.0***	25.28	27.65**	10.42	167.6***	19.79	195.2***	25.27
Between groups R²	0.593		0.581		0.603		0.589		0.581		0.602	
F	153.95***		301.17***		336.44***		129.46***		251.18***		281.17***	
Df	5		5		5		6		6		6	

Notes: Data from a pooled sample of the British Household Panel Survey, 1994–2005. For women, $N = 3655$ (number of groups = 1043).
[a]Defined as the difference between one's own potential hour wage and spouse's potential hourly wage divided by the sum of the two.
*$p < .05$. **$p < .01$. ***$p < .001$.

Table7.4a OLS models of domestic work time and relative potential earnings: men

	Routine housework		Care and non-routine housework		Total domestic work		Routine housework		Care and non-routine housework		Total domestic work	
	B	SE	B	SE	B	SE	B	SE	B	SE	B	SE
Age	0.530***	0.062	0.998***	0.125	1.528***	0.136	0.524***	0.064	1.019***	0.130	1.543***	0.141
Log (Household income)	−4.085***	1.095	−17.81***	2.542	−21.90***	2.931	−4.095***	1.095	−17.77***	2.543	−21.87***	2.936
Number of adults	−0.695	0.763	0.453	1.199	−0.242	1.553	−0.701	0.767	0.473	1.190	−0.228	1.541
Number of children	4.721***	0.737	35.26***	1.965	39.98***	2.115	4.710***	0.739	35.30***	1.967	40.01***	2.112
Relative potential earnings[a]	−15.01***	2.986	−12.84*	5.937	−27.85***	7.292	−15.77***	3.469	−10.21	6.889	−25.98**	8.432
Relative potential earnings[a] squared							4.315	9.016	−14.95	19.14	−10.64	23.31
Constant	40.92***	8.627	166.5***	20.21	207.4***	23.15	41.08***	8.636	165.9***	20.24	207.0***	23.23
R²	0.144		0.399		0.416		0.144		0.400		0.416	
F	29.79***		97.63***		123.01***		24.93***		81.38***		102.75***	
Df	5		5		5		6		6		6	

Notes: Data from a pooled sample of the British Household Panel Survey, 1994–2005. For men, $N = 3509$.
[a]Defined as the difference between one's own potential hour wage and spouse's potential hourly wage divided by the sum of the two.
*$p < .05$. **$p < .01$. ***$p < .001$.

Table 7.4b   Fixed-effect models of domestic work time and relative potential earnings: men

	Routine housework		Care and non-routine housework		Total domestic work		Routine housework		Care and non-routine housework		Total domestic work	
	B	Robust SE	B	Robust SE	B	Robust SE	B	Robust SE	B	Robust SE	B	Robust SE
Age	0.398*	0.188	1.222**	0.367	1.620***	0.436	0.405*	0.188	1.195**	0.368	1.600***	0.437
Log (Household income)	-3.691***	0.869	-8.594***	1.699	-12.29***	2.018	-3.702***	0.870	-8.554***	1.699	-12.26***	2.018
Number of adults	-0.430	0.690	-0.283	1.348	-0.713	1.601	-0.421	0.690	-0.317	1.348	-0.738	1.601
Number of children	5.953***	0.746	38.83***	1.457	44.79***	1.730	5.951***	0.746	38.84***	1.457	44.79***	1.731
Relative potential earnings[a]	-18.79***	3.912	-9.000	7.647	-27.79**	9.081	-17.90**	4.232	-12.25	8.271	-30.15**	9.823
Relative potential earnings[a] squared							-6.038	11.00	22.14	21.49	16.10	25.53
Constant	41.43***	7.434	86.35***	14.53	127.8***	17.26	41.48***	7.436	86.16***	14.53	127.6***	17.26
Between groups R²	0.159		0.441		0.473		0.157		0.440		0.473	
F	25.73***		186.64***		181.19***		21.48***		155.72***		151.02***	
Df	5		5		5		6		6		6	

Notes: Data from the British Household Panel Survey, 1994–2005. For men, $N = 3509$ (number of groups = 958).
[a] Defined as the difference between one's own potential hour wage and spouse's potential hourly wage divided by the sum of the two.
*$p < .05$. **$p < .01$. ***$p < .001$.

(the coefficients being −41.00, −59.15, and −100.1 for women, and −15.01, −12.84, and −27.85 for men). However, the squared term of relative potential earnings is significant only in the women's domestic time models but in none of the men's domestic time models. The coefficients are all positive in the models concerning the female partners, indicating that the relationship between bargaining power and domestic work is curvilinear (that is, there is some initial support to the 'doing gender' hypothesis). In the case of men, however, the squared term is insignificant in all of the three models. In particular, it goes in the opposite direction as predicted by the 'doing gender' hypothesis in the non-routine domestic work time model (−14.95). These findings concur with our earlier suggestion that care and non-routine domestic work are unlikely to be due to resource bargaining or the interaction between bargaining and expectations about gender roles.

The fixed-effect models in Tables 7.3b and 7.4b demonstrate striking results about the 'doing gender' hypothesis. A major advantage of these models is that they control for unobserved heterogeneity of individuals that may confound the relationship between potential relative earnings and domestic work time. When these unobserved characteristics are taken into account, the coefficients concerning relative potential earnings become much smaller in all of the female partners' models (the figures being −22.14, −26.15 and −48.29; c.f. Table 7.3a). In particular, the coefficient becomes insignificant in the male partners' model of care and non-routine domestic work time (the figure being −9.000; c.f. Table 7.4a). These findings show that earlier studies based on cross-sectional data have exaggerated the role of relative resources in determining one's housework hours.

Turning to the next set of fixed-effect models where both potential relative earnings and its square are included, we see that the squared term is insignificant in all models except in the case of women's routine housework. To put it simply, there is limited evidence of 'doing gender' (that is the relationship between women's routine domestic work time and their resource bargaining power is curvilinear) when unobserved heterogeneity over time and both routine and non-routine types of housework are taken into account. Together with our earlier findings, we have found that women's domestic work time is associated to a greater extent with relative potential earnings than men's. There is not much evidence to suggest that men 'bargain' for their housework time by their relative potential earnings. It is highly unlikely that men's time on care and non-routine domestic work is determined by their resource bargaining power or their expectations about a masculine gender role. Instead, it should be better explained by other possible factors such as expectations about parental roles, flexibility in work schedules, and so on.

DISCUSSION AND CONCLUSION

By employing longitudinal data of couples' time use on all the major daily activities, we have identified several important characteristics of the gender division of domestic labour. First, women are responsible for the major share of domestic work and increase their proportion of unpaid domestic work and to paid work continually after partnership. Second, men's paid work time and routine housework work time are relatively stable over the life course compared with women's. But we should note that they do increase their participation in care and non-routine types of domestic work significantly over the life course, and in particular, after partnership and after having a child. In sum, routine housework remains mainly 'women's work' throughout the conventional life course, while care and non-routine types of domestic work are less gendered in nature. Third, although women and men have more or less the same amount of work time (including paid work and all unpaid domestic work), the proportion of unpaid domestic work to all work in the case of women has increased steadily over the life course. This would certainly pose negative implications for their potential labour market income and hence bargaining power in the family (Kan and Gershuny 2009).

What explains the gendered division of domestic labour? This chapter has explored the role of resource bargaining power (estimated by relative potential earnings) and its possible interactions with one's gendered expectations. We surpass previous studies by analysing longitudinal data on time use that cover both routine housework, and care and more flexible types of domestic work. These data also enable us to take account of unobserved characteristics of individuals that may confound the relationship between resource bargaining and domestic work. The results show that relative potential earnings are negatively associated with women's and men's routine housework time, and particularly with further reduction in women's time just after partnership and men's time just after childbirth. But relative earnings are not effective predictors of women's and men's time on care and non-routine housework. In the case of male partners, some of the results even go against the predictions of the resource bargaining theory. In other words, it is seriously inadequate to explain the gendered division of domestic labour by relative economic advantages of men and women. Earlier studies based on cross-sectional data and stylised measures of routine housework have overestimated the role of relative resource level and bargaining in the domestic division of labour. In particular, men's domestic work time should be explained by factors other than resource bargaining, such as expectations about parental roles, flexibility in work schedules, gender role values and so on.

Is housework related to one's gender identity? There is some evidence to suggest that women who have a much higher potential labour market income than their partners tend to undertake more routine housework; that is, the relationship between their routine housework time and relative potential earnings is curvilinear. The curvilinear relationship between women's routine housework participation and their relative income represents a hurdle for women with high earning capacity to achieve gender equality in the family. But more research efforts are needed to substantiate this finding. Women who have a much higher earnings power than their partners are a small and highly selective group. Moreover, no parallel findings have been found for men's routine housework time and for both men's and women's care and non-routine housework time. Using non-parametric modelling techniques, Gupta and Ash (2008) argued that housework hours, especially women's, are better explained by individuals' own earnings rather than their share of earnings in the partnership. Furthermore, the curvilinear relationship between women's domestic work and their relative potential earnings in the present study disappear when both routine and non-routine types of housework and women's unobserved characteristics are taken into account. These findings further suggest that we need more complex social mechanisms to explain the gender division of routine housework and that of care and flexible types of household work respectively.

This chapter also underlines the importance of collecting high quality longitudinal time-use data for the understanding of trends in the domestic division of labour. These data will help us identify the difficulty in achieving gender equality in different types of household work, and the lifecycle events, for example marriage and childbirth, that will reinforce the gendered division of domestic labour.

NOTES

1. Stylised questions about time use are commonly collected in survey interviews. Respondents are requested to estimate and report the time they spent on, or the frequency they took part in, a particular activity in a given period.
2. For more details of the data calibration exercise, see Kan and Gershuny (2006a). We calibrate time-use estimates from Wave 4 (1994) of the BHPS, the first wave when major stylised time-use variables were collected.

REFERENCES

Becker, G.S. (1985), 'Human capital, effort, and the sexual division of labor', *Journal of Labor Economics*, **3**, S33–S58.

Becker, G.S. (1991 [1981]), *A Treatise on the Family*, Cambridge, Mass and London: Harvard University Press.

Bianchi, S.M., M.A. Milkie, L.C. Sayer and John P. Robinson (2000), 'Is anyone doing the housework? Trends in the gender division of household labor', *Social Forces*, **79**, 191–222.

Bittman, M., P. England, N. Folbre, L. Sayer and G. Matheson (2003), 'When does gender trump money? Bargaining and time in household work', *American Journal of Sociology*, **109**, 186–214.

Brines, J. (1994), 'Economic dependency, gender and the division of domestic labour at home', *American Journal of Sociology*, **100**, 652–88.

DeVault, M. (1990), 'Conflict over housework: a problem that (still) has no name', in L. Kriesberg (ed.), *Research into Social Movements, Conflict, and Change*, Greenwich, CT: JAI Press.

Gershuny, J. (1992), 'The domestic labour revolution: a process of lagged adaptation?', in N. Abercrombie and A. Warde (eds), *Social Change in Contemporary Britain*, Cambridge: Polity Press.

Gershuny, J. (2000), *Changing Times: Work and Leisure in Postindustrial Society*, Oxford: Oxford University Press.

Gershuny, J. and J.P. Robinson (1988), 'Historical changes in the household division of labor', *Demography*, **25**, 537–52.

Greenstein, T.N. (2000), 'Economic dependence, gender, and the division of labor in the home: a replication and extension', *Journal of Marriage and the Family*, **62**, 322–35.

Gupta, S. and M. Ash (2008), 'Whose money, whose time? A nonparametric approach to modelling time spent on housework in the United States', *Feminist Economics*, **14**, 93–120.

Kan, M-Y. (2008), 'Does gender trump money? Housework hours of husbands and wives in Britain', *Work, Employment and Society*, **22**, 45–66.

Kan, M-Y. and J. Gershuny (2006a), 'Human capital and social position in Britain: creating a measure of wage earning potential from BHPS data', *Institute for Social and Economic Research Working Paper 2006-3*, Colchester, UK: University of Essex.

Kan, M-Y. and J. Gershuny (2006b), 'Infusing time diary evidence into panel data: an exercise on calibrating time-use estimates for the BHPS', in *Working Paper of the Institute for Social and Economic Research Paper 2006-19*, Colchester, UK: University of Essex.

Kan, M-Y. and J. Gershuny (2009), 'Gender and time use over the life-course', in M. Brynin and J. Ermisch (eds), *Changing Relationships*, New York and Oxford: Routledge.

Layte, R. (1999), *Divided Time: Gender, Paid Employment and Domestic Labour*, Aldershot: Ashgate.

Manser, M. and M. Brown (1980), 'Marriage and household decision-making: a bargaining analysis', *International Economic Review*, **21**, 31–44.

McElroy, M.B. and M.J. Horney (1981), 'Nash-bargaining and household decisions: towards a generalization of the theory of demand', *International Economic Review*, **22**, 333–49.

Presser, H.B. (1994), 'Employment schedules among dual-earner spouses and the division of household labour by gender', *American Sociological Review*, **59**, 348–64.

Robinson, J.P. and G. Godbey (1997), *Time for Life: The Surprising Ways*

Americans Use their Time, Pennsylvania: The Pennsylvania States University Press.

Sorensen, A. and S. McLanahan (1987), 'Married women's economic dependency, 1940–1980', *American Journal of Sociology*, **93**, 659–87.

Sullivan, O. (2000), 'The division of domestic labour: twenty years of change?', *Sociology*, **34**, 437–56.

West, C. and S. Fenstermaker (1993), 'Power, inequality, and the accomplishment of gender: An ethnomethodological view', in P. England (ed.), *Theory on Gender/ Feminism on Theory*, New York: Aldine de Gruyter.

West, C. and D.H. Zimmerman (1987), 'Doing gender', *Gender and Society*, **1**, 125–51.

8. Family, class and gender 'strategies' in mothers' employment and childcare

Rosemary Crompton and Clare Lyonette

INTRODUCTION: SOCIETAL INEQUALITIES: ORIGINS AND POLICIES

As cross-national comparisons demonstrate, Britain is a highly unequal society, and indeed, class inequalities have considerably widened since the 1980s (Hills 2004). Sociologists with very different approaches to 'class analysis' would be in agreement on one important point – that the major 'transmission belt' for the reproduction of class inequalities is the family (Erikson and Goldthorpe 1993, Bourdieu 1996, Crompton 2006). However, there are important differences in emphasis. Whereas Goldthorpe (via the development of Rational Action Theory, RAT) has been emphatic that the 'drivers' of class reproduction via the educational system are entirely economic, Bourdieu and others influenced by his approach (such as Reay and Lucey 2003; Ball 2003) have also emphasised the parallel impact of cultural and social capital in the creation and reproduction of class *habitus* – 'things to do or not to do, things to say or not to say, in relation to a probable upcoming future' (Bourdieu, cited in Ball 2003: 16). In contrast to Goldthorpe's approach, therefore, these authors emphasise that both economic *and* cultural factors are significant in the reproduction of class inequalities.

In general, we would be in agreement with those who have emphasised the dual significance of economic and cultural factors in the reproduction of class inequalities (Crompton 2008). However, the question of the *relative* importance of one or the other factor is an important issue in policy debates. If class inequalities are seen as a 'problem' to be tackled, then the question of their origins becomes crucial. In particular, as critics of 'culturalist' approaches have always argued, if structured social inequality is seen to be in the larger part a consequence of 'cultural degradations', together with the subsequent behaviours of those groupings so degraded, then cultural, rather than material, solutions to the problems of social inequality are indicated (Fraser 2000; Frank 2000). Goldthorpe in particular is well aware of this problem. In making his argument against the significance of the 'inertial forces' of 'habitus' in the reproduction of educational inequalities, Goldthorpe argues that on the contrary, it is the 'unequal distributions of opportunities and constraints that characterise a class society [that] contribute to their own perpetuation through quite rational adaptive strategies that they induce on the part of those who must act under their influence' (2000: 178). It follows from this argument that policies to reduce inequality should be directed at the *structures* of opportunities and constraints. Here, Goldthorpe cites the example of Sweden, a society in which, as a consequence of political action, state policies have contributed to the narrowing of income differentials, and class inequalities in educational attainment have been reduced.

However, current government policies relating to inequality do not primarily address these external structures of opportunities and constraints (HMSO 2007).[1] Rather, they have a focus on removing prejudice and changing individual and family behaviours. If inequalities are understood as primarily an outcome of inadequate socialisation and/or damaging cultural 'preferences', then even well-meaning attempts to address the problem of social inequality can become focused on attempts to reshape individual attitudes, and/or attack the roots of cultural disadvantage, rather than to address the broader structures of social and economic inequality in which these cultures are embedded. Increasingly, these kinds of criticisms have been directed at 'New Labour' policies concerned with inequality, many of which have been developed with the intention of overcoming childhood disadvantage. These strategies have been criticised by some authors for giving priority to 'middle class' values (Gillies 2005; Evans 2006).

In this chapter, we will focus on decision making within the family in respect of the division of market work between men and women (in particular, the question of mothers' employment), as well as in relation to childcare. We shall argue that although there are indeed what might be described as 'cultural' differences associated with decision making in respect of these important issues, nevertheless, the most important factors shaping behaviours are in fact the structures of constraints and opportunities within which decisions are taken and 'choices' are made.

FAMILY BEHAVIOURS AND CLASS OUTCOMES

The relatively recent (re)entry of mothers, particularly mothers of young children, into the labour force has been class differentiated. Mothers with higher levels of qualification, who are likely to be in partnerships with similar men, are more likely to remain in employment than mothers with only low levels of qualification (Rake et al. 2000). Furthermore, women in 'routine and manual' and 'intermediate' occupations are more likely to work part-time than professional and managerial women. This pattern of couple employment behaviour will serve to deepen material inequalities. There is also evidence to suggest that working-class women are more traditional in their attitudes to the mothers' caring role than professional and managerial women (see Crompton and Lyonette 2008). Indeed, in a series of attitudinal questions, professional and managerial respondents emerge as less traditional on average in their attitudes to both gender roles and the impact of mothers' employment on family life (Crompton 2006) – although as we shall see, this is largely because of very low levels of gender traditionalism amongst professional and managerial women in employment.

This kind of evidence adds to a sociological strand that, as we have seen above, has long emphasised the impact of different cultures of class. In the past, one feature that was said to distinguish 'working' from 'middle' class perspectives was the capacity to plan for the future – to develop a family strategy. Middle classes were argued to be characterised by deferred gratification – investing in further training and qualifications, saving for the future, and so on, whilst the working classes 'lived for today': 'working-class life puts a premium on the taking of pleasures now, discourages planning for some future good' (Hoggart, cited in Goldthorpe et al. 1969: 119). Although this contrast of class perspectives might seem quaint and old-fashioned today, as noted above, Goldthorpe suggests that material class differences crucially affect the 'capacity to plan' in respect of education, and authors such as Ball and Reay have suggested that these capacities are underpinned by variations in cultural resources.

Ball and his colleagues have suggested that changes in education policy – in particular, the creation of a 'quasi-market' in education through an emphasis on parental choice, the creation of school league tables, and so on – have increased the scope for middle-class strategising, understood as a deployment of means to an end (Ball 2003). This argument has been extended to research on nursery care: 'Childcare may not, at first sight, seem to be a key arena of class reproduction but we suggest that that is exactly what it is. Childcare opportunities and choices are strongly stratified and very closely tied to family assets' (Vincent and Ball 2006: 63).

An emphasis on 'strategising' is, of course, perfectly compatible with a RAT-based approach. 'Cultural' approaches might argue, however, that 'strategies' are affected not only by structures of opportunities and constraint, but also by culturally embedded differences (habitus) that positively or negatively influence the choices that are made.

Debates as to the nature of the class-based origins and persistence of family strategies, however, would be seen as largely irrelevant by those who have argued that in contemporary societies, 'class' is no longer an appropriate concept as far as sociology is concerned (Giddens 1991; Beck and Beck-Gernsheim 2002). In respect of the family, it has been argued that the replacement of the 'standard biography' by the 'choice biography' is part and parcel of the way in which the 'traditional' family, which was a 'community of need', has become, increasingly, an 'elective relationship' (Beck and Beck-Gernsheim 2002: 86). These processes, it is claimed, are closely bound up with the emancipation of women. No longer bound to a life of domesticity, women have themselves become individualised and increasingly able to exercise their choices. As a consequence, family relationships are in flux and 'there is no given set of obligations and opportunities, no way of organising everyday work, the relationship between men and women, parents and children, which can just be copied' (Beck and Beck-Gernsheim 2002: 203). In respect of mothers' employment, one of the most contentious developments of the individualisation thesis has been in the work of Hakim, who has argued that the patterning of mothers' employment reflects the impact of the 'choices' made by different 'types' of women, and their individual 'preferences' for particular combinations of employment and family life. In common with the individualisation thesis, Hakim discounts the relevance of class and claims that the three lifestyle preference groups she identifies 'cut across social class, education, and ability differences' (Hakim 2003: 247).[2]

The persisting class differences in couple employment strategies suggest, however, that the exercise of women's individual 'choices' is not a sufficient explanation as far as mothers' employment is concerned.[3] Although critics of individualisation theses have challenged the over-emphasis on agency in explanations of family behaviours, they do not seek to replace agency with structure. Rather, they emphasise that one 'side' cannot be understood without reference to the other (Brannen and Nilsen 2005; Crompton 2008). This is the position that we take in this chapter. Drawing on both quantitative and qualitative data, we will first examine the question of whether family 'strategies' can be identified in respect of mothers' employment. Next, we will explore the childcare arrangements made by our interviewees, and the varying rationales associated with 'choosing' particular kinds of childcare.

DATA AND METHODS

We draw upon two sources of quantitative data: (i) the British Social Attitudes (BSA) surveys of 2002 and 2006, which included repeat questions on family and gender roles, and (ii) wave 14 (2005) of the British Household Panel Study (BHPS), which incorporates some of the questions included in the BSA surveys. Our major data source in this analysis, however, is over ninety work-life interviews.[4] All interviewees had at least one child under 14. For comparative purposes,[5] we interviewed qualified doctors, accountants (all members of the Institute of Chartered Accountants of England and Wales), and employees in finance and retail. Our interview 'sample', therefore, is not representative of all parents and will be particularly biased towards professional and managerial employees, as well as employed mothers (all women interviewed were in paid work to some degree, although some of the men interviewed had non-working partners).

Our finance interviews (we interviewed in an insurance company, a retail bank and an international bank) included a number of very highly-paid and qualified managerial and professional respondents, although the majority would be classified as 'intermediate' in occupational class terms (that is, lower managerial and administrative employees).[6] Similarly, most of the retail respondents (we interviewed in a large department store) were on supervisory grades and therefore in the 'intermediate' occupational class category, and only four could be described as 'working class' (routine/manual) – in that they were both unqualified and unpromoted.[7] In occupational class terms, therefore, our interviews are not representative of the whole. In terms of income, the differences between our respondents were very wide, with individual incomes ranging from £10000 to over £100000 a year, and household incomes from £23000 to over £250000.

FAMILY STRATEGIES AND 'CHOICE'

The last three decades have seen extensive changes in the patterning of family lives and family arrangements. The increase in the paid employment of mothers of relatively young children is one of the most striking manifestations of these changes. As we have seen above, some authors (Beck and Beck-Gernsheim 2002; Hakim 2003) have linked these changes to increasing 'individualisation' (particularly amongst women) and the decline of 'class'. However, in families, 'choices' about mothers' employment will rarely be taken on an individual basis. Rather, in couple households, both parents will be involved (Moen 2003: 19).

In order to explore the extent of family strategy, we asked all of our interviewees whether or not they had 'planned ahead' when they had children – that is, whether they had discussed childcare, sharing domestic work, and so on. A substantial minority (28) said that they simply hadn't planned ahead: 'Goodness, no . . . A bit of a shock, isn't it, when it arrives, oh my God.' (A15, male accountant, professional/managerial). However, the majority of those interviewed had had such discussions, and in many cases had made quite complex changes to their working lives in anticipation of parenthood. One of our interviewees (R2, male retail, intermediate), for example, had changed his job to one with more regular hours (although it paid less), and his wife had retrained as a driving instructor while pregnant. A job with regular hours enabled him to get home in time to care for the children so that his wife could work in the evenings – a case of 'shift parenting' (Warren 2003; La Valle et al. 2002).

However, although plans varied, in our interviews there was no obvious class, or occupational, pattern in whether or not couples had 'planned ahead'. In respect of mothers' employment, therefore, class differences in *propensity* to plan were not evident. Rather, what was apparent was that intermediate and manual interviewees felt much more materially constrained as far as their planning was concerned. In particular, intermediate and manual interviewees were more than four times as likely as professional and managerial interviewees to mention that the woman's income was vital as far as family finances were concerned. For example:

> We knew, she knew she had to go back to work because that's what happened, that's what you had to do, because there was no money (R5, male retail, intermediate).

> I know lots of people like that, where they need to have two incomes, particularly if someone's job is completely unstable, . . . I think I was under no illusions when I had a baby that I would have to work and I'd have to have some form of income coming in (F16, female finance, intermediate).

> I knew before I went on maternity leave what I wanted to come back to do. Financially it was never a case of I'm going to give up work, I knew I had to come back (R1, female retail, intermediate).

In these (and many other similar instances), the female partner's income is crucial to family finances, as was concisely expressed by one of our interviewees in retail:

> Getting the mother or that second earner back to work, I think can be key . . . I think that's where families live on the breadline, where that second earner has to look after the children (R16, male retail, intermediate).

In contrast, professional and managerial women were more likely to emphasise the importance of paid work to themselves as individuals, when taking the decision to work:

I do sometimes feel guilty myself . . . but I know I'd be a dreadful stay-at-home mum. I'd be really awful, and I'm a much better mum for not being there . . . And my mum didn't work, and I think I always resented her for that whole martyr being at home, running around after the men all the time . . . and I just looked at her and went 'I don't want any of that, thank you' (F12, female finance, professional/managerial).

Even though I've got two children, I'm not an earth mother at all, really. Like I couldn't survive without my job and that's why I carried on being a full-time, really. I tried the part-time for a year and didn't like it, so I decided to just go full-time and sort of work things around it really (M20, female GP, professional/managerial).

Rather than any differences in 'strategising', or abilities to plan ahead, therefore, the kinds of sentiments we have summarised reflect the very different patterns of class constraints and opportunities available to our interviewees. Professional and managerial women were more likely to emphasise their own need for self-fulfilment in describing their decisions to continue in employment; whereas intermediate and manual interviewees were more likely to stress the need for a second income. Many intermediate and manual women also found their jobs fulfilling on a day-to day basis, but none sought to explain their return to employment in these terms, however.

A similar pattern of 'constrained choice' by class was apparent in respect of childcare arrangements.[8] Apart from partners, interviewees used a large variety of childcare options, from friends and family to full-time nursery places and nannies. Professional and managerial interviewees were much more likely than intermediate and manual respondents to use the most expensive forms of childcare such as nurseries and nannies (66 per cent). Among intermediate and manual respondents, 14 per cent used nurseries, and none used nannies. Over half used grandparents, and a quarter used childminders. In the case of grandparents, these were frequently regular, unpaid childcare arrangements, facilitated by their family living close by, which often allowed the female partner to work.

We're very lucky in that we live very close to both sets of grandparents. So on the three days that she [wife] works, one set of grandparents has her two days and one has her for one day, and on Saturday mornings while [wife's] doing nails [a second part-time job as a manicurist], I have her, so we're spoilt really. . . . If we were paying for childcare, I don't know that we would have a child to be honest, because I *don't* think we could have made it work . . . Childcare probably wouldn't have made it worthwhile my wife carrying on working (R10, male retail, intermediate).

Her nan, which we've been very lucky with, because she's going to be able to (be) free when [wife's] going back to work, which is really a godsend because otherwise

I wouldn't know what else to do, because obviously paying for childcare, it's just *so* expensive, and we've looked into that and it's just astronomical. And we've worked it out that she'd most probably be better off not going to work, being honest, but her nan's come to the rescue (R13, male retail, intermediate).

For those without this kind of regular help from grandparents (usually due to old age, the grandparent still working or not living close by), it was evident that many intermediate and manual interviewees often had difficulties with struggling to combine work and childcare:

Yes, before I came back to work at six months, and from six months really until the . . . end of 2004, we relied on family, . . . not to look after her, but to pick her up and drop her off. . . . But my mother can't do that now and my husband's mother she's, she doesn't want to do, she's getting on, so it was a case of, come the beginning of 2005 we had to decide well look, what *are* we going to do because, you know, I used to be able to drop her off to the child minder but I can't pick her up as well just because of how I work the hours, so [the husband changed his working hours] (R1, female retail, intermediate).

For intermediate and manual interviewees, grandparental care was not a matter of preference, but rather, necessity. A substantial minority of professional and managerial interviewees also drew upon grandparental help, but in only two cases was this as a direct support for parental employment. In many cases, grandparents simply lived too far away:

They live in C, so whilst they do help out and they're very good and from time to time the children go and stay with them, and have a great time, but it's difficult to say, 'I'm not going to get home for half past six, can you pop round', because by the time you know that, there's no way they can do it (M13, male doctor, professional/managerial).

Rather, for professional and managerial interviewees the grandparent's care was seen to be of benefit to the child, and not a regular support system for the parent. Professional and managerial interviewees who lived close to grandparents tended to use them on an occasional basis for childcare:

Yes, my husband's mother lives not too far away, and my eldest loves going there, so probably once every two or three weeks she'll stay overnight on the Saturday, but it's not regular, she doesn't drive, so it's more emergencies or just a bit of space at the weekend (F12, female finance, professional/managerial).

And do your parents-in-law help out at all? I mean you said they live just . . . Not on that basis. They did take two of them on a Wednesday morning just for, I don't know, it was just for sort of special granny time. And they also certainly help out with babysitting in the evenings and things like that if we ever go out (M1, male GP, professional/managerial).

It is not being suggested that professional and managerial interviewees had no problems with childcare. For example:

> The difficulty I have with that is that my son's school is in [London suburb], it's just over there, my daughter's nursery is in [other London suburb], and both will finish at six o'clock, it will be quite difficult to get to both places, so I am thinking that I might have to resort to a nanny, which I never wanted to do (A18, female accountant, professional/managerial).

Rather, what we are arguing is that although the logistics of childcare might present problems, as in the example above, being unable to pay was not one of them. However, more limited choices were available as far as the intermediate and manual respondents were concerned, because of their inability to pay for certain types of care. The pattern of childcare arrangements amongst our interviewees, therefore, (and not surprisingly) reflected in large part the ability of parents to pay, and inability to pay for certain types of childcare obviously restricts the choices available to many couples.[9] Recent data available from the Families and Children Study (FACS) shows that in 2005, 55 per cent of couples where both work more than 16 hours per week use some form of childcare (both formal and informal). Reflecting our discussion of the types of childcare used by couples where both partners worked, the FACS findings show that 39 per cent of families in the highest income quintile used formal childcare compared with only 20 per cent of families in the lowest quintile. These figures correspond with the class differences in childcare use found amongst our interviewees. As Butt and her colleagues (2007: 54) have argued: 'there are two distinct childcare markets in operation. More affluent areas are mainly served by private providers . . . Deprived areas have been reliant on government intervention (and) particular concerns remain about the viability of provision in . . . deprived areas, once the start-up funding provided by government initiatives runs out'.

In this section we have examined the strategies used by our interviewees in respect of mothers' employment and childcare. We argue that it is not the presence or absence of 'strategising', or the nature of the strategy itself, that is the major issue, but rather the kinds of material constraints that couples face in relation to the necessity for mothers' employment and the kind of childcare that can be afforded. As we have seen, these vary systematically by class. Furthermore, we would suggest that class-related 'cultural' variations (for example, a greater 'familialism' amongst intermediate and manual interviewees) have not, in fact, played a major part in shaping couples' strategies. As we shall see, this does not mean that issues of choice or 'preference', or class variations in cultural capital, were not relevant at all to the decision-making process. For example, in our interviews, one theme that emerged was that professional and managerial women seemed to have had considerably more freedom to exercise their 'choices' to take up employment or not. This finding lends support to an argument we have already developed in a previous analysis of the BSA data. We found that professional and managerial women who had stayed at home when their children were young were (statistically) significantly more likely to emphasise the importance of maternal care for young children than professional and managerial women who had gone out to work. In contrast, although women in intermediate and routine and manual class categories who had been in paid employment when their children were young were less likely to emphasise the importance of maternal care than stay-at-home mothers, the attitudinal difference between working and non-working mothers in these class groupings was much less than that amongst professional and managerial mothers (Crompton and Lyonette 2008).

CLASS, GENDER AND ATTITUDES TOWARDS MATERNAL EMPLOYMENT

In a similar vein, there were systematic class differences in interviewees' attitudes regarding the impact of non-maternal care on children. Here, however, we also found substantial gender differences. As we shall see, in aggregate, men are rather more 'traditional' than women in their views about maternal care for pre-school children.

The question of childcare is a very emotive issue. However, it is also a topic where changes in attitudes seem to follow changes in behaviour. Using longitudinal data from the BHPS survey, Himmelweit and Sigala (2003) have demonstrated that as the employment rate of mothers of pre-school children rose (between 1991 and 1999), so the proportion of mothers of pre-school children 'agreeing' that such children are likely to suffer if their mother works, declined.

Data on this question were available from the 2002 and 2006 BSA surveys. However, numbers were small, given the requirement to work with a subsample reflecting the demographic characteristics of our interviewees (in a partnership, with at least one child under the age of 14). We therefore turned to the British Household Panel Survey, in which we were able to locate over two and a half thousand respondents who met our broad criteria. Table 8.1 summarises the BHPS findings for 2005 by sex and class, using the five-category ONS-SEC classification.[10]

The first point to note about Table 8.1 is the rather high (nearly a third) proportion of respondents who 'neither agree nor disagree' on this question – an ambivalence that, as we shall see, was also very evident amongst

Table 8.1　　*'A pre-school child suffers if his or her mother goes out to work'*
(men and women in a partnership with a child under the age of
12)

		Prof/ manage-rial	Interme-diate	Small employ-ers and own account workers	Lower supervi-sory and technical	Semi-routine and routine	Total
Men	Agree/strongly agree	36	39	46	33	35	37
	Neither agree nor disagree	28	24	28	27	32	28
	Disagree/ strongly disagree	36	37	26	40	34	35
	Total	590 100%	102 100%	203 100%	165 100%	324 100%	1384 100%
Women	Agree/strongly agree	20	27	31	28	29	26
	Neither agree nor disagree	25	26	34	30	34	29
	Disagree/ strongly disagree	55	47	35	43	37	45
	Total	455 100%	354 100%	94 100%	40 100%	458 100%	1401 100%

Source:　BHPS 2005 (weighted percentages).

our interviewees. We know that in aggregate, professionals and mana-
gerials are less 'traditional' in their attitudes to family and gender roles
(Crompton 2006). We also know that opinions about the impact of the
employment of mothers on young children are rather sensitive to whether
the woman works or not (Himmelweit and Sigala 2003). As far as women
are concerned, therefore, Table 8.1 demonstrates the expected variation
by class – professional and managerial women (who are more likely to be
in employment) are significantly more likely to 'disagree' that a pre-school
child suffers than are women in the other occupational class categories (χ^2
37.027; d.f.=8; p<0.001).

Much research on childcare, and childcare choices, has, not surprisingly, tended to focus on mothers alone (Himmelweit and Sigala 2003;

Vincent and Ball 2006; Duncan 2005). Although it is true that mothers – even mothers in employment – take the major responsibility for childcare (and this was also the case amongst the great majority of our interviewees), as we have argued, and as is demonstrated by many of our interviewees (see R1 above, for example), fathers often play a crucial role in holding the childcare 'package' together, and decisions about couples' employment strategies will often be taken in relation to the needs of the family unit, rather than the individual. The attitudes of fathers, therefore, are of some interest.

It is well established that men are more gender-traditional than women in their attitudes (Inglehart and Norris 2003; Crompton and Lyonette 2008). This is borne out in Table 8.1, in that 37 per cent of fathers, as against only 26 per cent of mothers, think that a pre-school child will suffer if the mother is in employment (χ^2 48.303; d.f.=4; p<0.001). Another gendered contrast within Table 8.1 is that whereas the class differences in women's attitudes are relatively large (and run largely in the 'expected' direction), the class differences in fathers' attitudes do not reveal any distinct pattern. Small employers and own account workers are rather more 'conservative' on this issue than other men – reflecting, perhaps, the political conservatism of the self-employed (χ^2 9.939; d.f. =2; p<0.01). In respect of this rather sensitive topic, therefore, gender and class cut across each other.

Given the pattern of results described in Table 8.1, we carried out a similar analysis of the 1991 BHPS data. The proportions thinking that a child suffered as a consequence of maternal employment were higher in all categories in 1991, as we would have expected. However, the pattern of variation in attitudes by class and gender was rather similar in 1991 to that in 2005. That is, in 1991, more men (52 per cent) than women (36 per cent) thought that a child would suffer, and managerial and professional women (44 per cent) were more likely to disagree than routine and manual women (36 per cent). In 1991, there was some class variation in men's attitudes, but nevertheless, our comparisons suggest that the broad pattern of attitudinal variation by class and sex revealed in Table 8.1 has been evident for well over a decade. Looking at change over time, the two groups amongst whom attitudes have changed the most are managerial and professional women, and routine and manual men.[11]

In the 2005 BHPS sample, of mothers with a child under 12, only 14 per cent of professional and managerial women reported their current economic activity as 'family care', as compared to 25 per cent of intermediate, and 30 per cent of routine and manual, women. Amongst employed mothers, there were significant class differences in attitudes – 61 per cent of employed professional and managerial women 'disagreed' that a pre-school child would suffer, as compared to 45 per cent of routine and manual women. This finding confirms our arguments, drawing on quantitative data (see Crompton and Lyonette 2008), as well as the qualitative data already presented in this chapter, that professional and managerial women are better placed to exercise their 'choices' (in so far as these choices are reflected in attitudes) in respect of employment.

Not surprisingly, women with children under 12 who were not in employment were much more likely (46 per cent) to agree that maternal employment was damaging to a pre-school child than mothers in employment (only 18 per cent, both 2005 figures). However, in 2005 there were no class differences at all in attitudes amongst non-employed mothers. Although, as noted above, only a small minority of professional and managerial women were stay-at-home mothers, those who had opted for full-time motherhood held virtually identical views to intermediate, and routine and manual, women in the same position.[12]

The evidence summarised so far suggests that occupational class is a major determinant of whether a mother is (a) in employment and (b) considers her children will not suffer as a consequence. Middle-class women are more likely to be working for 'self-fulfilment'; women in the lower occupational categories are more likely to be working for extra income. Nevertheless, a small minority of professional and managerial women would seem to have a preference for motherhood over employment. The attitudinal pattern amongst men (which appears to have persisted over time) presents intriguing problems of interpretation. Everywhere, men have more traditional attitudes to gender roles than women (perhaps because they fear the loss of their 'patriarchal dividend', see Connell 2002), but this does not explain why there would seem to be a tendency for routine and manual men to become *more* tolerant over time of mothers' employment at a greater rate than professional and managerial men – even though their partners are less likely to be in paid work. We can only speculate. It might be that, as interviewee R16 (male retail, intermediate) argued above, routine and manual men are feeling increasingly aware of the need for a second income, and are therefore in the process of changing their views quite rapidly on the necessity for maternal care.[13] In the case of managerial and professional men (whose partners are much more likely to be in employment, and working longer hours, than either intermediate or routine and manual women), it is possible that the family pressures to which this gives rise are keeping attitudes rather more 'traditional'.[14]

We also asked our interviewees whether or not they thought a pre-school child suffers if his or her mother goes out to work. Gender differences on the topic were very evident. Twenty men agreed that a lack of maternal care was harmful to young children, as against only six women, and 22 mothers held that non-maternal childcare was definitely *not* damaging, as compared to only seven men. Our number of interviews was simply too small to explore the interactions of gender and class revealed in the quantitative data. What the answers to this question did reveal, however, were class (cultural) differences in the rationales offered by respondents to explain their opinions.

CLASS AND ATTITUDES TOWARDS PAID CHILDCARE

Most of the parents, from all classes, who had used paid childcare emphasised the social benefits that their children had gained in the process, particularly as far as interactions with other children were concerned:

> I mean I would say he's a very confident little boy, argues like mad and he's only four, it drives me mad. And he's got his confidence I would say 50% from nursery really, from interacting with the other kids, and he's been in nursery since he was four months old (M20, female GP, professional/managerial).

> I look at [daughter], she's always been around my child minder and her three kids. In our family, my brother has twins which are a year older than [daughter] . . . if I look at [daughter] and I look at like my brother's kids before they went to school, they were very shy, you know, they were at home at lot whereas [daughter's] very social, you know, she's not a shy girl and she interacts very well (R1, female retail, intermediate).

However, the professional and managerial interviewees were much more likely to refer to 'scientific' evidence in explaining their views. This might be seen as an artefact of having so many doctors amongst our interviewees, but the recourse to scientific explanation was by no means limited to our medical interviewees:

> I look at all these studies that people do about, you know, one says that they're more intelligent if they go to nursery earlier and one says they're less intelligent, and I think it's horses for courses. I really do think that (A1, female accountant, professional/managerial).

> It's a group of child psychologists, I think it said, who believe that children suffer if their mother goes out to work and they're put into childcare. And I don't think so, providing the childcare that they are receiving is high quality and that the parents have adequate input around the childcare (A18, female accountant, professional/managerial).

Another theme that emerged amongst the professional and managerial interviewees (and reinforcing their arguments about a woman's own personal need for the satisfactions of employment) was that maternal care is not necessarily the best for children:

> I think it's a very bad thing to be where the mother at home who's depressed or who isn't able to stimulate children or doesn't have a choice, you know I think that can be worse. I think if you got a depressed mother – I don't want to stereotype – a mother who's not equipped at the current time for whatever reason not to be a great mum, I think there some nursery support or nursery education can be very positive, because it gives them more stimulation, it gives them a different environment (F12, female finance, professional/managerial).

> But I also think the child suffers if, if somebody is full time at home, it's vital that whoever's at home recognises the child's needs for social development and, and probably slightly more creative play . . . I'm reassured by the fact that, that she does actually do painting at nursery. . . . I think, I think, I've seen a lot of stay-at-home mums who I think do actually choke their child's development by not exposing them to a sufficient variety of environments (M15, male GP, professional/managerial).

In short, professional and managerial respondents, in discussing the impact of pre-school care on their children, were considerably more likely to draw on rational, 'scientific' arguments in arguing for the absence of a negative impact (and vice versa) as far as non-maternal care was concerned. This kind of reasoning reflects 'ways of thinking' that demonstrate the 'academic' approach characteristic of middle-class *habitus* (Ball 2003), that underpin the class differences in attitudes – particularly amongst women – revealed in Table 8.1.

DISCUSSION AND CONCLUSIONS

In this chapter, we have, from a class perspective, explored in some depth the closely-related topics of the employment of mothers of young children, and the childcare 'choices' of the couples involved. Our interviews supplied concrete evidence of what may be broadly described as differences of class *habitus* in the dialogues that surrounded their decision-taking, particularly in relation to childcare. What was more striking about our interviews, however, was that in the main, the major factors shaping outcomes were the *structures* of opportunities and constraints faced by the parents involved. Here, therefore, we would incline to Goldthorpe's 'materialist' explanation of class inequalities. More particularly, it was the professional and managerial interviewees who had most clearly been able to exercise their personal 'choices' – whether for mothers to work out of a sense of personal fulfilment, or to 'choose' – and switch – into and out of expensive childcare.

These findings have implications for current government policy. In present-day Britain, the government argues that inequalities are *not* socially desirable. As noted in our introduction, however, contemporary policies focus more on individual and family choices and motivations, rather than the structural opportunities and constraints we have emphasised. For example, a recent review (HMSO 2007: 14–15) argues for a 'new approach' to inequality, drawing on Sen's (1999) 'capabilities' approach, which focuses on process and worth, rather than outcomes. Prejudice against individuals, as reflected in organisational and institutional constraints, must be removed, but: 'A large part of what will unseat entrenched inequalities will lie in what communities and families do for themselves', and 'barriers to aspiration' must be removed (HMSO 2007: 45). The sharp rise in income inequality and job polarisation in Britain in recent years is acknowledged (HMSO 2007: 32), but it is not acknowledged that rising income inequality (and changes in the employment structure) were themselves a consequence of changes in economic policy following the turn to neoliberalism from the 1980s (Harvey 2005).

It is certainly a positive step to introduce policies that aim to develop the practical capacities for individuals to realise their 'capabilities', but this does not mean that approaches to the problem of inequality that focus on resources and outcomes can simply be discarded. If the 'class structure', as reflected in the occupational structure, remains highly unequal, then extensive inequalities will endure. In short, it is being argued here that parallel efforts should be made to improve the overall 'quality' of *employment*, as well as the 'quality' of the people taking up employment. This would imply some narrowing of income differentials. The provision of high quality, universal childcare would also serve to narrow class inequalities. The extent of childcare provision in Britain has been much improved, but much of this is supplied by the private sector. Our evidence suggests that the capacity to pay for childcare remains crucial in facilitating mothers' employment, and is a major class factor differentiating childcare use, as Vincent and Ball (2006) have argued.

Finally, gender differences – which have not been explored much in the past as discussions of maternal employment and childcare have focused mainly on women – have emerged around this important topic. Professional and managerial men are as traditional as other men as far as their views on maternal care are concerned – although they have significantly less traditional attitudes than men in other occupational classes as far as 'general' gender roles are concerned. This may possibly be an indication of a potential gender conflict *within* the professional and managerial grouping, and is certainly an area that merits further research.

NOTES

1. Indeed, the tax and benefits system was defined as 'outside the scope' of their enquiry (HMSO 2007: 14).
2. Hakim has argued that: 'the only cleavages that will matter within the workforce in the twenty-first century will be the continuing differences between primary and secondary earners . . . Sex and gender will cease to be important factors and are already being replaced by lifestyle preferences as the only important differentiating characteristic in labour supply' (Hakim 2003: 261).
3. Debacker (2008), on the basis of a survey of nearly 3000 Flemish households, has also demonstrated the wide variation in parental work-care strategies by class.
4. The wider project 'Class, gender employment and family' was part of the Network on 'Gender inequalities in production and reproduction' (GeNet) that is funded by the Economic and Social Research Council.
5. See Crompton and Lyonette (2010).
6. Using the ONS-SEC 3-category classification.
7. Work forces are stratified by both age and stage of family formation, and our interviewing strategy made the recruitment of routine and manual employees problematic. Doctors and accountants are clearly professionals, and the majority of employees in finance would be classified as 'Intermediate'. In retail, the majority of employees would be classified as 'routine and manual' according to the NS-SEC classification. We interviewed in a large London department store, where the majority of all employees were on lower grades. However, the vast majority of these were young. All of our interviewees had to have a child under the age of 14. Had we interviewed in, say, a supermarket, most of the shopfloor employees would have been either women with children, or young part-timers, often students (see Crompton et al. 2003).
8. We had 85 usable respondents for this part of the analysis (that is heterosexual, coupled). Of these, 37 were men (19 prof/managerials, 17 intermediates and 1 manual) and 48 were women (31 prof/managerials, 14 intermediates and 3 manuals).
9. Figures from The Daycare Trust (2007) show that the typical cost of a full-time nursery place for a child under two is £152 a week (over £7900 per year), and that the costs in the south-east are much higher (typically £205 a week in inner London or £180 a week in the south-east, where most of our interviews were conducted). Typical cost with a childminder for a child under 2 is £141 per week. Nannies cost anything between £250 and £500 per week, with families also responsible for the nanny's tax and NI contributions. Debacker (2008: 543) also emphasises the importance of reasonable childcare costs for low-educated mothers.
10. Occupational class was allocated on an individual basis. Men and women in employment were allocated the class category of their current job; those not in employment ('looking after the home', or unemployed) were allocated the class category of their last job. We use the 5-category ONS-SEC classification. In the 3-category ONS-SEC classification, occupational segregation has a marked impact on the 'Intermediate' category. Whereas women cluster in the 'Intermediate' grouping (lower level clerical and administrative employment), men cluster in the 'small employers and own account workers' and 'lower supervisory and technical' categories. Thus gender/class breakdowns using the 3-category ONS-SEC do not compare like with like in occupational terms.
11. Although our numbers are small, the BSA 2002 and 2006 surveys also indicated a larger shift in attitudes, in a more liberal direction, amongst routine and manual men.
12. This finding lends confirmation to the findings of Duncan's (2005) qualitative research. That is, the group he identified as 'suburban wives' (non-employed professional and managerial women), identified themselves as 'primarily mothers' and placed a very high value on maternal care. In this respect, their views were closer to the 'peripheral working class' mothers (who were also not in employment) than other middle-class women ('gentrifying partners') who were more likely to identify themselves as 'workers'.
13. Support for this interpretation may be found in the fact that, in 2005, 55 per cent of

semi-routine and routine manual men 'agreed' that both the man and woman should contribute to the household income, as compared to only 34 per cent of professional/managerial men.

14. In this discussion, we concentrate on one question only. However, an analysis of other family and gender role questions in the BHPS revealed that, although professional and managerial men were *more* gender-liberal on questions relating to gender roles, they (and the self-employed) tended to be similarly *less* liberal on other attitudinal questions relating to the impact on the family of mothers' employment.

BIBLIOGRAPHY

Ball, S.J. (2003), *Class Strategies and the Education Market: the Middle Classes and Social Advantage*, London: Routledge Falmer.

Beck, U. and E. Beck-Gernsheim (2002), *Individualization*, London: Sage.

Bourdieu, P. (1996), 'On the family as a realised category', *Theory, Culture and Society*, **13**, 19–26.

Brannen, J. and A. Nilsen (2005), 'Individualisation, choice and structure', *The Sociological Review*, **53**(3), 412–28.

Butt, S., K. Goddard and I. La Valle (2007), *Childcare Nation?*, London: Daycare Trust.

Connell, R.W. (2002), *Gender*, Oxford: Blackwell.

Crompton, R. (2006), 'Class and family' *Sociological Review*, November, 658–76.

Crompton, R. (2008), *Class and Stratification*, 3rd edn, Cambridge: Polity.

Crompton, R. and C. Lyonette (2008), 'Mothers' employment, work–life conflict, careers and class', in J. Scott, S. Dex and H. Joshi (eds), *Women and Employment*, Cheltenham, UK and Northampton, MA, USA: Edward Elgar.

Crompton, R. and C. Lyonette (2010), 'Women's career success and work–life "balance" in the accountancy and medical professions in Britain', *Gender, Work & Organisation*, **17**(2), forthcoming.

Crompton, R., J. Dennett and A. Wigfield (2003), *Organisations, Careers and Caring*, Bristol: Policy Press.

The Daycare Trust (2007), http//www.daycaretrust.org.uk.

Debacker, M. (2008), 'Care strategies among high and low skilled mothers', *Work, Employment and Society*, **22**, 527–45.

Devine, F. (2004), *Class Practices: how Parents Help their Children get Good Jobs*, Cambridge: Cambridge University Press.

Duncan, S. (2005), 'Mothering, class and rationality', *Sociological Review*, **53**, 2.

Erikson, R. and J.H. Goldthorpe (1993), *The Constant Flux*, Oxford: Clarendon Press.

Evans, G. (2006), *Educational Failure and White Working Class Children in Britain*, Houndmills, Basingstoke: Palgrave Macmillan.

Frank, T. (2000), *One Market under God*, New York: Doubleday.

Fraser, N. (2000), 'Rethinking recognition', *New Left Review*, May/June, 107–20.

Giddens, A. (1991), *Modernity and Self Identity*, Cambridge: Polity Press.

Gillies, V. (2005), 'Raising the "meritocracy": parenting and the individualisation of social class', *Sociology*, **39**(5), 835–53.

Goldthorpe, J.H. (2000), *On Sociology: Numbers, Narratives and the Integration of Research and Theory*, Oxford: Oxford University Press.

Goldthorpe, J.H., D. Lockwood, F. Bechhofer and J. Platt (1969), *The Affluent Worker in the Class Structure*, Cambridge: Cambridge University Press.

Hakim, C. (2003), *Models of the Family in Modern Societies*, Aldershot: Ashgate.

Harvey, D. (2005), *A Brief History of Neoliberalism*, Oxford: Oxford University Press.

Hatcher, R. (1998), 'Class differentiation in education: rational choices?', *British Journal of Sociology of Education*, **19**(1), 5–24.

Hills, J. (2004), *Inequality and the State*, Oxford: Oxford University Press.

Himmelweit, S. and M. Sigala (2003), 'Internal and external constraints on mothers' employment', working paper no 27, ESRC Future of Work Programme.

HMSO (2007), *Fairness and Freedom*, London: HMSO.

Inglehart, R. and P. Norris (2003), *Rising Tide: Gender Equality and Cultural Change around the World*, Cambridge: Cambridge University Press.

La Valle, I., S. Arthur, C. Millward, J. Scott and M. Clayden (2002), *Happy Families? Atypical Work and its Influence on Family Life*, Final report, York: Joseph Rowntree Foundation.

Moen, P. (ed.) (2003), *It's About Time: Couples and Careers*, Ithaca and London: Cornell University Press.

Rake, K., H. Davies, H. Joshi and R. Alami (2000), *Women's Incomes over the Lifetime*, London: The Stationery Office.

Reay, D. and H. Lucey (2003), 'The limits of "choice": children and inner city schooling', *Sociology*, **37**(1), 121–42.

Sen, A. (1999) *Development as Freedom*, Oxford: Oxford University Press.

Vincent, C. and S. Ball (2006), *Childcare, Choice and Class Practices*, London: Routledge.

Walker, A. (1990), 'Blaming the victims' in C.A. Murray (ed), *The Emerging British Underclass*, London: IEA Health and Welfare Unit.

Warren, T. (2003), 'Class and gender-based working time?, *Sociology*, **37**(4), 733–52.

9. Perceptions of quality of life: gender differences across the life course

Jacqueline Scott, Anke C. Plagnol and Jane Nolan

INTRODUCTION

The study of quality of life is in the ascendancy. As the evidence becomes clearer that increasing the purchasing power of citizens does not automatically increase their sense of well-being, there is new interest in how quality of life is perceived. If it is not merely money and good health that matter, then what else is important for the 'good life'? Recent decades have seen a convergence of interest in quality of life research by economists, psychologists, sociologists and philosophers (for example Sirgy et al. 2006). Philosophers have tended to focus on the abstract principles or, more often, the difficulties of arriving at principles that might help guide people's pursuit of happiness. A crude summary of the philosophers' position is that it is tough for people to know what makes a good life. Social scientists are more modest in their aims and tend to focus on the range of so-called 'goods' that may contribute to quality of life. The economists and sociologists are interested in not only how these are distributed across the population, but also how they change across time. The range of possible 'goods' is very wide and includes health (Wilkinson 1996), employment (Gallie 1996), money (Easterlin 2001), time (Gershuny and Halpin 1996), status (Marmot 2004), environment (Bliss 1996) and so on.

Among the most important of these 'goods' are those that are found in the private sphere, particularly in terms of relationships with friends and family. The notion that it is not merely the existence of family relationships but also the quality of family relationships that affect individual well-being is well established (Elliott and Umberson 2004). What is also clear is that trade-offs in the balance between family and work are very different for men and women. The traditional gender division of labour, in which men do the paid work of winning the bread for their loved ones and women busy themselves with unpaid labour of love within the home, may seem anachronistic. Nevertheless, in the UK, women's increasing involvement in paid work has not had as much of an impact on gender roles as might have been expected: women still do the bulk of unpaid work, regardless of their employment status. Such gender role differences mean that men and women are starting from somewhat different viewpoints in assessing what matters for their quality of life.

If love and work, as Freud asserted, are the cornerstones of our humanness, and if the balance of family and work are very different for men and women, then it would follow that there may be important gender differences in how quality of life is perceived. Yet, with some notable exceptions, quality of life research often lacks a gender perspective. One exception is Plagnol and Easterlin (2008) who show that aspirations and attainments play an important role in shaping well-being. Early in adult life, women are more likely than men to fulfil their aspirations concerning family life and material goods and express greater satisfaction in these domains than do men. In later life these gender differences are reversed and men come closer than women in satisfying their family and material aspirations and are the happier of the two genders. The question that Plagnol and Easterlin are unable to address, given the constraints of their data, is whether there are qualitative differences in what family life or material goods *mean* for men and women. This matters because if the goods aspired to are viewed differently, then how men and women best achieve quality of life may also be different.

It is important to take a life course perspective when examining people's perceptions of quality of life. It is not just the case that younger people's perceptions are likely to differ from older age groups, but also that people's perceptions of quality of life will change with important life course transitions, such as the move into a new job, becoming parents, retiring and so on. Another crucial insight of the life course perspective is that lives are interlinked. As psychologists have noted, people tend to live their lives in convoy (Antonucci and Akiyama 1987). What happens to one member of the household crucially affects the lives of other household members. This relational dimension is often ignored in quality of life research because most national surveys only interview one person from the household. Household panel surveys that interview all members of the household allow for the possibility of not only exploring how a person's own quality of life is dependent on what is happening in the lives of significant others, but also how quality of life is perceived differently by different household members.

Our aim in this chapter is to explore what people say matters for their own quality of life. This is a somewhat novel focus, because while there is much research exploring the influences on people's well-being or happiness, far less is known about how people perceive what is important for their own quality of life. Yet, as the Thomas theorem states, perceptions do matter: 'If men define situations as real they are real in their consequences' (Thomas and Thomas 1928: 572).

Our exploration of perceptions has four main analytical goals. The first is to explore both quantitatively and qualitatively how men and women differ in what they say is important. Second, we explore whether there are gender differences in the way men and women see their quality of life as bound up with others. There is a psychological literature suggesting that women are more relationally orientated than men. Recognition of the significance of intimacy and relationships with others, is something that Gilligan claims is gendered and 'is something women have known from the beginning' (Gilligan 1982: 17). Following Chodorow (1978), Gilligan sees the gender difference originating in early childhood with the different patterns of attachment and separation of girls and boys from mothers. For girls, identification with the mother leads to attachment being a more prevalent aspect of later relationships; whereas separation is the equivalent experience for males, who have to establish a distinct gender identity from the mother. Whatever the merits of such psychoanalytical theorising, the question of whether significant others play a more important role for women than for men in perceptions of quality of life is open to empirical investigation. Third, we investigate how perceptions of quality of life change with the transition to parenthood. Parenthood is perhaps the most important life course change in terms of its effect on the gender division of labour. Thus we expect gender differences in what matters before and after parenthood to be marked. Finally, we consider how the transition to retirement influences perceptions of quality of life. Retirement is likely to affect perceptions of quality of life differently for men and women, given the different gender balance in paid and unpaid work across the life course.

Before we present the results of our analysis we first describe the data used and explain the detailed coding exercise that was required to reach a descriptive understanding of quality of life. In an earlier study, we have used the example of perceptions of quality of life to argue that there is room for methodological advancement in panel surveys by including at least some qualitative elements in questionnaires through the use of open-ended questions (Scott et al. 2009) and have examined more generally what matters for wellbeing (Plagnol and Scott 2008). Here we extend this work to show that perceptions of quality of life are not fixed but change over time. Moreover, we demonstrate that men and women have different perceptions of what matters, in ways that are bound up with their different gender roles across the life course.

PERCEPTIONS OF QUALITY OF LIFE: BRITISH HOUSEHOLD PANEL SURVEY

Our data are from the British Household Panel Survey which began in 1991 and is a multi-purpose study whose unique value resides in the fact that it: a) follows the same individuals over time, interviewing all household members on an annual basis; b) is household-based, interviewing every adult member (16 and over) of the sample households; c) contains sufficient cases for a meaningful analysis of sub-population groups such as different age groups, or different family types. The first wave of the panel consisted of some 5500 households and 10 300 individuals, drawn from a proportionate representative sample of 250 postal areas in Great Britain (Taylor et al. 2007).

An open-ended question is routinely included at the end of the individual questionnaire. In Wave 7 (1997) and Wave 12 (2002), the question asked about people's quality of life was:

> The final question asks you to think about things that are important to you. There is a lot of discussion these days about quality of life, yet that means different things to different people. Would you take a moment to think about what quality of life means to you, and tell me what things you consider are important for your own quality of life?

The interviewer was instructed to probe each mention in more detail with the prompt: 'In what ways is that important to you?'

Our development of a coding scheme for these verbatim responses proceeded as follows. As we were manipulating thousands of responses, some initial coding of themes was necessary in order to aid the development of our qualitative analysis. First, a detailed descriptive coding scheme was developed by the first author, which captured the full range of mentions across different domains such as health, family, finances, friends, home comforts, leisure, employment, freedom, time for self, environment and community. Each domain often had several sub-codes, for example, family is subdivided into four – partner/marriage, children and grandchildren, other family members and mentions of family in general. In all, the original BHPS coding frame lists 77 substantive codes (see Taylor et al. 2007: Appendix 3.18). Up to four mentions were coded in the verbatim responses. We then carried out extensive new qualitative analysis, using both the original verbatim responses and re-grouping the pre-coded material to better reflect the main themes that people mentioned (see the Appendix).

The next stage was to unpack precisely *what* things people considered to be important for their own quality of life. The descriptive results of our

Table 9.1   Rank order of things which are important for your quality of life

Item	1997			2002		
	% first mention	combined %	combined n	% first mention	combined %	combined n
Health	36.6	53.1	4803	38.3	52.7	4361
Family	11.0	40.3	3646	15.4	44.2	3660
Finance	9.8	37.7	3414	8.2	33.9	2808
Happiness	9.9	28.5	2580	9.2	25.6	2116
Friends	3.6	20.5	1854	2.8	16.7	1379
Home comforts	5.3	15.7	1417	4.0	12.0	989
Leisure	3.1	15.4	1394	3.7	17.8	1474
Employment	4.2	14.2	1287	2.7	9.6	795
Freedom	2.8	7.3	659	3.0	8.8	730
Time for self	3.1	7.2	651	3.6	9.9	818
Miscellaneous other	1.9	7.2	648	2.1	8.4	693
Other material benefits	1.2	6.6	595	1.1	5.8	478
Environment, community	1.5	6.6	594	1.5	5.3	442
Other personal	1.8	6.4	578	0.7	3.3	272
Negative mentions	2.1	5.2	469	1.8	3.4	282
Spiritual, moral	1.2	4.6	412	0.8	3.6	300
Don't know	1.0	1.0	93	1.0	1.0	82
N	9047			8272		

Source: BHPS (with cross-sectional weights).

substantive re-grouping of the more detailed coding scheme are shown in Table 9.1. The first column and the fourth column show the responses people cited first in 1997 and 2002 respectively, with percentages adding to 100 per cent. Thus, in 1997, 37 per cent of people mention health as the first (or the only thing) they cite, and in 2002 the figure was 38 per cent. The second column (on which the rank order of the table is based) and the fifth column show the percentage of the samples who mention a particular response *at all*. Thus in 1997 53 per cent of our sample mention health (the most frequently mentioned concern) whereas 47 per cent (not shown) do not. Similar figures are found for 2002, with 53 per cent again mentioning health. As up to four mentions were coded, these columns do not add to 100 per cent. We can see that three domains are mentioned by more than one third of participants: health (53 per cent both waves), family (40 per cent in 1997, 44 per cent in 2002) and finance (38 per cent in 1997 and 34 per cent in 2002). There are interesting things to be said about other domains mentioned, like, for example, the relatively low mentions of environment and community, which the literature suggests is a more prominent concern (Rapley 2003). However, this result may simply be due to the phrasing of the question, which may seem to give a steer towards more personal issues.

In our subsequent analysis we first consider the extent to which there are gender differences in what people perceive as important for quality of life. We then present further analysis of the three most mentioned categories in order to explore whether, regardless of whether or not there are quantitative differences in quality of life, men and women show qualitative differences in the way different domains matter. The graphs below are based on the combined data from 1997 and 2002 and we draw on both waves for illustrative quotes. We will return to examine the qualitative data longitudinally later in the chapter but, in the section that follows, our aim is to investigate gender similarities and differences in the range of meanings attached to each key domain.

QUANTITATIVE AND QUALITATIVE ANALYSIS OF QUALITY OF LIFE

Our analysis suggests that concepts of quality of life change at different stages of the life course. Both men and women mention health as being an important part of their own quality of life more often than any other item overall. However, at young ages both genders are more likely to mention family and finances than health (Table 9.2). Mentions of friends, home comforts and employment also are less pronounced among the older age groups, whereas the importance of leisure and freedom is more marked among older respondents. Here we focus on younger (15–25) and older (65 and over) age groups, in order to contrast the widest spread of generations. The full age-range responses are shown under 'all' (in columns 3 and 6). However, in the next section, we unpack how responses varied across the entire range of age groups. Almost all categories display significant gender differences, with women more likely than men to mention health, family, happiness and friends and less likely to mention finance, leisure and employment. The gender difference in mentions of home comforts is slight (although with these large numbers still statistically significant at p<.05).

Table 9.2   *Quality of life mentions by gender and age, pooled data 1997 and 2002*

Age	Women			Men		
	15–25	65 and over	all	15–25	65 and over	all
Health	35.84	61.10	57.41	29.57	60.97	50.29
Family	51.92	35.84	49.30	36.22	27.60	38.44
Finance	39.72	20.86	33.30	43.72	27.60	38.83
Happiness	32.23	17.68	29.71	26.28	17.38	24.96
Friends	35.58	19.49	19.14	32.39	11.86	15.29
Home comforts	18.10	13.64	14.39	16.82	11.43	13.45
Leisure	11.36	22.45	15.15	19.21	23.78	19.66
Employment	19.82	0.69	9.87	24.37	1.45	14.94
Freedom	5.11	11.04	6.94	5.45	10.17	7.69
Time for self	4.89	3.97	7.82	6.02	5.47	9.75
Miscellaneous other	7.62	9.74	7.93	6.26	7.31	7.16
Other material benefits	11.71	6.39	6.68	10.61	7.07	6.81
Environment, community	2.47	3.72	3.86	4.83	7.02	6.86
Other personal	6.47	4.58	4.90	6.98	4.31	4.91
Negative mentions	1.98	5.20	3.83	3.01	5.13	4.57
Spiritual, moral	2.11	8.19	4.28	2.68	6.44	3.90
Don't know	1.59	0.90	0.80	2.05	1.26	1.07
N	2271	2771	14291	2093	2065	12037

Source: BHPS (no weights).

Because our data are from two surveys of only five years apart, it is important to note that the percentages reported in Table 9.2 are based on individuals who belong to very different birth cohorts. Thus the observations for the lower age group (15–25 years) are from people who were born between 1972 and 1987, whereas members of the 65 and over age group were all born before 1937. It is possible that members of the younger cohort will place considerably less importance on health once they reach 65 than the older cohorts shown here, but the qualitative responses presented below make it apparent that there are pronounced life course differences. Similarly, it is possible that gender differences might diminish for future cohorts, but again, as our qualitative analysis shows, there are pronounced gender differences in what matters for quality of life across the life course.

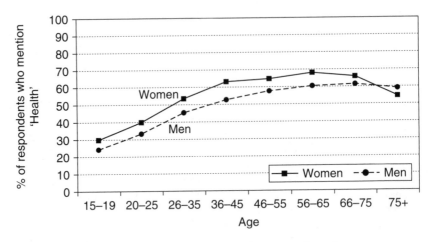

Figure 9.1 Percentage mentions of health by age and gender

QUALITATIVE ANALYSIS OF KEY DOMAINS

Health

There is a large body of literature on preference-based measures of quality of life that focuses on health (for example Lenert and Kaplan 2000). In our study, too, we found that the majority of statements in this domain showed a keen sense of the importance of good health as a foundation from which to build a reasonable quality of life, and examples of this awareness can be found across all groups: Josh,[1] 17, notes that 'without health you're nothing', likewise Lily, 67 notes 'If you've got your health that's all that's important'.

As Figure 9.1 makes clear, health is a more important factor for some age groups than others in assessing quality of life. It is a particular priority from the mid-30s onwards, which may reflect a growing awareness of decreasing energy levels as well as increasing functional difficulties. It may also, as we will discuss later, indicate that health becomes more salient for people when they have children themselves.

While younger participants tend to discuss health in the generic sense outlined above, older participants are more likely to mention specific ailments or declines in cognitive functioning. Older people focus on having their 'marbles' or keeping their 'mobility'. Thus our data confirm an emphasis that is already well documented in the health-related quality of life literature (Bowling 1995). Joan, 61, said: 'I suffer from sciatica and high blood pressure so I know how much illness can affect my life and social activities.' Similarly, Will, 76, tells us: 'You need to have all your marbles; mobility is important and to have all your thinking facilities.'

However, while deterioration in the participant's *own* health becomes more pronounced in older age groups, another interesting finding was the way in which the role of the older person as the *carer* of a partner in ill-health also has a bearing on their assessment of their *own* quality of life. June, 75, reflects on the impact of her husband's illness on her own quality of life: 'I haven't got any quality [of life] at the moment as my husband has Alzheimer's.' Similarly, men in the caring role also note the importance of the health and well-being of significant others: Phillip, 63, tells us: 'If Ann [participant's wife] was better it would help. Ann is still waiting for her operation.'

While the strains of being an older carer are well known, we find some examples of this *relational* aspect of health echoed by both women and men in all age groups. Jack, 20, notes the importance of 'My family's health and well-being, including my own' to his quality of life. Sarah, 38, answers, 'Children's health: because life is tough when they're not well – everything goes much smoother when they're well.' This 'other orientation' in the importance of health for well-being is something that is easily overlooked in the quality of life literature, which tends to focus solely on the individual.

Family

Our next domain, family, continues the theme of the relationship between self and others in understanding lay evaluations of quality of life. Some argue that demographic changes, coupled with social and economic changes, such as geographical mobility, increased divorce rates, single-parenthood, women's increased involvement in paid work, and supposed increases in individualism make 'family' less important to people, both emotionally and materially, than in previous eras (Beck 1992; Giddens 1992). However, there is a significant amount of literature which critiques and problematises these claims (Crompton 2006; Duncan and Smith 2006; Nolan and Scott 2006; Williams 2004). In our study, too, we find further empirical evidence of the continuing importance of family, particularly for women. As Figure 9.2 shows, in all age groups women are more likely than men to mention family as important for their quality of life (though we would not wish to over-emphasise the difference, as family is clearly important to men too). Interestingly, however, for women in particular, it is the under-46s, those who are most likely to live in households with two generations, who are most likely to mention family.

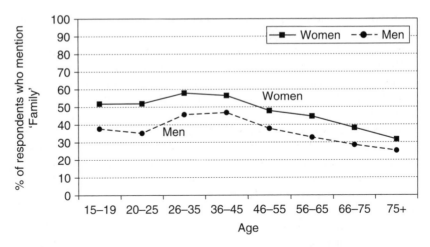

Figure 9.2   Percentage mentions of family by age and gender

But what precisely do people talk about in relation to family and quality of life, and what differences do we find between women and men in different age groups? First, we find a common generic appreciation of family that echoes across gender and age groups: Paul, 27, notes: 'The family's the most important part of my life' and June, 61, describes the importance of 'Having family around you'. That said, however, there are, of course, differences in the *kinds* of support given and received by different family members across the life course and, not surprisingly, in the under-25s we find reference to families as the *providers* of moral and material support: Edward, 19, notes that family is important to his quality of life because: 'My family looked after me for a lot of my life'. Similarly Cindy, 21, values family because 'They give me moral support'.

There were also some fairly gender-stereotypical responses in relation to family and quality of life. In the 26–45 age group, we find more women than men mentioning the importance of children's well-being, and men more likely than women to link the importance of family to their role as breadwinners. There were, of course, occasions when women discussed the importance of their breadwinning role for their family (see the following section on finance) and when men mentioned their concern with their children's well-being, but the following are typical statements illustrating gender differences: Amber, 28, for example, tells us that what is important for her quality of life is: 'My children. How they are, how they eat and dress. Their education.' And Luke, 41, notes that for him, quality of life means: 'A secure job [which] enables me to buy things for my family'. We see further examples of this breadwinning theme as we turn to mentions of finance.

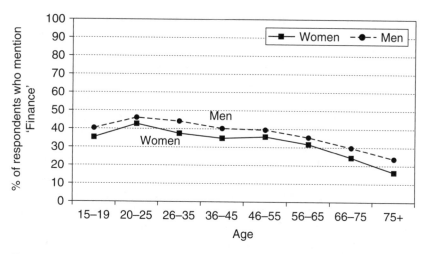

Figure 9.3   Percentage mentions of finance by age and gender

Finance

It is sometimes claimed that consumerism and lifestyle aspirations increasingly govern values and quality of life (Rapley 2003). However, while over a third of our sample mentioned finance-related matters as important for their quality of life, the key theme to emerge from our qualitative analysis highlighted the importance of 'not worrying about money' or 'not struggling'. We don't find people dreaming of winning the lottery, nor do we find responses that emphasise the importance of buying luxury cars, designer clothes or other consumer goods to ensure a good quality of life. Rather, typical quotes include: 'Not having to struggle financially' (Duncan, 33); 'To not worry about paying bills and have money for extra meals and holidays' (Mandy, 38); 'Having enough money not to have to struggle' (Ralph, 51).

Examining group differences in this category, Figure 9.3 illustrates that, in all age groups, men are more likely than women to mention finance, although the frequency of mentions across the life course is very similar for men and women. Interestingly, however, qualitative analysis shows that men in the 20–35 age range discuss finance in relation to quality of life in the sense of being free from debt. From 36 to 54, however, an additional theme emerges which illustrates, once again, the importance of the relationship between finance and breadwinning identity. Rhys, 43, discusses finances in terms of 'Earning a decent wage; to support my family financially'. Likewise Roy, 38, notes, 'I would say not having to struggle. Being able to provide for the children and ourselves.'

It is important to highlight the ways in which each of our core themes are interlinked. While counting the number of mentions of each theme provides us with a stronger base from which to make generalisations, this form of 'chunking' qualitative data can gloss over important information about processes. For example, our qualitative analysis shows that health is often important because individuals need good health to care for others, both financially and emotionally. To illustrate the point further, men in mid-life mentioned health as important for work, which, in turn, was central to their breadwinning role. As Sebastian notes, quality of life consists of 'My health, so I can run my business and provide for my family'. Likewise Phillipa, when asked *why* her health was important to quality of life, noted the importance of good health for fulfilling her caring roles, 'I need to keep my health to look after my mam and my husband'. Aged 26, and following a divorce, Lily notes the importance of being healthy because she needed to be 'able to look after the children by myself'. Similarly, Charlie, 39 and divorced, says, 'I need my health as I have 4 children to look after'. In the following section we examine the influence of key life transitions – family formation and retirement – on perceptions of quality of life.

LIFE COURSE TRANSITIONS AND CHANGING EVALUATIONS OF QUALITY OF LIFE

Family Formation and Changing Evaluations of Quality of Life

As indicated in the quotations above, the way people evaluate the well-being of *others* is, in fact, central to their assessment of their *own* quality of life. In this section, we will focus specifically on how the transition to partnership and parenthood influences an individual's perception of what matters for quality of life. This is mainly because it seems likely that 'other orientation' becomes more significant at this point in the life course. Not surprisingly, however, we find that this transition is somewhat different for women and men.

There were 51 women who were single and under 40 in 1997 and who were living with both a partner and a child five years later in 2002. There are clear indicators in the qualitative data of the way in which family formation brings changes to evaluations of what is important for quality of life. For example, in 1997, Olive emphasises 'financial security, health and peace of mind'. In 2002, however, while she still emphasises financial security, she also notes the importance to her quality of life that 'my son and immediate family are happy'. Likewise, Sally mentioned financial and emotional security in 1997, but, in 2002, the first thing she discusses is 'spending time with family at home'.

The change in definitions of quality of life brought on by motherhood can be illustrated by the following examples. Eleanor's priorities in 1997 were 'health and work'; 'giving up smoking, health generally, expanding my career, making myself money, my future generally'. In 2002, however, her concerns are: 'my son and a good family life – that's all that's important to me'. For Mary her priorities in 1997 were 'happiness and standard of living'. In 2002, she emphasises the importance of 'the health of my child and family – they're my whole life, what would I do without them'. Similarly, Carol undergoes a shift from placing importance on 'good friends and a steady income' in her first interview, to 'being with family, see baby grow up and being with partner'.

Forming a family also changes the way in which men evaluate their quality of life. There were 79 men who were single and aged under 40 in 1997 and in a couple with at least one child in 2002. Predictably, the way priorities change for men is often linked to becoming the 'breadwinner'. For example when Andrew was aged 26, what was important to his quality of life was that he could 'go out and enjoy myself'. Aged 31, as a father, he now wants to be 'comfortable, not struggling as we do at the moment. If I could get a better job, everything will be fine'. Billy, 23, was interested in a 'comfortable income, nice food, nice place to live, nice clothes, spending time with my girlfriend'. But aged 28 he is focused on 'making a living to keep us all happy'. Likewise, aged 22, Martin noted the importance of 'going to work, money is important, a stable family'; five years later he defines quality of life as 'providing for my family, make sure they are happy. If the family is happy, that's all we need.'

But the transition to family did not just influence quality of life in relation to the importance of 'providing'. The intimacy and companionship of family life were also now more salient to definitions of quality of life. Aged 29, Ian first described quality of life as 'being able to go out and enjoy yourself'; later he focuses on 'being with my family; they keep me happy; make me laugh'. Similarly, Darren, 24, wants 'money, friends, [good] neighbourhood, health, socializing and confidence'. Aged 29, he lists 'my daughter, my wife, money, health: now Hannah and Vanda are in my life I couldn't be without them'.

Of course, there were both men and women who remained consistent in their views across the waves, or whose perceptions changed in ways which are not linked with their change in family status. Nevertheless, for most people the transition to partnership and parenthood brings different priorities, and quality of life had become more 'other orientated'.

Quality of Life before and after Retirement

Our final analysis examines whether people's perceptions of quality of life shift before and after retirement, which is, like entering parenthood, an important life stage transition. We also explore qualitatively how men and women differ in their perceptions of quality of life, before and after retirement, and how this might relate to the different gender roles concerning priorities given to the breadwinner role and to family care. In addition, we examine the claim of Laslett (1989) that the map of life has to be redrawn, and that the 'third age' – the period when employment has ended and children have grown – should be 'the crown of life', when people have greater freedom to realise their own personal objectives. The theory has been criticised, not least because Laslett is seen as giving undue focus to the elite group who benefit from lifelong learning and self-improvement. Our findings on the Laslett hypothesis can be summarised very briefly. Not surprisingly, in our representative sample, there are a handful of mentions from both women and men of the benefits they accrue from time for reading and travel and education – but these are the exception, not the rule.

As can be seen in Table 9.3, there are systematic differences between men and women in how perceptions of what matters for quality of life changes in the years before and after retirement. Among the 157 women who retired between 1997 and 2002, the dominant quality of life mentions in both years are health and family. However, health mentions decline, whereas family mentions slightly increase. For the 149 men who retired in the same period, health mentions increase, but family mentions slightly decrease. Health and finance are the two main mentions for men following retirement. When asked to elaborate on why these are important, a common response is that the reasons are so obvious that they hardly need elaboration – after all 'it's no good being ill or poor'. As we saw in Figure 9.3, more men mention finance than women throughout the life course, and this gender difference continues post-retirement.

However, men's mentions of finance often display a continuity with their former breadwinner role, and the focus of their response is about maintaining a reasonable standard of living or about sufficient financial support for other family members. Previously published analyses using BHPS data show that men are more likely than women to provide financial help to adult children, while women are more likely than men to provide regular care for grandchildren (Nolan and Scott 2006). In the current analysis it is quite clear that for many men and women, taking care of others is perceived as being important. In other words, people perceive relationships as mattering hugely for one's own quality of life.

Both women and men talk of the importance of grandchildren for quality

Table 9.3 *Quality of life mentions by men and women who were self-employed or in paid employment in 1997 and retired in 2002*

Mention	Women		Men	
	1997	2002	1997	2002
Health	71.34	63.06	52.35	69.80
Family	38.22	45.22	37.58	30.87
Finance	38.85	26.11	35.57	44.30
Happiness	36.31	21.66	25.50	18.12
Friends	22.93	17.20	14.77	13.42
Leisure	14.01	19.11	24.16	18.79
Home comforts	12.10	10.83	16.78	11.41
Freedom	7.64	12.10	10.74	9.40
Employment	10.19	1.27	18.12	1.34
Misc other	5.10	12.10	7.38	9.40
Spiritual	5.10	5.10	3.36	4.03
Negatives	3.18	1.27	7.38	3.36
Environment	5.73	7.01	12.75	12.75
Time self	6.37	6.37	8.05	9.40
Other personal	3.18	1.91	6.04	2.68
Other material	1.27	8.28	5.37	4.03
N	157	157	149	149

Source: BHPS (no weights).

of life, albeit with some important gender differences. A typical male response is from Mike, aged 62, who spoke of his grandchildren as 'taking years off me', and goes on to say, 'I have time for them that I didn't have for my own children'. This response captures succinctly the changing image of what a 'good father' involves. For men of Mike's generation a good provider was a good father. Today, good fathers are expected to spend time with children. Needless to say, there are no equivalent responses given by women; whatever their paid work hours, mothers are expected to provide care for children. Perhaps this helps explain an intriguing quantitative gender difference – for women, post-retirement mentions of the importance of leisure increase, whereas after retirement men's mentions of leisure decrease.

CONCLUSIONS

In this chapter we explore people's perceptions of what matters for their quality of life. The three most common themes mentioned are health, family and finance. One common aspect of health mentions was the very high degree of emphasis on the health of others. The importance of relationships, not surprisingly, comes through very clearly in mentions of family. Here there is strong evidence of gender-stereotypical responses. Men are more likely than women to link the importance of family to their role of breadwinner. Moreover, men's mentions of finance are often bound up with their breadwinner role. Thus one of our most important findings is that people see their own quality of life as strongly bound up with the quality of life of significant others. The existing literature often is overly individualistic and fails to give sufficient attention to the 'other orientation' that is frequently emphasised by both men and women.

A second finding of this study is that quality of life is a concept that changes as people age and move across different life course stages. For example, as people move into partnership and parenthood their perceptions of the importance of others become even more marked. Similarly, when people move from employment into retirement, quality of life perceptions shift once again. Moreover, they shift in ways that are crucially related to the distinctive gender roles of men and women.

Throughout our analysis we found strong gender differences in the way men and women talked about their family and work responsibilities and how these connect to quality of life. This has important ramifications for policy makers who are concerned to address the work–life balance issue, which has come to the fore both in the UK and in the rest of Europe. Often discourse on work–life balance and quality of life is framed in gender-neutral terms. However, any policy concerned with the allocation of paid and unpaid work must take into account the pronounced gender differences. Men and women's different caring and breadwinning roles lead to important differences in the way they perceive quality of life.

Yet both men and women perceive their own quality of life as being bound up with the well-being of others. Thus our data would support the view that one policy priority should be to tackle the so-called 'care deficit' which in part results from the long work-hour culture of men and the increased labour force participation of women. We argued at the outset that the Thomas theorem applies and that studying perceptions is important, because if people perceive something to be real, then it is real in its consequences. If this is the case, then steps taken to support both men and women's actions in caring for others will benefit the quality of life for all.

NOTE

1. For stylistic reasons we use pseudonyms when discussing quotations. To protect anonymity, participants can only be identified by a unique number in the data set.

REFERENCES

Antonucci, T. and H. Akiyama (1987), 'Social networks in adult life and a preliminary examination of the convoy model', *Journal of Gerontology*, **42**(5), 519–27.

Beck, U. (1992), *Risk Society: Towards a New Modernity*, London: Sage.

Bliss, C. (1996), 'Economics of the environment', in A. Offer (ed.), *In Pursuit of the Quality of Life*, Oxford: Clarendon Press, pp. 66–87.

Bowling, A. (1995), 'What things are important in people's lives: a survey of the public's judgement to inform scales of health related quality of life', *Social Science and Medicine*, **41**(1), 1447–62.

Chodorow, N. (1978), *The Reproduction of Mothering*, Berkeley: University of California.

Crompton, R. (2006), *Employment and the Family: the Reconfiguration of Work and Family Life in Contemporary Societies.* Cambridge: Cambridge University Press.

Duncan, S. and D. Smith (2006), 'Individualisation versus the geography of "new" families', *21st Century Society*, **1**(2), 167–89.

Easterlin, R.A. (2001) 'Income and happiness: towards a unified theory', *Economic Journal*, **111**, 465–84.

Elliott, S and D. Umberson (2004), 'Recent demographic trends in the US and implications for well-being', in J. Scott, J. Treas and M. Richards (eds), *Blackwell Companion to Sociology of Families*, Oxford: Blackwell.

Gallie, D. (1996), 'The quality of employment: perspectives and problems', in A. Offer (ed.), *In Pursuit of the Quality of Life*, Oxford: Clarendon Press, pp. 163–87.

Gershuny, J. and B. Halpin (1996), 'Time use: quality of life and process benefits', in A. Offer (ed.), *In Pursuit of the Quality of Life*, Oxford: Clarendon Press, pp. 188–210.

Giddens, A. (1992), *The Transformation of Intimacy: Sexuality, Love and Eroticism in Modern Societies*, Cambridge: Polity Press.

Gilligan, C. (1982), *In a Different Voice: Psychological Theory and Women's Development*, Cambridge: Harvard University Press.

Laslett, P. (1989), *A Fresh Map of Life*, London: George Weidenfeld and Nicolson Ltd.

Lenert, L. and R. Kaplan (2000), 'Validity and interpretation of preference-based measures of health related quality of life', *Medical Care*, Supplement II, **38**(9), 138–50.

Marmot, M. (2004), *Status Syndrome: How your Social Standing Directly Affects your Health and Life Expectancy*, London: Bloomsbury.

Nolan, J. and J. Scott (2006), 'Gender and kinship in contemporary Britain', in M. Richards (ed.), *Kinship: Relationships and Law in a Changing Society*, London: Hart.

Plagnol, A.C. and R.A. Easterlin (2008), 'Aspirations, attainments, and satisfaction: life cycle differences between American women and men', *Journal of Happiness Studies*, 9(4), 601–19.

Plagnol, A.C. and J. Scott (2008), 'What matters for wellbeing: individual perceptions of quality of life before and after important events', *GeNet Working Papers*, No. 33.

Rapley, M. (2003), *Quality of Life Research: A Critical Introduction*, London: Sage.

Scott, J., J. Nolan and A.C. Plagnol (2009), 'Panel data and open-ended questions: understanding perceptions of quality of life', special issue (edited by G. Crow, N. Bardsley, and R. Wiles), *21st Century Society*, 4(2), 123–35.

Sirgy, M.J., A.C. Michalos, A.L. Ferriss, R.A. Easterlin, D. Patrick and W. Pavot (2006), 'The quality-of-life (QOL) research movement: past, present, and future', *Social Indicators Research*, 76(3), 343–466.

Taylor, M.F., J. Brice, N. Buck and E. Prentice-Lane (eds) (2007), *British Household Panel Survey User Manual Volume A: Introduction, Technical Report and Appendices*, Colchester: University of Essex.

Thomas, W.I. and D.S. Thomas (1928), *The Child in America: Behavior Problems and Programs*, New York: Knopf.

Wilkinson, R.G. (1996), *Unhealthy Societies: the Afflictions of Inequality*, London: Routledge.

Williams, F. (2004), *Rethinking Families*, London: Calouste Gulbenkian Foundation.

APPENDIX: QUALITY OF LIFE PERCEPTION OF WHAT MATTERS*

Question:

'Would you take a moment to think about what "quality of life" means to you, and tell me what things you consider are important for your own quality of life?'

Coding of mentions: based on BHPS manual, Appendix 3.18

1. *Health*: good health, mobility, living and breathing, personal welfare.
2. *Family*: children and grandchildren, partner, marriage, other family members, family in general.
3. *Finance*: finances, money, standard of living.
4. *Happiness*: happiness, peace of mind, security.
5. *Friends*: friends, friendship.
6. *Leisure*: food, cooking, having a drink, music, radio, theatre, sports, walking, exercise, TV, gardening, nature in general, reading, writing, painting, travel, incl. holidays abroad, getting out and about (going places generally), other leisure/pleasure activities (not elsewhere codable), exercising.
7. *Home comforts*: home comforts, roof over head, regular meals, domestic hygiene.
8. *Employment*: employment, job satisfaction.
9. *Misc. other*: safety, lack of fear, neighbours, pets, other relationships, other positive mentions, other.
10. *Freedom*: freedom, independence.
11. *Time self*: time for self, not too overworked, life in balance, sleep, no stress.
12. *Other material*: consumption, shopping, getting new things, car, transport, education (own, children's, standard of system in general), other material benefits.
13. *Other personal*: other personal characteristics (not elsewhere specified), love, sense of humour, personal cleanliness.
14. *Spiritual*: religion, treating others well, equality, tolerance, helping others, voluntary work, community participation, political activities, other spiritual, moral, community aspects, law and order.
15. *Environment*: good recreational facilities, neighbourhood-specific rural/urban benefits, neighbourhood – general mention, likes area or neighbourhood, environment, lack of pollution, general mention of

environment, lack of crime, safe area, climate, weather, other local/ environment mentions (not elsewhere codable), news and current affairs.

16. *Negatives*: (this could be by implication, i.e. need more/better) need better personal characteristics – less worry, better health, more happiness; need better material characteristics – more money, better job; more leisure, recreation; more morality, spiritual, community spirit; better relationships; improvements in locality, environment, e.g. less crime, less crowds; other negative mentions (not elsewhere codable), need more time.

NOTE

* See Taylor et al. (2007), Appendix 3.18 for the full list of possible mentions.

PART IV

Understanding Inequalities

10. Within-household inequalities across classes? Management and control of money

Fran Bennett, Jerome De Henau and Sirin Sung

INTRODUCTION

Any analysis conducted at the level of the household obscures the effect of gender inequalities within households (Jenkins 1991; Himmelweit 2002). In particular, treating household income as pooled obscures women's 'hidden' poverty within households and the existence of gendered inequalities in the control of household resources. Gender-sensitive policy analysis is needed to go 'beyond the front door' to open up the 'closed box' of the family/household unit (Daly 2000; Lister 2000). The case for examining within-household inequalities is persuasive, not only on moral grounds but also to improve policy design (Jenkins 1994).

This chapter describes some results from a project which investigates how public policies in Britain may affect within-household inequalities in male/female couples, and how their effectiveness can be reinforced or undermined by such inequalities.[1] More precisely, the project as a whole aims to explore alternative approaches to understanding the behavioural and distributional impact of policy change which take account of gender inequalities in power and influence within the household, and to use such approaches to analyse the effects of actual and potential changes in fiscal, social security and associated labour market policies within the UK.

The focus of this chapter is money management and control over household resources. A growing range of literature has recently explored the intra-household allocation of resources and financial control (Pahl 1989; Goode et al. 1998; Vogler 1998; Vogler et al. 2008a and 2008b; Sonnenberg 2008). Results tend to show that when it comes to control over how resources are used within households, it is not only who contributes to what, and who receives the income, which matter, but also how resources are managed. Findings such as these may sometimes contradict the common vision of equal sharing (pooling of income) between household members, in particular male/female couples, that is usually (implicitly) assumed by policy makers, and is epitomised in the 'unitary household' view of coupledom (see Bargain et al. 2006 for a discussion).

A recent report from one financial services provider claimed that women are now taking control of the family finances (Norwich and Peterborough Building Society 2008). The claim was based on analysis of answers to survey questions about which partner in couples has the final say in major financial decisions. In addition, recent research into money management shows that female 'final say' is more likely to be found in working-class households than in others (Vogler et al. 2008a). This chapter investigates claims of growing female control over financial resources in couple households. In particular, it examines the concerns of money management researchers that female 'final say' in working-class households may not represent real control, but may instead be rather more nominal in nature.

We therefore first explore different patterns of financial management and their relationship to control over material resources in the household. This is important in order to understand how income inequalities within households can result in differences both in legitimate command over household resources for individuals living together – what Sen (1990) calls 'entitlements' – and in those individuals' degree of financial autonomy in the case of relationship breakdown. Understanding how couples manage their resources, and to what extent different types of management are related to financial control, is also key to uncovering the extent of individuals' command over household resources in order to be able to pursue their own objectives and interests (Sen 1990).

Our analysis is divided into two parts. First, we draw a general picture of financial management and control for male/female couples of working age and how these differ according to income levels and source, employment status, educational level and time (namely, the early to mid-1990s and 2005). Secondly, we look in more depth at the results of qualitative research involving a sample of 30 low- to moderate-income couples, to investigate issues that arise from the quantitative analysis. In particular, we discuss how management and control are (or are not) related, and the extent to which female control in households such as these is real or more nominal.[2]

QUANTITATIVE ANALYSIS: OVERVIEW OF BRITISH COUPLES' FINANCIAL MANAGEMENT AND CONTROL

Using data from the British Household Panel Survey (BHPS), we analyse the answers to two individual questions asked only in the years 1991–1995 and 2005, one on financial management and the other on financial control (or 'final say').[3] We have selected as our sample male/female couples of working age, both with and without children, in which both partners were asked these questions individually. The final sample includes 6714 observations of these couples in the years 1991 to 1995, and 1230 couples in 2005.

Money Management

The question on money management was phrased as follows: 'People organise their finances in different ways. Which of the methods on this card comes closest to the way you organise yours?' We have grouped the possible answers[4] into six main types of money management, to fit the typology developed by Pahl and Vogler (Pahl 1989; Vogler and Pahl 1993; 1994): (i) female management or female whole wage (the woman looks after all the money except male personal expenses – this includes cases in which the man is given a housekeeping allowance); (ii) male management or male whole wage; (iii) the woman is given a housekeeping allowance; (iv) finances jointly managed (also called income pooled); (v) partial pooling (some money pooled, with the rest separate); and (vi) separate management (and other).

In both periods, more than half of the partners report pooling their resources and jointly managing them, while a quarter of couples report that their money is mostly managed by the female partner (Table 10.1). Very few couples use a system of completely separate finances or other arrangement, though in recent years this proportion has increased (also noted by Pahl 2008). Housekeeping allowance systems are used much less in 2005 than in the earlier period. Men and women seem to agree overall by reporting comparable proportions of different management arrangements.[5]

Other studies have also identified the main correlates to these management styles – mainly income level, education, employment status and receipt of benefits, which may together be seen as indicators of socioeconomic class (Vogler and Pahl 1993; 1994; Vogler et al. 2008b; Pahl 1995). Univariate analysis of our data provides similar results (Appendix Table 10A.1), in that:

Table 10.1   Reported systems of money management (1991–95 and 2005) – male and female answers (%)

		F. manag.	M. manag.	House-keep.	Pool.	Part. pool.	Separate
Male	1991	25.3	10.5	7.8	54.0	0.0	2.4
answer	1995	24.0	8.7	6.4	56.2	0.0	4.7
	2005	25.3	12.1	2.8	46.8	8.1	4.9
Female	1991	25.2	9.6	9.9	52.5	0.0	2.9
answer	1995	24.2	9.7	7.2	54.0	0.0	5.0
	2005	22.0	11.8	3.4	47.7	9.3	5.8

Source: Own calculations using BHPS 1991, 1995 and 2005.

i.   female management is more associated with:
- low income (and with a high proportion of income coming from benefits),
- low educational level (either partner), high female share of income (in turn associated with low income), and
- lower socioeconomic status (measured by the Essex score[6]);

ii.   male management and housekeeping allowance are more associated with
- a higher share of income from the man,
- a low level of female education, and
- the woman not being employed;

iii.   partial pooling and separate management are more associated with
- higher household income,
- higher educational levels and higher Essex scores (either partner) – which is also true for joint management – and
- female full-time employment.

'Final Say' in Big Financial Decisions

The question asked to identify financial control was: 'In your household who has the final say in big financial decisions?', to which each respondent could answer (i) themselves; (ii) their partner/spouse; (iii) both; or (iv) other (negligible numbers). According to both respondents (Table 10.2), both partners having the final say predominates in both periods – around two-thirds of answers – and male final say is reported by around 20 per cent of respondents of both sexes. Slightly more women report that they have the final say than the proportion of men who say that their partner does, and vice versa. However, between the early 1990s and 2005 female

Table 10.2 Final say in big financial decisions by money management
system (1991–95 and 2005) – male and female answers (%)

	Male answer			Female answer		
	Female say	Both say	Male say	Female say	Both say	Male say
1991–1995						
F. manag.	14.8	71.8	13.3	18.9	69.6	11.6
M. manag.	3.4	55.2	41.3	6.2	52.4	41.5
Housekeep.	3.5	49.4	47.1	7.1	48.6	44.3
Joint	5.9	72.4	21.8	8.7	73.0	18.3
Separate	11.9	59.8	28.3	11.6	69.5	18.9
All couples	8.0	68.7	23.4	11.0	68.2	20.9
2005						
F. manag.	25.9	65.4	8.6	29.8	64.5	5.7
M. manag.	5.8	47.1	47.1	6.6	47.4	46.1
Housekeep.	2.8	72.2	25.0	6.8	61.4	31.8
Joint	11.0	71.7	17.2	11.6	69.3	19.1
Part. pool.	13.6	70.9	15.5	13.7	71.8	14.5
Separate	14.8	57.4	27.9	28.2	50.7	21.1
All couples	14.3	66.4	19.3	16.0	64.6	19.5

Source: Own calculations using BHPS 1991–1995 and 2005.

final say over big financial decisions increased substantially according to
male answers (almost doubling from 8 per cent to 14 per cent).

We have compared 'final say' with management types, to investigate
whether the association between management and control measured in
this way, as described in the money management literature, holds for these
couples – and if so, whether this is the case over the entire period (Table
10.2).

As expected, female management is more associated than other management styles with female final say, especially in the most recent period,
according to both respondents. Both female and joint management
systems are more associated with female final say in the more recent period
than before. In addition, the association between claiming sole final say
and sole management seems to vary according to sex: in 2005, for example,
the man claims the final say in 47 per cent of couples in which the money is
managed by the man, while the woman claims the final say in only 30 per
cent of couples in which the money is managed by the woman. This shows
that men may keep control (at least partially, in the case of both partners
having the final say) in most couples, and that money management can

only be associated to some extent with financial control, especially in the case of women.

'Final say', like management types, is associated with socioeconomic factors, such as the couple's education and employment. Thus, we need to account for these factors as well, in order to get a clearer picture of whether differences in who has the final say are partly associated with specific management styles *per se*, over and above differences in the distribution of income, employment, family status, education, age and gender-role attitudes (as in Vogler et al. 2008b).[7] For example, if we look at the association between management and 'final say' for low- and high-income couples separately, female 'final say' is much more associated with female management in low-income couples than in higher-income couples (in which this type of management is instead associated with both having the final say).

The regression analysis shown in Table 10.3 focuses on couples who gave the same answer about who had the final say, which gives 5068 observations in the first period (1991–1995) and 886 observations in 2005. We use a multinomial logistic regression, assuming no particular hierarchical ranking of the three types of answers.[8] Table 10.3 gives the results of the *relative risk ratios* for each period. The way to read the table is as follows: we can see from the first column that those reporting female management are 5.39 times more likely to have final female say than is the case for those reporting joint management (joint management is the reference category and therefore has a relative risk of 1.0 by definition). Similarly, belonging to the highest quintile of the distribution of household income reduces the odds of having female final say over both having the final say by a factor of 0.39 compared with belonging to the lowest quintile.

The categories of management systems have been regrouped to account for the differing views of partners. In particular, 'female (male) management/joint' refers to one partner reporting female (male) management and the other a joint system; 'opposing views' stands for partners having opposing views on individual management (male versus female). 'Partial pooling' includes separate management (and partners reporting joint and separate systems).

Table 10.3 reveals that individual share of household income and management systems significantly influence who is described as having the final say in big financial decisions (alongside other characteristics such as age, education and marital situation), in line with findings from Vogler et al. (2008b). Women are more likely to have the final say (rather than both, or men) if they have higher income than their partner (compared with more even income distribution), whatever the couple's income level, though this result stands for 2005 only (in fact, surprisingly, the opposite is true

Table 10.3 Results of multinomial logistic regression of final say over big financial decisions (1991–95 and 2005) – relative risk ratios

		2005			1991–1995		
		Female control/ both	Male control/ both	Male control/ female control	Female control/ both	Male control/ both	Male control/ female control
Share of hh inc.	Equal share (40–60%) – ref.	1.00	1.00	1.00	1.00	1.00	1.00
	M. share > 60%	1.30	1.59	1.22	0.74*	1.81***	2.46***
	F. share > 60%	2.26**	0.58	0.25**	0.52***	1.02	1.95**
Managt system	Joint management – ref.	1.00	1.00	1.00	1.00	1.00	1.00
	F. management	5.39***	0.10***	0.02***	4.15***	0.38***	0.09***
	F. managed/joint	3.77***	0.67	0.18***	2.75***	0.61***	0.22***
	Partial pooling	2.37*	1.45	0.61	2.84	1.29	0.46**
	M. managed/joint	1.19	3.83***	3.21*	1.37	2.27***	1.66*
	M. management	0.41	4.49***	11.02**	1.17	3.75***	3.22***
	Opposing views (m. vs f.)	8.15**	5.98***	0.73	0.34	1.42	4.19
Level of hh inc.	1st income quintile – ref.	1.00	1.00	1.00	1.00	1.00	1.00
	2nd income quintile	0.57	0.52	0.91	0.53***	0.90	1.71**
	3rd income quintile	0.49*	0.57	1.18	0.56***	0.87	1.57*
	4th income quintile	0.49	0.75	1.53	0.27***	0.89	3.34***
	5th income quintile	0.39**	1.00	2.59	0.48***	0.90	1.87**

Table 10.3 (continued)

		2005			1991–1995		
		Female control/ both	Male control/ both	Male control/ female control	Female control/ both	Male control/ both	Male control/ female control
Education	Both low educ. – ref.	1.00	1.00	1.00	1.00	1.00	1.00
	M. high/f. low educ.	0.67	0.74	1.11	0.86	1.05	1.22
	M. low/f. high educ.	0.95	0.46**	0.48	0.94	0.71**	0.75
	Both high educ.	0.76	0.38***	0.50	0.62**	0.66***	1.06
Male empl.	M. not in employment – ref.	1.00	1.00	1.00	1.00	1.00	1.00
	M. manager/prof.	0.57	1.16	2.01	0.35***	1.19	3.45***
	M. intermediate job	0.81	0.85	1.05	0.57***	0.97	1.68*
	M. low skill./manual job	0.62	1.33	2.14	0.51***	0.92	1.80***
Female empl.	F. full-time job – ref.	1.00	1.00	1.00	1.00	1.00	1.00
	F. part-time job	0.82	1.45	1.78	1.19	1.15	0.96
	F. not in employment	0.93	0.96	1.03	1.15	1.19	1.03
Gender role att.	Av. tradi1 (f work/fam)	1.13*	1.29***	1.14	0.98	1.18***	1.21***
	Av. tradi2 (f work/ind)	0.82**	0.92	1.12	0.83***	0.95*	1.15***
	Difference tradi1 (m–f)	1.12	1.00	0.90	1.00	0.98	0.98
	Difference tradi2 (m–f)	1.02	1.04	1.01	1.03	1.08**	1.05

Demographics						
Married	0.88	1.07	1.21	0.69**	1.02	1.46*
Average age	0.95***	0.96***	1.02	0.99*	0.97***	0.99*
Difference in age (m–f)	1.00	1.13***	1.14**	0.95**	1.11***	1.17***
# Observations		886			5068	
Prob.>ch^2		0			0	
Log likelihood		–511			–2935	
Pseudo-R^2		0.217			0.147	

Notes:
*** p-value < 0.01; ** p-value < 0.05; * p-value < 0.1.
Standard errors (clustered for 1991–95) are available upon request from the authors.

Source: Own calculations using BHPS 1991–1995 and 2005.

223

for the early 1990s). Women are also more likely to have the final say if they live in low-income couples, have a non-working partner (though this is not significant in 2005) and manage most of the household income. By contrast, men are more likely to have the final say (rather than both, or women) if their income or their age is higher than their partner's (but only in 1991–1995), and in couples with more traditional gender-role attitudes, as well as where money is mostly managed by the man. The connection between money management and having the final say is much stronger for women than for men, especially in 2005. Finally, results from Table 10.3 also allow us to conclude that some characteristics are independently associated with a greater likelihood of both having the final say rather than either doing so, such as female higher educational attainment and couples being older.[9]

Disagreement about 'Final Say'

Conflicting views about who has the final say are not negligible and appear to be related to systematic factors such as disagreement about management style, in addition to being more prevalent in lower-income couples and amongst older couples. Moreover, it appears that disagreement is asymmetric by sex. In 2005, 13 per cent of female respondents who claimed that they had the final say had a partner who reported that he had the final say instead, whereas only 7 per cent of female respondents who said their partner had the final say had a partner claiming the opposite. This indicates that men may be more reluctant to give up final say to their partner, and will tend to report more control on average. This result illustrates that answers to questions about who has the final say may not necessarily be an accurate indicator of overall financial control, given the large proportion of conflicting views. This could be a sign of different meanings being given to 'final say' by each partner. It may also be the case that women tend to report more male final say (or both having the final say), even if they are in charge of most of the finances, to abide by traditional gendered patterns of power and behaviours ('doing gender' – West and Zimmerman 1987).

This quantitative analysis showed contrasting results. On the one hand, we can find some clear patterns in terms of the factors which seem to determine who is said to have control over financial decisions within male/female couples in Britain, such as income level, employment status, gender-role attitudes and especially money management styles. On the other hand, our analysis could not entirely uncover the meaning of control reported by these couples, using one indicator (who has the final say over big financial decisions). It is possible, for example, that there are differences in the notion of control in different socioeconomic groups: women seem to be more likely to be identified as having the final say in situations of scarce resources, though this seems to be more subject to disagreement, whereas men are more likely to do so in couples on higher joint incomes, when their partner is in a lower status position. The qualitative analysis presented below will attempt to clarify these issues, as well as discussing the notions of control and management, and why categories used in typologies may give us only an incomplete description of what really goes on within households in terms of allocation systems and decision making.

QUALITATIVE ANALYSIS: A CLOSER LOOK AT LOW- TO MODERATE-INCOME COUPLES

The Sample

For the qualitative research, semi-structured, separate interviews were carried out during 2006 with each individual in 30 male/female couples across England, Wales and Scotland. The couples were selected purposively to be those who had at some point had a child or children – with both partners of working age if possible (though there were a few pensioners). In so far as this could be ascertained, they were living on low to moderate incomes, with the vast majority in receipt of means-tested benefits or tax credits at the time of interview and/or in the past (see Appendix Table 10A.2 for demographic and employment information about the sample). In practice, the interviewees were virtually all married, though for a significant proportion this involved remarriages, and were all white – although neither of these features was an intentional choice. These couples had already been interviewed annually from 1997 to 2001, as members of a booster sample of low- to moderate-income households added to the BHPS for inclusion in the European Community Household Panel. The data were analysed with the aid of Nvivo software and direct use of the transcripts.

Money Management[10]

The interviews were intended to go beyond analysis by category within a money management typology (Ashby and Burgoyne 2008), to investigate instead the elements that go to make up such categories (such as access, management versus control and the degree of sharing), the meanings which individuals may give to these elements, and how the couples had come to organise their household finances in various ways.

We found strong evidence amongst these low- to moderate-income couples of loyalty to an ideal of marriage entailing pooling of resources. 'All in one pot' was a common description of family finances.[11] This could be due to a variety of reasons, including the low to moderate level of the couples' income, their ages, the relative stability of their relationships and the fact that they had all had children at some point. There was also some continuity of traditional gendered patterns in the management of money (Sung and Bennett 2007). One woman, for example, when asked about the couple's financial arrangements, described them as: 'he earns, I spend' (case 8, female). Vogler et al. (2008b) argue that idea(l)s about women's traditional role in the home appear to have changed less than those supporting the idea(l) of the male as the breadwinner. This seemed to be true for many of these couples. Women's continuing responsibility for domestic tasks often included managing the family budget day to day, which in a surprising number of cases included doling out regular small amounts of pocket money to the man.[12]

A common pattern was for the man's income to be paid into the couple's joint account, where they had one, whilst the woman's was paid into her own account (for example case 11). Individual accounts were more common amongst women than men, as found in previous research (Pahl 1999). Men's income was more likely to be seen as the income for family needs (case 18, case 20) (Pahl 1989). A few men asserted with some pride that they did not 'interfere' with any income brought in by their partner – that she could do what she liked with 'her' income.

> Whatever she wants she gets, I don't interfere, you know, I mean her money is hers and what comes out of mine, well I buy food and whatever we want, it's out of my wage, like. (Case 22, male)

(In this case, however, it was the woman's (small, part-time) wages which were paid into the joint account, with the man's wages being kept in cash and used by the woman to pay various bills.)

This distinction seemed to have ambiguous implications for women, however, with the potential for positive and negative connotations – conferring a degree of desirable autonomy, and/or suggesting that their contribution to the household was 'pin money', of little account, and potentially unreliable.

What might be described by the couple as joint management of money could often involve a traditional division of labour in terms of spending too (Pahl 2000), usually involving the man paying the less frequent bills, whilst the woman did the more frequent shopping for food and other needs ('I'm bills, she's food' (case 17, male)). However, changing employment patterns seemed to affect this; in several cases, the women had white-collar, salaried jobs, and were therefore paid monthly, whereas the men were in manual, weekly-paid jobs (cases 10, 13, 14, 16 and 24). In couples such as these, spending responsibilities were sometimes (though not always) reversed. The man might also buy the food in situations in which he was effectively the house-husband (for example, because he was on benefit).

The research revealed the dangers in relying on the existence of joint and/or individual accounts as an indicator of the degree of jointness or independence in money management (Ashby and Burgoyne 2008). Eight couples had no joint account; but the degree of jointness in their finances varied widely (for example case 2, female) (Sung and Bennett 2007). It was hard to discern in these low- to moderate-income couples' money management firm evidence of increasing individualism (Pahl 2008). However, mutuality in financial matters can be used in very different ways in practice – for example, by one partner to safeguard resources for the family, or by another to justify the sharing of debts acquired before marriage. One man argued that a joint account was important because his wife got more money than he did:

> Because my wife gets more money than me . . . I don't get a Family Allowance, it's basically we're married and I believe we should, everything is together. But the latter reason is a good reason. (Case 31, male)

In addition to being more likely to have individual accounts, women in our sample seemed to be more aware of the tensions involved in jointness, especially in terms of how it might limit autonomy. Women were more likely to express a wish for a degree of independence, whereas many men claimed not to see the need for anything other than joint finances.

Management versus Control

In the quantitative findings described earlier, female management of finances (more precisely, the woman 'looking after' the household money, except for the man's personal spending money) appears to be increasingly likely to lead to female control (measured by which partner is said to have the final say in big financial decisions). But Vogler et al. (2008b) suggest that management of money in this sense is often in practice delegated responsibility, rather than the exercise of real control. Other research has also found that the day-to-day management of finances in low-income families, typically carried out by the woman, does not necessarily result in control; it may be experienced instead as a burden and a source of anxiety – though paradoxically it can also result in a sense of pride when carried out well, and so may be difficult to give up (see, for example, Goode et al. 1998). So how real was any female financial control in the low- to moderate-income couples in our sample?

At first sight, many women in our sample certainly did appear to have a degree of control over the family finances. In several couples, for example, as already noted, women gave their partner a small amount of pocket money each week. Some women retained the debit card for their partner's individual account (case 7, case 13) and/or used his personal identification number when he did not know it (case 15, case 25). One woman kept the chequebook for the joint account (case 12); another had the only debit card, so if her partner wanted to draw some money out, he had to ask her for it.

In many of these families, however, financial control (by one partner or the other) may be more about achieving peace of mind in terms of balancing the finances than about wielding disproportionate power over resources within the relationship:

> I think one person needs to be in control because if they're not then they could easily overspend, you know, I think one person needs to organise everything and work out the budget, or work out what your bills are and what you've got left. (Case 10, female)

However, one woman who gave her husband small amounts of money regularly said that, if the situation were the other way round,

> it would be like pocket money and I'd feel like one of the children, I wouldn't feel as if I had any control over anything. So I like the fact that I get a certain amount . . . [i.e. a housekeeping allowance system, with household and personal money together] (Case 29, female)

But did one partner have real control in any case? We looked at various potential indicators of control over household finances, including responses from our interviewees about how big financial decisions were made and who had the final say; access to and management of joint accounts; and whether individuals felt they had to justify their personal spending to their partners (see Sung and Bennett, 2007, for more detailed information).

Vogler et al. (2008b) argue that financial decision making is important because expenditure decisions have been found to be one of the main sources of conflict between partners in couples. The men and women in our sample did not necessarily give very clear answers when they were asked about how big financial decisions were made in their household, followed by a question asking them to specify which of them had the 'final say'. In findings similar to those of the quantitative research analysed earlier, more respondents said that such decisions were joint than those who identified one partner or the other as having the final say. In some cases, however, the respondents hesitated or changed their minds about whether they usually make joint decisions or whether one of them tended to dominate (for example case 17, male), making it difficult to place them unambiguously in one category or another. Of those who did identify a lead partner, about twice as many said that the man rather than the woman had the final say.[13] More couples gave differing answers (either straight away, or when prompted further) than those who said the same, however. The prevalence of disagreements in this area, also seen in the quantitative research, is one of the reasons why researchers have increasingly begun to argue that answers about what goes on within couples cannot just be read off in an uncomplicated way as representing reality in either quantitative or qualitative research (see, for example, Sonnenberg 2008).

Some individuals' answers appeared to depend on what item(s) they were thinking of when they were asked about 'big financial decisions', and in particular the relative depth of knowledge, and/or strength of feeling, of each partner about such item(s). Sometimes, for example, men were more likely to be responsible for decisions about computers, cars and other technical equipment. One woman said that if it concerned 'a really, really want' (rather than 'just a want') of hers, she would have the final say (case 1, female); another said about her partner that 'if it was something that he wanted in particular, he wouldn't think as long and as hard about it' (case 7, female). For others, it might depend on whose money was used for what. For example, in one couple (case 20), the woman's money was seen as additional and was used for holidays and exceptional items, whereas the man's was seen as the main family income to be used for everyday bills and needs. He argued that she made the decisions on big items, such as buying a new motorbike for him to use (but recognised that this could be because of his guilt about having a new motorbike).

In the study by Vogler et al. (2008b), within working-class households in particular each partner had autonomy in terms of spending joint money in their area of gendered spending. This may help to explain the recent findings cited earlier from the Norwich and Peterborough Building Society (2008) (see also Womack 2008), which claimed to find women appearing to 'take the lead' in family finances. Their spokesperson asserted that the findings put the myth of the father as the financial head of the family to rest. However, the survey lists more items in the areas that are usually the preserve of women in more traditional couples, resulting in women appearing to take more financial decisions in those cases where decisions were not joint.

In addition, the meaning which different individuals give to the phrase 'final say' is not necessarily always clear. For example, the decision about whether an item is affordable (or not), or how to pay for it, is different from the decision about whether to buy that particular item as opposed to another (see Kirchler et al. 2008), as one couple in our sample illustrates:

> If she likes different furniture I go with her. (Case 30, male)

> He would know more about the finances but we both need to like it. (Case 30, female)

It is also possible that individuals in low-income families may see many more decisions as 'big financial decisions', just because of the relative paucity of the resources at their disposal. If this is the case, issues about management of money may shade more easily into issues of financial control, as whether to pay out on larger household items or to go without may be the only kinds of big financial decisions that they usually take. What answer is given about who has the 'final say' may depend on who has to find the money with which to buy something – including who is in charge of managing the household finances (for example case 10). In addition, even if one partner is the one to make the decision, this does not always mean that they will benefit more than the other partner from the outcome of that decision; who has the final say may have a direct relationship with individual welfare or well-being, but this is not necessarily the case.

Researchers have also queried whether questions such as this really capture the essence of control over household finances (Vogler 1998), and in particular the nature of ongoing power within a relationship on a day-to-day basis. We therefore explored other possible indicators of financial control (and potentially also wider inequalities), including access to and management of joint bank/building society accounts. In most cases, couples who had joint accounts both said that they managed the joint account together, and in general both also said they had access to it. Where only one partner did so, this was usually the woman, who tended to deal with cash on a day-to-day basis, thus on the surface at least seeming to bear out the link between female management and female control explored in the quantitative research above. Women appeared to have greater access to income for household purposes – although they might have less for personal spending. (We did find several women who were reluctant to access the couple's joint account, however, especially if their own children from a previous relationship were living with the couple) (case 4, female; case 11, female):

I never do, no never do [draw money from the joint account]. (Case 4, female)

In most cases, neither men nor women said that they felt they had to justify their personal spending to their partner. Those who feel they have to do so could arguably be said to have their spending controlled by the other partner. For some of these couples, there was no opportunity to circumvent any such control via the use of credit cards and other forms of 'new' money such as debit cards, smart cards, and telephone and Internet banking (Pahl 1999), because neither partner had them (case 29); some households in fact appeared to operate a largely or wholly cash-based economy. For others, personal spending was severely limited in any case ('I don't spend on myself' (case 1, female)), and seemed to consist of little more than spending gifts of cash from family at birthdays or Christmas time (Sung and Bennett, 2007). However, it could also be argued that the absence of any felt need to justify personal spending to a partner may indicate firm control of the household's resources and freedom to spend these on oneself. One man in our sample (in a family living on benefits) had a credit card (whereas his partner did not), bought items on e-bay, and felt no need to justify his spending to his wife. However, he was annoyed if she spent without telling him, and said that she was more responsible for paying a household debt (case 31, male).

The issue of control of individual spending is affected by the definition of personal versus household spending, which can be just as important as the definition of personal versus household income (Goode et al. 1998). It may amount to a kind of control by categorisation (though the person doing so may not realise this). For example, one man (case 14, male) equated the provision of a new kitchen floor (prior to a hoped-for sale of the house) as equivalent, for his partner, to his own desired purchase of a DVD recorder. One woman (case 8, female), on the other hand, said that the decisions about (spending on) the car were made by her partner; this was because, rather than seeing the car as a household item, she saw it as his, as she did not drive. The claims by some men that their purchases of various 'gadgets' were intended for the household as a whole sometimes seemed to be doubtful (case 24, male), as found by Goode et al. (1998). There were also one or two examples amongst our sample of women who said they had felt so strongly about the need for a household item (such as a dishwasher, for example) that they had bought it out of their 'own' money (case 2, female).

Finally, even joint 'final say' may have different meanings, both between and within couples. The woman in one couple in which both partners said they had joint final say nonetheless made clear (when asked whether they agreed on money issues) that they had vigorous discussions, with strongly held views on both sides, before reaching agreement (case 19, female); and her partner said that they both listened to each other's point (case 19, male). Another couple were clear that they had a discussion (case 17, female) and came to a compromise (case 17, male). Thus, arriving at joint final say may not be a simple or straightforward process, and may differ between couples.

Research carried out for the Poverty and Social Exclusion Millennium Survey in the UK (Adelman et al. 2000) suggested that women who do have control of the family finances tend to suffer deprivation, whereas those women without control tend to worry. In our sample, some women appeared to be using their (constrained) agency to try to deal with this apparent 'no win' situation. Women told us, for example, that because their partner was in control of the money they were able to avoid any blame for (for example) letting the money run out (case 31, female); or alternatively that, because the finances were their own responsibility instead, they could avoid having to ask their partner for money – or having to worry: 'There is probably an element of control because I wouldn't sleep if we were in debt' (case 26, female). This example also reflects the fact that some women (as well as men, for example case 31, male) themselves used the word 'control' to describe their management of the household's money (for example case 2, female; case 10, female). One woman claimed that she knew where 'every single penny' went in the household (case 26, female); another said: 'I quite like the control' (case 14, female). In the latter case, the context suggested that this did involve at least some restraint of the behaviour of this woman's male partner, who had had a bad debt record prior to the marriage. In another case (8), it was clear from the man's response that his partner gave him limited amounts of pocket money to keep in check his tendency to spend money if he had it, for which he seemed grateful. He did add in a joking way that his partner gave him his pocket money 'because I've been a good boy . . . if I'm bad I don't get it' (case 8, male). But if the man acquires his sense of control from elsewhere, being restrained in everyday spending may not represent a loss of control to him in the same way that it might for his partner.

CONCLUSIONS

This analysis of intra-household allocation of resources and control has shown that different systems of money management are associated with which partner has the final say over big financial decisions in male/female couples. Having the final say is positively associated with both managing the household's money and having a higher share of income, especially for men. Female management and female final say are both highly associated with living on a low income. This may not, however, have the same implications in terms of control and autonomy as it does for higher-income couples (in which both partners having the final say and partial pooling of money are both more widespread).

The quantitative analysis of BHPS data uncovered strong associations between 'final say' and the main theoretical predictors of financial control (such as share of income, management style and gender-role attitudes). In addition, both the quantitative and qualitative analysis showed, as in previous research, that couples may disagree strongly over who has the final say; in the quantitative analysis, this is in turn associated with disagreement over money management (and with cases in which the man handles the money). Those disagreements revealed that 'final say' may not in itself be a sufficient indicator of effective control over household financial decisions. This is due not only to contestation of decision-making 'power' but also to different understandings, both between and within the couples interviewed, of the meaning of 'final say', as shown in the qualitative analysis.

The existence of disagreements over who has the final say is further evidence of possible different meanings of control within the couple, which were explored in relation to low- to moderate-income couples through the qualitative analysis. Our findings suggest that most women in these low- to moderate-income families still have the primary domestic role, often including management of the finances, even if the male breadwinner role is no longer unquestioned. Nevertheless, if we are to take seriously what some women themselves say about their role in relation to the household finances, it is difficult to dismiss entirely their perceptions of a degree of control, albeit within a restricted and highly gendered (separate) sphere. This fits with the finding from the quantitative research about the link between female management and female control, and their particular prevalence in low-income families.

However, control of household finances has been shown to be a complex and multifaceted issue. There may be different levels of control, from the micro to the macro, or from the day-to-day to the more strategic. Each will have different implications for individuals' autonomy and sense of entitlement. For low-income couples, 'big financial decisions' may have a different meaning, and the most important meaning of 'control' for them is likely to be managing the weekly budget so that the money lasts. In order to do this successfully, some women in particular will aim to control their partners' personal spending, as well as limit the amount which is spent jointly, and/or go without themselves. In this situation, some women use their (constrained) agency to avoid blame by ceding financial control, or alternatively take control and thereby try to avoid worry.

Results have shown that, even when women exercise full control over major spending decisions (for example couple 20, in which the woman decided to buy a motorbike for her partner), the main beneficiary of the purchase may not be themselves. Thus control over household resources in one partner's hands may not necessarily coincide in the end with an increase in well-being for that partner, particularly with a persistent traditional division of roles.

Our findings taken together therefore suggest that the notion of control, rather than being a criterion which can be easily applied with a stable meaning to men and women in different money management systems, is itself socially constructed in a gendered way, and may have different meanings under different systems (as well as in different couples' relationships). This chapter contributes to the arguments for supporting the complementarity of quantitative and qualitative approaches, the former to uncover systematic effects over a large sample of the population, and the latter to refine and deepen categories of variables used as proxies for underlying concepts such as control and decision-making power.

NOTES

1. RES-225-25-2001 Gender Equality Network project No. 5: 'Within-household inequalities and public policy', with Fran Bennett (University of Oxford), Prof. Holly Sutherland (University of Essex), Prof. Susan Himmelweit and Dr Jerome De Henau (Open University) and Dr Sirin Sung (Queen's University, Belfast). GeNet (www.genet. ac.uk) is funded by the Economic and Social Research Council.
2. We recognise that the categories of low to moderate income and working class are not synonymous.
3. The questions were dropped from the BHPS after 1995 and not reintroduced again until 2005. This was reportedly because the answers to these questions did not show much change from one year to another.
4. Possible answers were: '(i) I look after all the household money except my partner's spending money; (ii) my partner looks after all the household's money except my personal spending money; (iii) I am given a housekeeping allowance and my partner looks after the rest of the money; (iv) my partner is given a housekeeping allowance and I look after the rest of the money; (v) we share and manage our household finances jointly; (vi) we pool some of the money and keep the rest separate [only in 2005]; (vii) we keep our finances completely separate; (viii) some other arrangement'.
5. Most differing views relate to confusion between sole (male or female) and joint management systems, or between male management and housekeeping allowance, or joint management and partial pooling. Very few had opposing views (such as male versus female management). We have accounted for these differences in a new typology used in the regressions on financial control later in the chapter (Table 10.3).
6. The Essex score, developed and computed by Gershuny (2002) and Gershuny and Kan (2006), is the log of an estimated hourly wage based on the individual's educational level, employment status for each of the last four years, and the average occupational wage of their most recent occupation. It is used as a measure of social position.
7. We did not include the presence of children in our analysis, after having verified that this

factor did not add any information to the model (that is it had no association with either who had the final say or what style of money management the couples reported).

8. In the sense that determinants of equal say, for example, may be different from those of male say and of female say. See Greene (2008) for further explanation of the method.
9. This latter result may indicate more stable couples, though it is not possible to verify the duration of the relationship with our data.
10. There is more detail about the money management practices of these couples in Sung and Bennett (2007).
11. Other research has suggested, however, that this phrase can be more figurative than real (see Sonnenberg 2008).
12. However, Burns et al. (2008), investigating money management in same sex couples, found that invariably amongst those couples who pooled their money, the lower earner was the one with more day-to-day responsibility for managing the household's money, including in one case providing cash for minor expenses for the higher earning partner.
13. Both the man and woman in one couple (case 3) whose two adult daughters had returned to live with them said that all four people in their household participated in taking big financial decisions. A significant proportion of the couples in our sample had adult children living with them. There is a pressing need for research into the role of such additional household members in financial decision making, which is often – in our view, mistakenly – seen as being carried out by a couple isolated from any other influences. Our own study, however, unfortunately could not extend to exploring this.

BIBLIOGRAPHY

Adelman, L., S. Middleton and K. Ashworth (2000), 'Management of household finances and intra-household poverty: evidence from the Poverty and Social Exclusion Survey of Britain', CRSP Working Paper 23, Loughborough: Centre for Research in Social Policy.

Ashby, K.J. and C.B. Burgoyne (2008), 'Separate financial entities?: Beyond categories of money management', *Journal of Socio-Economics*, 37(2), 458–80.

Bargain, O., M. Beblo, D. Beninger, R. Blundell, R. Carrasco, M.-C. Chiuri, F. Laisney, V. Lechene, N. Moreau, M. Myck, J. Ruiz-Castillo and F. Vermeulen (2006), 'Does the representation of household behavior matter for welfare analysis of tax-benefit policies? An introduction', *Review of Economics of the Household*, **4**, 99–111.

Burns, M., C.B. Burgoyne and V. Clarke (2008), 'Financial affairs? Money management in same-sex relationships', *Journal of Socio-Economics*, **37**(2), 481–501.

Daly, M. (2000), *The Gender Division of Welfare: The Impact of the British and German Welfare States*, Cambridge: Cambridge University Press.

Gershuny, J. (2002), 'A new measure of social position: social mobility and human capital in Britain', ISER Working Paper 2002-02, Colchester: Institute of Social and Economic Research.

Gershuny, J. and M.Y. Kan (2006), 'Human capital and social position in Britain: creating a measure of wage-earning potential from BHPS data', ISER Working Paper 2006-03, Colchester: Institute of Social and Economic Research.

Goode, J., C. Callender and R. Lister (1998), *Purse or Wallet? Gender Inequalities and Income Distribution within Families on Benefits*, London: Policy Studies Institute.

Greene, W.H. (2008), *Econometric Analysis*, 6th edn, New York: Prentice Hall.

Himmelweit, S. (2002), 'Making visible the hidden economy: the case for gender impact analysis of economic policy', *Feminist Economics*, **8**(1), 49–70.

Jenkins, S. (1991), 'The measurement of income inequality', in L. Osberg (ed.), *Economic Inequality and Poverty. International Perspectives*, New York: M.E. Sharpe, pp. 3–38.

Jenkins, S. (1994), 'The within-household distribution and why it matters: an economist's perspective', in C. Badelt (ed.), *Familien Zwischen Gerechtigkeitsidealen und Benachteiligungen*, Vienna: Bohlau-Verlag.

Kirchler, E., E. Hoelzl and B. Kamleitner (2008), 'Spending and credit use in the private household', *Journal of Socio-Economics*, **37**(2), 519–32.

Lister, R. (2000), 'Gender and the analysis of social policy', in G. Lewis, S. Gerwitz and J. Clarke (eds), *Rethinking Social Policy*, London: Sage/Open University, pp. 22–36.

Norwich and Peterborough Building Society (2008), Press release, 7 March.

Pahl, J. (1989), *Money and Marriage*, London: Macmillan.

Pahl, J. (1995), 'His money, her money: recent research on financial organisation in marriage', *Journal of Economic Psychology*, **16**, 361–76.

Pahl, J. (1999), *Invisible Money: Family Finances in the Electronic Economy*, Bristol: The Policy Press.

Pahl, J. (2000), 'The gendering of spending within households', *Radical Statistics*, **75**, 38–48.

Pahl, J. (2008), 'Family finances, individualisation, spending patterns and access to credit', *Journal of Socio-Economics*, **37**(2), 577–91.

Sen, A. (1990), 'Gender and cooperative conflict', in I. Tinker, (ed.), *Persistent Inequalities: Women and World Development*, New York and Oxford: Oxford University Press, pp. 123–49.

Sonnenberg, S. (2008), 'Household financial organisation and discursive practice: managing money and identity', *Journal of Socio-Economics*, **37**(2), 533–51.

Strategy Unit (2008), *Realising Britain's Potential: Future Strategic Challenges for Britain*, London: Cabinet Office.

Sung, S. and F. Bennett (2007), 'Dealing with money in low-moderate income couples: insights from individual interviews', in K. Clarke, T. Maltby and P. Kennett (eds), *Social Policy Review 19: Analysis and Debate in Social Policy 2007*, Bristol: The Policy Press in association with Social Policy Association, pp. 151–73.

Vogler, C. (1998), 'Money in the household: some underlying issues of power', *Sociological Review*, **46**(4), 687–713.

Vogler, C. and J. Pahl (1993), 'Social and economic change and the organisation of money in marriage', *Work, Employment and Society*, **7**, 71–95.

Vogler, C. and J. Pahl (1994), 'Money, power and inequality within marriage', *Sociological Review*, **42**(2), 263–88.

Vogler, C., M. Brockmann and R.D. Wiggins (2008a), 'Managing money in new heterosexual forms of intimate relationships', *Journal of Socio-Economics*, **37**(2), 552–76.

Vogler, C., C. Lyonette and R.D. Wiggins (2008b), 'Money, power and spending decisions in intimate relationships', *Sociological Review*, **56**(1), 117–43.

West, C. and D.H. Zimmerman (1987), 'Doing gender', *Gender and Society*, **1**, 125–51.

Womack, S. (2008), 'Women taking control of family finances', *Daily Telegraph*, 8 March.

Table 10A.1 *Distribution of money management systems by household characteristics (2005) – male and female answers (%)*

	Male answer						Female answer					
	F. manag.	M. manag.	House-keep.	Pool.	Part. pool.	Separate	F. manag.	M. manag.	House-keep.	Pool.	Part. pool.	Separate
By household income quintile												
1	31.8	12.9	3.9	40.0	5.5	5.9	28.1	11.3	3.9	48.4	3.9	4.3
2	33.5	10.5	3.1	44.4	5.1	3.5	30.0	10.9	4.7	42.8	5.8	5.8
3	23.7	12.1	2.0	51.8	5.8	4.7	21.0	13.6	2.3	52.5	6.2	4.3
4	17.9	14.4	1.6	49.4	10.9	5.8	15.2	12.1	3.1	49.8	13.2	6.6
5	19.5	10.6	3.5	48.4	13.3	4.7	15.6	11.3	3.1	45.1	17.1	7.8
By proportion of household income from benefits												
0%	22.5	10.2	2.1	47.7	11.6	6.0	16.6	12.2	1.4	50.6	12.5	6.7
0–50%	26.4	12.8	2.9	47.2	6.7	4.1	23.8	11.8	4.1	47.2	8.0	5.2
50–100%	30.5	17.0	6.8	35.6	1.7	8.5	36.1	9.8	9.8	34.4	3.3	6.6
By female share of household income												
0–40%	23.1	14.3	4.2	48.0	6.2	4.3	19.8	15.7	5.3	46.9	7.6	4.8
40–60%	26.5	10.2	1.2	46.8	10.6	4.7	21.9	6.4	1.5	53.7	10.6	5.9
60–100%	31.9	7.4	0.6	41.7	10.4	8.0	31.7	8.5	0.0	36.6	13.4	9.8
By individual Essex score (median)												
low	32.0	10.5	2.7	43.6	6.3	5.0	24.5	14.5	5.5	44.5	6.1	5.0
high	18.5	13.7	3.0	50.0	10.0	4.8	19.4	9.2	1.4	51.0	12.4	6.5

Table 10A.1 (continued)

	Male answer						Female answer					
	F. manag.	M. manag.	House-keep.	Pool.	Part. pool.	Separate	F. manag.	M. manag.	House-keep.	Pool.	Part. pool.	Separate
By educational group (A-level or more)												
both low	35.0	9.5	2.3	44.2	5.8	3.2	28.0	9.3	5.5	48.6	4.3	4.3
m high/f low	20.3	17.7	5.5	46.0	5.1	5.5	21.6	19.9	5.1	42.8	7.2	3.4
m low/f high	27.7	10.4	2.5	50.5	5.9	3.0	28.2	7.4	2.0	48.0	8.4	5.9
both high	19.5	11.9	1.9	47.5	12.5	6.8	14.4	11.6	1.9	49.9	14.6	7.6
By female employment status												
full-time	24.4	8.7	1.0	48.3	11.4	6.3	21.1	9.1	1.2	49.7	12.0	7.1
part-time	25.0	14.6	3.7	46.5	6.2	4.0	21.5	13.9	3.2	46.0	9.7	5.7
inactive	29.3	15.4	6.3	42.8	2.9	3.4	23.1	15.4	9.6	47.6	1.9	2.4
unemployed	8.7	21.7	0.0	52.2	8.7	8.7	21.7	21.7	0.0	43.5	8.7	4.4
disabled	30.0	15.0	5.0	45.0	5.0	0.0	34.2	9.8	9.8	39.0	2.4	4.9

Source: Own calculations using BHPS 2005.

Table 10A.2   Demographic information for couples in qualitative research sample

No.	Couple case	Gender	Education	Employment	Housing	Marital status
1	M 1A	Male	O Level	Employed	Mortgage	Married
2	F 1B	Female	A Level	Employed	Mortgage	Married
3	M 2A	Male	No qual	Retired	Mortgage	Married
4	F 2B	Female	O Level	Employed	Mortgage	Married
5	M 3A	Male	No qual	Disabled	Owned outright	Married
6	F 3B	Female	CSE	Family care	Owned outright	Married
7	M 4A	Male	Other higher qual	Employed	Owned outright	Married
8	F 4B	Female	Other higher qual	Carer	Owned outright	Married
9	M 5A	Male	Other higher qual	Retired	Council rent	Married
10	F 5B	Female	No qual	Disabled	Council rent	Married
11	M 6A	Male	CSE	Employed	Council rent	Married
12	F 6B	Female	O Level	Employed	Council rent	Married
13	M 7A	Male	CSE	Self-employed	Mortgage	Married
14	F 7B	Female	CSE	Employed	Mortgage	Married
15	M 8A	Male	A Level	Employed	Rented Private	Cohabiting
16	F 8B	Female	O Level	Not employed	Rented Private	Cohabiting
17	M 9A	Male	A Level	Not employed	Mortgage	Married
18	F 9B	Female	CSE	Employed	Mortgage	Married
19	M 10A	Male	O Level	Employed	Owned outright	Married
20	F 10B	Female	CSE	Employed	Owned outright	Married

239

Table 10A.2 (continued)

No.	Couple case	Gender	Education	Employment	Housing	Marital status
21	M 11A	Male	CSE	Employed	Mortgage	Married
22	F 11B	Female	O Level/NVQ	Employed	Mortgage	Married
23	M 12A	Male	O Level	Employed	Rented Council	Married
24	F 12B	Female	No qual	Family care	Rented Council	Married
25	M 13A	Male	CSE	Employed	Mortgage	Married
26	F 13B	Female	CSE	Employed	Mortgage	Married
27	M 14A	Male	CSE/NVQ	Employed	Mortgage	Married
28	F 14B	Female	O Level	Employed	Mortgage	Married
29	M 15A	Male	No qual	Employed	Rented	Married
30	F 15B	Female	Other higher qual	Employed	Rented	Married
31	M 16A	Male	O Level	Self-employed	Mortgage	Married
32	F 16B	Female	Missing	Employed	Mortgage	Married
33	M 17A	Male	No qual	Employed	Rented	Married
34	F 17B	Female	No qual	Employed	Rented	Married
35	M 18A	Male	A Level	Employed	Owned outright	Married
36	F 18B	Female	Other higher qual	Employed	Owned outright	Married
37	M 19A	Male	A Level	Employed	Owned outright	Married
38	F 19B	Female	O Level	Family care	Owned outright	Married
39	M 20A	Male	O Level	Employed	Mortgage	Married
40	F 20B	Female	A Level	Employed	Mortgage	Married

41	M 21A	Male	A Level	Disabled	Mortgage	Married
42	F 21B	Female	No qual	Disabled	Mortgage	Married
43	M 22A	Male	Other higher qual	Employed	Mortgage	Married
44	F 22B	Female	No qual	Employed	Mortgage	Married
45	M 24A	Male	No qual/NVQ 4	Employed	Mortgage	Married
46	F 24B	Female	O Level	Employed	Mortgage	Married
47	M 25A	Male	Other higher qual	Employed	Mortgage	Married
48	F 25B	Female	Other higher qual/HNC	Employed	Mortgage	Married
49	M 26A	Male	Other higher qual	Disabled	Mortgage	Married
50	F 26B	Female	First Degree	Employed	Mortgage	Married
51	M 27A	Male	O Level	Employed	Mortgage	Married
52	F 27B	Female	O Level	Not employed	Mortgage	Married
53	M 28A	Male	A Level/NVQ	Self-employed	Rented	Married
54	F 28B	Female	First Degree/NVQ	Self-employed	Rented	Married
55	M 29A	Male	O Level	Disabled	Rented Private	Married
56	F 29B	Female	Other higher qual	Not employed	Rented Private	Married
57	M 30A	Male	Apprenticeship	Retired	Council rent	Married
58	F 30B	Female	No qual	Retired	Council rent	Married
59	M 31A	Male	O Level	Not employed	Rented	Married
60	F 31B	Female	A Level	Disabled	Rented	Married

11. Restructuring gender relations: women's labour market participation and earnings inequality among households

Gunn Elisabeth Birkelund and
Arne Mastekaasa

INTRODUCTION

In most Western countries, in the decades following World War II, the male breadwinner model was dominant among married couples: husbands went to work and earned a family income, whereas women stayed at home as housewives and took care of children and housework (Crompton 1999). This traditional division of labour within the households coincided with a period of lower household income inequality than earlier (Aaberge et al. 1997). From the 1960s and onwards, in many countries married women's labour market participation increased, resulting in a decline in the male breadwinner model and a restructuring of gender relations and work (Crompton 2006; Ellingsæter 2001). In what seems to be a parallel process, income inequalities between households have increased in most Western countries (Alderson and Nielsen 2002: 1248). This process (from higher to lower to higher levels of economic inequality) has been termed 'the great U-turn'. As argued by Esping-Andersen (2007: 641), the rise in income inequality was first restricted to the United Kingdom and the United States, yet later most countries have followed, including the Scandinavian countries, otherwise known for their egalitarian income distributions: 'The growth in market income Ginis between 1980 and 2000 ranges from a 6% to 7% increase in Denmark and Italy to a 20%-plus jump in the United Kingdom, the United States, Germany, and most surprising, Sweden' (Esping-Andersen 2007: 641).[1]

Increasing household inequalities may be caused by a number of factors, such as technological change, restructuring of industries, globalisation and migration, and other institutional changes (Alderson and

Nielsen 2002). The growth of dual earner families might also be part of the explanation. Certainly, we would expect married women's earnings to have a bearing on household economic inequalities; the question would be if their earnings contribute to greater household inequality or have an equalising effect.

Recently a number of studies on the impact of wives' earnings on earnings inequality among households have been undertaken. Their conclusions are diverse. Most studies have found an equalising effect of wives' earnings (see Pasqua 2008, for a cross-national study of fourteen European countries; Esping-Andersen 2007, for a cross-country study of USA and seven European countries; Amin and DaVanzo 2004, for Malaysia; Harkness et al. 1996 and Harkness et al. 1997, for the UK; Bjørklund 1992, for Sweden; Pong 1991, for Hong Kong; Gronau 1982, for Israel). Several US studies have also found an equalising effect (Cancian and Reed 1999; Reed and Cancian 2001), yet Karoly and Burtless (1995), including all households (not just married couples), find that changes in wives' earnings have led to more inequality after 1979. One study also found no effect of wives' earnings (Barros and Mendonca 1992, for Brazil). Esping-Andersen (2007) found an equalising effect of wives' earnings in Denmark, Sweden and the United States, whereas wives' earnings contributes to greater household inequalities in the other countries including, France, Germany, Italy, Spain and United Kingdom. This may sound puzzling, and certainly calls for a better understanding of the mechanisms involved.

Taking Norway as our case, we will explore the impact of women's earnings on households' earnings inequality. We follow much of the previous work in this area (for example, Esping-Andersen 2007) by focusing on household earnings, thus disregarding capital income and income from transfers. We will analyse a 30-year period, going back to the 1970s, when most married women in Norway were housewives. Using Norwegian Labour Force Surveys with added information from public income registers we will first describe trends in inequalities in earnings among married-couple households from 1974 to 2004, a period characterised by rising female labour force participation. Second, we also consider unmarried cohabitation, since this has increased considerably in the period we cover, and may introduce a (time-varying) selection bias in our data if we only include married couples. For the period 1993–2004, we also have register information on cohabiting couples, and we will therefore be able to compare the impact of women's labour market participation on household inequality in earnings for both married and cohabiting couples.[2]

In both analyses we include dual earner couples (where both spouses participate in the labour force) as well as couples where the wife is not gainfully employed. Inclusion of the last group, which more appropriately could be termed single earner couples, is important since we want to measure the impact of housewives entering – in accelerating speed – the labour market.

A SCANDINAVIAN CASE

Norway still has smaller socioeconomic differences than most other Western countries and a very compressed income distribution (Atkinson et al. 1995), a factor that is often mentioned as important for the legitimacy and maintenance of the Scandinavian welfare states' policies of redistribution (Listhaug and Aalberg 1999; Esping-Andersen 2000). It is also the case that the gender gap in earnings is smaller in Scandinavia than in most Western countries (Blau and Kahn 1996).

Comparing a number of countries, Chaftez and Hagan (1996) have documented that Norway, starting from a very low level in the 1960s, together with Canada, Australia, Israel and New Zealand, had the largest increase from 1960 to 1990 in women's labour force participation. At the turn of the century, Norwegian women's labour force participation was at about the same level as men's: 89 per cent of all men and 82 per cent of all women aged 25–54 were gainfully employed. Thus, together with the other Nordic countries, Norway is among the countries with the highest female labour force participation in the world, yet about 40 per cent of Norwegian women work part-time (Rosenfeld and Birkelund 1995; Torp and Barth 2001; Birkelund and Sandnes 2003), a figure that has remained remarkably stable for several years. Women's labour market participation has risen since the 1970s, yet women with low education systematically have lower labour market participation: in 1976 40.8 per cent of women with lower secondary education were gainfully employed as compared to 72.6 per cent of women with higher education (university level). In 1991 the same figures were 39.8 per cent and 81.9 per cent, respectively (Statistics Norway 2009a).

The period we cover in this chapter also coincides with substantial changes in family types. Cohabitation in Norway has become widespread, in particular, since the mid-1980s. In 2008 cohabiting couples comprised 22 per cent of all couples, an increase from 10 per cent in 1990 (Statistics Norway 2009b). Looking at first union formation, Wiik (2009) documents that, for persons entering their first unions between 1970 and 2002, about 90 per cent choose cohabitation as their first union.

From the early 1970s to today, women's educational level has increased, women's labour market participation has increased, marital selection has changed and cohabitation has increased, marital instability has increased

(Lyngstad and Engelhardt 2009) and women's fertility rates have changed (Lappegård 2000). These demographic changes in household, structure and women's choices might be important for earnings inequality among households, and changes in household inequality over time.

WOMEN'S LABOUR SUPPLY AND HOUSEHOLD INEQUALITIES IN EARNINGS

In a cross-national study of changing income distributions, Esping-Andersen argues that three main demographic factors are important for households' income distribution (Esping-Andersen 2007: 643). The first factor is related to partner choice. If marital homogamy is increasing, we could expect more inequality to follow.[3] Second, since the 1960s–1970s, married women have increased their labour force participation, thus contributing to the growth in dual earner families. The third factor is related to rising instability in marriage/partnerships. In particular, single-mother households are in general more vulnerable than other households. A growth in single-parent households could also increase inequality among households (see also Jenkins 1995).

Looking at couples only (married or cohabiting with common child) we will not discuss the third factor above. Inequality in household (husband plus wife) earnings would then be a function of inequality in husbands' and wives' earnings taken separately, the relative size of husbands' and wives' earnings, and the association between two spouses' earnings (Cancian and Reed 1999). There are two main mechanisms determining the husband–wife earnings correlation. The first is related to marriage patterns and the second is related to couple's allocation of time. Looking at marriage patterns first, if men with a high earnings potential marry women with high earnings potential, and men with low earnings potential marry women with low earnings potential, the husband–wife correlation in earnings will be positive.

The second mechanism determining the husband–wife earnings correlation is related to the spouses' allocation of time. If men are regarded as the main breadwinners and women adjust their labour force participation to the financial needs of the family, women married to low-earning men would work more, to compensate their husbands' low earnings, compared to women married to high-earning men. The two mechanisms therefore have opposite effects: the homogamy effect implies high husband–wife correlation in earnings; the compensation effect implies low (or even negative) husband–wife correlation in earnings.

Esping-Andersen's (2007) results suggest that husband–wife earnings correlations are typically quite low; therefore, it is unlikely that they have a strong impact on between-household inequality. Wives' share of household earnings and the degree of inequality in wives' earnings are likely to be more consequential, and a high share of household earnings and low inequality can only be realised simultaneously if most wives are occupationally active. Thus, Esping-Andersen summarises his cross-national analysis by arguing that the main mechanisms are related to wives' labour supply and the distribution of labour supply across households: 'The conditions required for an equalizing effect are quite steep: namely, maximum, Nordic-type female labour force participation with a fairly symmetric distribution of work intensity across households' (Esping-Andersen 2007: 646).

Esping-Andersen's conclusions on the impact of women's labour market participation are based on comparing countries over a limited period of time (1993–2001). In this chapter, we will be able, by going more than 30 years back in time, to document the impact of rising female labour force participation, from a low level in the 1970s to the present-day high level.

DATA AND METHODS

For the period 1974–2004, we use data produced by merging the Norwegian labour force surveys (LFS) with administrative data on earnings (as reported by employers and the self-employed to the compulsory national health and pension insurance scheme). We include all married couples in which the husband is in the 26 to 65 age range and is occupationally active (defined by non-zero earnings from employment or self-employment). We thus exclude young people who are often students, as well as age groups in which pensioners dominate. For each year we have approximately 2000 to 4600 cases.

In order to compare married couples with cohabiting couples, we supplement the LFS data with a register-based data set comprising the complete birth cohorts 1955 to 1990, which includes annual earnings data for the 1993 to 2004 period. (This data set was originally prepared for a research project named Educational Careers, and we refer to it as EC data.)[4] For each year 1993 to 2004 we have selected couples in which the husband is between 35 and 39 years of age (38 in 1993) and have earnings above zero. We concentrate on this age range to get comparable data for the whole period 1993 to 2004 (in 1993 the oldest individuals in our data are 38 years of age). In these data cohabitants with a common child are also included.[5]

Earnings are measured by register-based information provided by employers to the national pension scheme (LFS data) or to the tax authorities (EC data). This means that we measure annual earnings (from employment or self-employment) before tax and before public or private transfers.[6]

We follow much of the previous literature on household earnings inequality by using the Coefficient of Variation (CV) as our measure of inequality. The CV is defined as the standard deviation divided by the mean. A problem with the standard deviation is that it will increase over time merely as a result of a declining value of money. This is corrected in the CV by the division by the mean. Thus, the CV can be considered as a standardised version of the standard deviation, which secures the important property of scale insensitivity (Allison 1978). Since the CV is based on the standard deviation, it is, however, quite sensitive to households with extreme earnings. We have therefore excluded households in the top 0.5 percentile (in the LFS data) or 0.1 percentile (EC) of the earnings distribution.[7] We also include confidence intervals based on bootstrapped standard errors with 200 replications.[8]

TRENDS IN HOUSEHOLD EARNINGS INEQUALITIES, 1974–2004

Figure 11.1 shows trends in earnings inequality among households (both spouses), as well as trends in earnings inequality among husbands taken separately, for the period 1974–2004.

The inequality in husbands' earnings was stable with a CV of about 0.4 in the 1970s, yet since the early 1980s inequality in married men's earnings has increased to about 0.55, with some fluctuations. The lower line in Figure 11.1, showing the CV for total household earnings, is comparatively flat, indicating stability over time in household inequalities in earnings. We also note that the levels of inequality in husbands' earnings and in household earnings are very close in the earliest part of the period (cf. also the overlapping confidence intervals). From about 1983, however, inequality in earnings among husbands started increasing substantially whereas economic inequalities between households remained at the same level, at least until the end of the 1990s. Thus, wives' earnings did not have a noticeable effect on the economic inequalities among households until the early 1980s. From about 1983 wives' earnings have had an equalising effect on households' earnings; in fact, as inequality among husbands increased, women's earnings have had an increasing equalising effect on household inequality, as can be seen in the increasing gap between the two lines. Yet from 1996 and onwards, the difference between the CV for

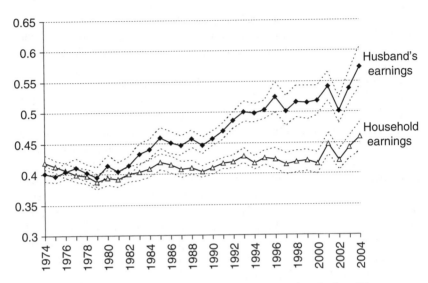

*Figure 11.1   Coefficient of variation for husband's earnings and household
(husband plus wife) earnings, 1974–2004*

households and for husbands has changed very little, indicating that the
equalising impact of wives' earnings may have reached its maximum.

Thus, for the period 1974 to 2004 we find three patterns regarding the
impact of wives' earnings on household's inequalities: In the first period,
from 1974 to about 1983, married women's labour force participation
was increasing, yet still at a low level, and their earnings were not enough
to have a significant impact on the overall level of household inequality
in earnings. Thus, in this 10-year period, we find no significant effect of
wives' earnings on household inequalities. In the second period, from 1983
to about 1996, we find an increasing equalising effect of wives' earnings
on household inequalities. In this period, in our data, married women's
labour force participation increased from 68 per cent in 1983 to nearly
80 per cent in 2004. Third, after 1996 wives' labour supply has remained
stable at about 80 per cent, and wives' earnings have likewise had a stable
and strong equalising effect on inequality in earnings among households.

Analyses not shown here reveal that the equalising effect of women's
labour market participation to a large extent is due to the fact that more
women have entered the labour market (Birkelund and Mastekaasa 2009).
With fewer housewives over time, the variation in women's earnings
decreases. Women's share of household earnings also increases, from less

than 20 per cent in 1974 to 35 per cent in 2004 (Birkelund and Mastekaasa 2009). The overall conclusion therefore is that after the early 1980s women's earnings have had a significant equalising effect on household inequalities in earnings.[9]

MARRIED AND COHABITATING COUPLES, 1993–2004

As Table 11.1 shows, the populations of married couples we have had information about from the LFS in the period 1974 to 2004 have grown more and more selected over the years; in 1974 about 70 per cent of all men between 25 and 65 years of age were married and gainfully employed, whereas in 2004 this figure was only 54 per cent of all men in the same age span.

Thus, it would be of interest to see if cohabiting couples differ from married couples in terms of economic inequality. Since we have access to register data on cohabitants for the period 1993–2004, we can compare these with married couples. As noted above, we have here selected men aged 35–39 and their partners (married or cohabitants). For each year, we have about 100000 individuals in our sample. Due to the very large N and the resulting very low sampling variability, we have omitted confidence intervals in this figure.

In Figure 11.2, we see slightly different trends for the two groups. For the married couples we find a small increase in inequality for husbands' earnings in the 1993 to 2004 period, which is in line with the findings in the analysis of the LFS data. Also, wives' earnings have a quite stable equalising impact, the inequality in household earnings being 82 to 84 per cent of the inequality in men's earnings. For cohabiting couples, too, there is no clear trend in inequality for men's earnings, but there is a slight decline in household inequality. This means that the equalising impact of the women's earnings increases slightly, with the inequality in household earnings being about 85 per cent of male earnings in the beginning of the period and 81 per cent in the end. Overall, however, the equalising impact of women's earnings is of very similar magnitude for married couples and cohabitors.

The slight differences between the married and the cohabiters notwithstanding, the period 1993–2004 has been characterised by *considerable stability* in household earnings inequality among the households we have investigated. It is too early to conclude that the homogamy effect and the substitution effect are both found invalid. They may both be valid mechanisms, but operate against each other so that the end result at the aggregate level is stability.

Table 11.1   *Men by marital status and earnings: percentage of all men*
            aged 26–65 within each year

	Not married		Married		Sum	N
	With earnings	Without earnings	With earnings	Without earnings		
1975	16.4	4.9	67.6	11.1	100.0	11093
1976	14.6	4.6	70.4	10.5	100.0	6051
1977	15.8	3.7	70.7	9.8	100.0	6408
1978	14.9	3.8	67.0	14.3	100.0	6893
1979	17.3	4.4	70.7	7.6	100.0	6570
1980	17.2	4.5	70.8	7.6	100.0	6464
1981	17.3	3.8	66.9	11.9	100.0	6954
1982	18.7	3.6	66.2	11.5	100.0	7081
1983	19.5	4.1	66.1	10.3	100.0	6448
1984	19.9	4.8	62.4	12.8	100.0	6951
1985	21.6	4.6	62.6	11.1	100.0	7093
1986	21.1	4.3	64.0	10.6	100.0	7328
1987	22.1	3.9	64.7	9.4	100.0	7233
1988	22.9	4.5	63.3	9.2	100.0	9933
1989	24.8	4.4	62.2	8.6	100.0	13949
1990	25.6	4.4	62.0	8.0	100.0	14436
1991	27.3	4.5	60.4	7.8	100.0	14638
1992	29.0	4.7	58.2	8.1	100.0	15242
1993	29.5	4.6	57.8	8.1	100.0	15401
1994	30.4	5.0	57.3	7.3	100.0	15495
1995	32.6	5.0	55.5	6.9	100.0	15596
1996	32.6	4.7	56.0	6.6	100.0	7742
1997	34.9	4.3	54.8	5.9	100.0	7753
1998	34.3	4.1	55.2	6.4	100.0	7657
1999	34.1	4.1	56.1	5.7	100.0	7586
2000	35.2	3.9	55.2	5.7	100.0	7550
2001	34.9	4.5	54.2	6.5	100.0	7495
2002	36.0	3.8	55.0	5.2	100.0	7906
2003	36.6	4.0	53.8	5.6	100.0	7677
2004	37.1	3.9	53.6	5.3	100.0	7736

Source: Labour Force Surveys 1975–2004.

CONCLUDING COMMENTS

Economic inequality among households has increased in most Western
countries, including, but from a lower level, Scandinavian countries. At

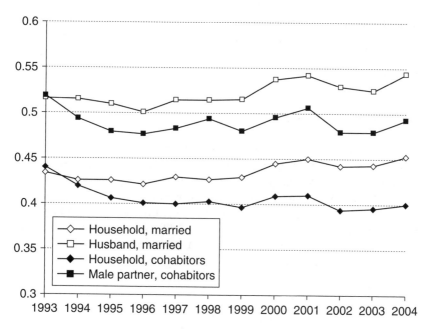

*Figure 11.2   Coefficient of variation for husband's and household earnings
            for married and cohabiting couples: households with
            occupationally active husbands aged 35–39, 1993–2004*

the same time gender relations have changed, from a male breadwinner
model, where men earned money and women were housewives, to a dual
earner family model, where both spouses/partners are gainfully employed.
A vital question for all interested in household inequalities and women's
work would be if married women's increasing labour market participation
has contributed to 'the great U-turn' in economic inequality. The time
span covered in this chapter is deliberately chosen to reflect the period
under which dual income families emerged in Norway, that is, when
married women gradually entered the labour market.

We have seen that since 1983 married women's earnings have had an
equalising effect on household inequalities in earnings. This equalizing
effect increased considerably until about 1996, and has since been stable and
strong. Looking more specifically at the period 1993–2004, including data on
cohabiting as well as married couples, we found slightly different inequality
levels and trends for married couples and cohabiters. Again, however, the
equalising effect of women's earnings is very similar in both groups.

The restructuring of gender relations has had implications for a number
of issues related to work and family (such as lower birth rates and higher

divorce rates); also, higher female labour market participation has had an equalising effect on economic inequalities among households. The 'great U-turn' in economic inequality, it seems, would have been stronger without women's work.

ACKNOWLEDGEMENT

An earlier version of this chapter was presented at a meeting of the International Sociological Association's Research Committee on Social Stratification and Mobility, Brno, Czech Republic, 24–27 May 2007, at an AIAS Lunch seminar, University of Amsterdam, 18 June, 2007 and at 'Gender, Class, Employment, and Family. An International Conference', City University, London, 27–28 March, 2008. We would like to thank participants at these meetings for their valuable comments, as well as the referee of this anthology.

NOTES

1. See also OECD (2006: Table A13).
2. For simplicity, we will sometimes use the terms 'husband', 'wife' and 'spouse' to include partners in cohabiting couples.
3. See Birkelund and Heldal (2003) and Wiik (2009) for studies of educational homogamy in Norway.
4. These data were originally prepared by Statistics Norway for the project Educational Careers, funded by the Norwegian Research Council, 2003–2007.
5. Cohabitants without common children are not registered, and can not be included.
6. Our measures are close to *pretax-pretransfer income*, also referred to as market income (Kenworthy 2007), but we do not have information on capital income (which is also included in the *pretax-pretransfer income measurement*).
7. Even in large samples like ours, a few observations with incomes of tens or even hundreds of millions may have a strong impact on the results.
8. Bootstrapping is used since common estimators of the standard error of the CV appear to be quite sensitive to distributional assumptions (Curto and Pinto 2009).
9. See Harkness et al. (1997: Table 8) for a similar finding based on British data.

REFERENCES

Aaberge, R., S. Strøm and T. Wennemo (1997), *Inntektsulikhet i Norge 1973–1990* (*Income Inequality in Norway, 1973–1990*), Report no. 17, Statistics Norway, 1–97.

Alderson, A.S. and F. Nielsen (2002), 'Globalization and the great U-Turn: income inequality trends in 16 OECD countries', *American Journal of Sociology*, **107**, 1244–99.

Allison, P.D. (1978), 'Measures of inequality', *American Sociological Review*, **43**, 865–80.

Amin, S. and J. Da Vanzo (2004), 'The impact of wives' earnings on earnings inequality among married-couple households in Malaysia', *Journal of Asian Economics*, **15**, 49–70.

Atkinson, A.B., L. Rainwater and T.M. Smeeding (1995), *Income Distribution in OECD Countries: Evidence from the Luxembourg Income Study*, Paris: OECD.

Barros, R.P. and R.S. Mendonca (1992), 'A research note on household and income distribution: the equalizing impact of married women's earnings in metropolitan Brazil', *Sociological Inquiry*, **62**, 208–19.

Birkelund, G.E. and J. Heldal (2003), 'Who marries whom? Educational homogamy in Norway', *Demographic Research*, **8**, 1–29.

Birkelund, G.E. and A. Mastekaasa (2009), 'Female labour force participation and household inequalities in earnings and income', Paper, Department of Sociology and Human Geography, University of Oslo.

Birkelund, G.E. and T. Sandnes (2003), 'Paradoxes of welfare states and equal opportunities: gender and managerial power in Norway and the USA', *Comparative Social Research*, **21**, 201–41.

Bjørklund, A. (1992), 'Rising female labour force participation and the distribution of family income – the Swedish experience', *Acta Sociologica*, **35**, 299–309.

Blau, F.D. and L.M. Kahn (1996), 'Wage structure and gender earnings differentials: an international comparison', *Economica*, **63** (Supplement), S29–S62.

Cancian, M. and D. Reed (1999), 'The impact of wives' earnings on income inequality: issues and estimates', *Demography*, **36**, 173–84.

Chaftez, J.S. and J. Hagan (1996), 'The gender division of labour and family change in industrial societies', *Journal of Comparative Family Studies*, **27**, 187–219.

Crompton, R. (1999), *Restructuring Gender Relations and Employment. The Decline of the Male Breadwinner*, Oxford: Oxford University Press.

Crompton, R. (2006), *Employment and the Family. The Reconfiguration of Work and Family Life in Contemporary Societies*, Cambridge: Cambridge University Press.

Curto, J.D. and J.C. Pinto (2009), 'The coefficient of variation asymptotic distribution in the case of non-random variables', *Journal of Applied Statistics*, **36**, 21–32.

Ellingsæter, A.L. (2001), 'Scandinavian transformations. Labour markets, politics and gender divisions', *Economic and Industrial Democracy*, **21**, 335–59.

Esping-Andersen, G. (2000), *Social Foundations of Postindustrial Economies*, Oxford: Oxford University Press.

Esping-Andersen, G. (2007), 'Sociological explanations of changing income distributions', *American Behavioral Scientist*, **50**, 639–58.

Gronau, R. (1982), 'Inequality of household income: do wives' earnings matter?', *Population and Development Review*, **8** (Suppl.), 119–36.

Harkness, S., S. Machin and C. Meghir (1996), 'Women's pay and household incomes in Britain, 1979–1991', in J. Hills (ed.), *New Inequalities: The Changing Distribution of Income and Wealth in the United Kingdom*, Cambridge: Cambridge University Press, pp. 158–81.

Harkness, S., S. Machin and J. Waldfogel (1997), 'Evaluating the pin money hypothesis: the relationship between women's labour market activity, family income and poverty in Britain', *Journal of Population Economics*, **10**, 137–58.

Jenkins, S.P. (1995), 'Accounting for inequality trends: decomposition analyses for the UK, 1971–86', *Economica*, **62**, 29–63.

Karoly, L.A. and G. Burtless (1995), 'Demographic change, rising earnings inequality, and the distribution of personal well being, 1959–1989', *Demography*, **32**, 379–406.

Kenworthy, L. (2007), 'Inequality and sociology', *American Behavioral Scientist*, **50**, 584–602.

Lappegård, T. (2000), 'New fertility trends in Norway', *Demographic Research*, **2**, Article 3, available at http://www.demographic-research.org/volumes/vol2/3/.

Listhaug, O. and T. Aalberg (1999), 'Comparative public opinion on distributive justice: a study of equity ideals and attitudes toward current politics', *International Journal of Comparative Sociology*, **40**, 117–40.

Lyngstad, T.H. and H. Engelhardt (2009), 'The influence of sex and age at parents' divorce on the intergenerational transmission of divorce, Norwegian first marriages 1980–1999', *Population Studies*, **63**, 1–13.

OECD (2006), 'Labour market performance, income inequality and poverty in OECD countries', ECO/WKP (2006) 28/ANN.

Pasqua, S. (2008), 'Wives' work and income distribution in European countries', *The European Journal of Comparative Economics*, **5**, 197–226.

Pong, S. (1991), 'The effect of women's labour on household income inequality: the case of Hong Kong', *Economic Development and Cultural Change*, **40**, 131–52.

Reed, D. and M. Cancian (2001), 'Sources of inequality: measuring the contributions of income sources to rising family income inequality', *Review of Income and Wealth*, **47**, 321–33.

Rosenfeld, R.A. and G.E. Birkelund (1995), 'Women's part-time work: a cross-national comparison', *European Sociological Review*, **11**, 111–34.

Statistics Norway (2009a), 'Persons in the labour force, by sex and level of education', available at http://www.ssb.no/histstat/tabeller/9-9-11t.txt, accessed 8 April 2009.

Statistics Norway (2009b), 'Family trends', available at http://www.ssb.no/norge/fam.pdf, accessed 28 April 2009.

Torp, H. and E. Barth (2001), *Actual and Preferred Working Time*, Report 2001: 3, Oslo: Institute for Social Research.

Wiik, K.A. (2009), '"You'd better wait!" Socioeconomic background and timing of first marriage versus first cohabitation', *European Sociological Review*, **25**, 139–55.

PART V

Confronting Complexity

12. Feminist policies and feminist conflicts: daddy's care or mother's milk?

Anne Lise Ellingsæter

Gender relations of work and family are changing all over the Western world, accentuating the question of gender equality. The goal of gender equality and how to proceed politically is an unrelenting subject of feminist dispute (Orloff 2009). How to restructure work and family is no exception. For some, the dual earner/dual carer model, where women and men engage symmetrically in paid work and unpaid caregiving is the vision of a gender egalitarian society (for example Fraser 1994; Gornick and Meyers 2008). Gender egalitarianism will require transformations in gender divisions in employment and at home (Crompton 2009). Others question the underlying premise of this position, that women's emancipation above all demands the dissolution of the gendered division of labour, and that asymmetry is associated with inequality, and symmetry with equality (Orloff 2009). Goals that expand choice or decisional autonomy are seen a better alternative for a multiplicity of gender arrangements among diverse citizens.

The policy institutions of the Nordic welfare states have come a long way toward the dual earner/dual carer model (Ellingsæter and Leira 2006). That is why the Nordic countries serve as notable 'exemplars' in current debates of institutional reform for gender equality (for example Gornick and Meyers 2008). The only partial transformation of asymmetrical gender relations in families and labour markets is seen as a paradoxical – and problematic – outcome of the Nordic policy model (for example Mandel and Semyonov 2006). When policy institutions are close to the dual earner/dual carer model, why, asks Orloff (2009), are those countries not much closer to gender symmetry? While most attention is directed at assessing the gender equality outcomes of Nordic policy arrangements, I shall argue that in understanding change, it is important also to consider the ongoing political struggles over gender equality in these countries. The potential for moving policies further along a dual earner/dual carer path is crucial in that respect. This chapter investigates recent controversies over parental leave reform in Norway, and important insights about *obstacles* to the strategy of gender symmetry can be drawn from these conflicts. Paid parental leave is an essential element of the dual earner/dual carer model, and a particularly important measure in transforming the gender division of labour within the family. I examine a new tension emerging in the 2000s, between proposals to reserve more of the existing parental leave for fathers and an expansion in breastfeeding policy insisting on mothers' lengthy intensive breastfeeding.

PARENTAL LEAVE: TRANSFORMATIVE POTENTIAL

Domestic sharing is crucial to gender equality – inequalities within the family around the domestic division of labour, especially caregiving, are a significant obstacle to achieving gender symmetry (Crompton 2009). Statutory parental leave policies are widespread, but the forms they take vary considerably depending on eligibility criteria, length of leave provision, wage replacement level, job security guarantees, flexibility in uptake, and last, but not least, whether entitlements are individually or family based (Moss and Deven 2006). Policy rationales differ, reflecting various social assumptions of childhood, motherhood and fatherhood (Deven and Moss 2002). The aims of leave policies may be pro-natalist, family welfare, children's right to parental care or gender equality – or even conflicting combinations of these. Parental leave may be considered more a welfare policy for children than a policy promoting gender equality, argues, for instance, Björnberg (2002). Most advocates of policy arrangements that allow more family time simply ignore the issue of gender equality because they view full-time care of infants by their own mother as more important than gender equality, according to Bergmann (2008).

Various parental leave arrangements have different potential to transform the private realm of inequality. Brighouse and Wright (2008) distinguish between three kinds of publicly supported parental caregiving leaves, based on their gender egalitarian transformative ability:

1. *Equality-impeding* policies, that is, leaves given only to mothers, but also unpaid leaves. Such leaves may increase the quality of life of families, but do not contribute to reducing inequality within the gendered division of labour within the family.
2. *Equality-enabling* policies, that is, paid leaves given to families, which reduce the obstacles of women combining employment and children,

and make it easier for men to engage in caregiving activities. The policies enable egalitarian strategies within families, but put no pressures on families to adopt such strategies.

3. *Equality-promoting* policies, that is, paid leaves given to mothers and fathers individually, incentives putting pressures on families to share caregiving activities more equally. Only the latter policies support 'strong gender egalitarianism', 'a structure of social relations in which the division of labour in housework and caregiving within the family and occupational distributions within the public sphere are unaffected by gender' (Brighouse and Wright 2008: 360).

Gornick and Meyers' (2008) recent proposal falls in the latter category: they advocate the individual (non-transferable) right to six months' paid leave each for the mother and the father. They argue that trade-offs among gender equality, family time and child well-being are not inevitable, and that their proposal will support gender-egalitarian caregiving and ample time for children and thus child well-being. Some take a different position regarding long paid parental leaves as measures to increase gender equality – even if they are symmetrically divided among mothers and fathers. Balancing gender equality with other concerns may represent a real conflict, where the interests of women, men and children may be at odds. Based on the experience of the Nordic countries among other things, Bergmann (2008) argues that more time at home for parents means in reality more time for mother.

THE NORDIC REFORM PATH

Paid leave arrangements for parents in the Nordic countries have converged through continuous reforms over the past three decades (Ellingsæter 2009). Four major trends are emerging: shift from maternal leave to parental leave, extended length of leave (converging at about one year), earmarking of non-transferable leave for fathers, and more flexible regulation of leave take-up.[1] Timing of the introduction of the various policy elements has varied considerably among the countries, however.

The 1970s saw the first step toward *equality-enabling* policies, when maternity leave was transformed into parental leave. The change implied that parents could divide most of the leave days between them, at their own discretion. This early reform signalled the expansion of men's responsibility as fathers to include also practical and emotional care for children. It was part of the rise of Scandinavian 'state feminism' – feminist policy directed by the state but generated by women from 'below' – producing legislation and policy reforms with the aim of promoting gender equality in society (Hernes 1987; Leira 2006). Politically the dual-earner/dual-carer model is a 'state feminist' innovation – advocated by social democrats and parties on the left.

The expected increase in fathers' leave uptake did not ensue, however, and the 1990s became the decade of *equality-promoting* policies, introducing elements of mandated equal sharing of the by now lengthy parental leaves. Fathers' negligible use of parental leave sparked off a policy innovation: the introduction of the 'daddy quotas', reserving parts of the parental leave for fathers on a use it or lose it basis.[2] A more symmetrical division of labour within the family was a main goal, but improving the father–child relationship has also been emphasised. Infancy represents a short period of parenthood, but has been accorded great political significance for gender equality in the Nordic countries. If gendered employment-care practices are allowed to settle at an early stage, they assumedly will be reproduced at later stages of parenthood. Daddy quotas were again 'state feminism' at work – pushed forward by social democrats.[3] Norway was the first country to introduce a quota in 1993, Sweden followed suit in 1995, Demark in 1998 (removed in 2002, however, see Borchorst 2006) and Iceland and Finland in early/mid-2000s.

Until recently daddy quotas have been a distinct Nordic leave policy element. At the end of the 2000s, the length of the daddy quota varied significantly, however: 2–4 weeks in Finland, 2 months in Sweden, 2.5 months in Norway and 3 months in Iceland. The quotas have had undisputable effects on fathers' leave take-up: the proportion of the total leave taken by fathers is proportional to the length of the national daddy quotas – the longer the quota, the longer fathers' leave take-up (Ellingsæter 2009). Almost all eligible fathers use their quota, but few fathers take more leave. Nordic mothers continue to take up most of the total leave days. In Norway, for instance, mothers take 89 per cent of the available leave days. Rather than reconciling work and family, long parental leaves to a significant extent have re-established separate spheres of work and family, and full-time mothering for women (Ellingsæter 2006). A common assumption is that the fathers' leave uptake will be more costly to the family, as fathers earn more than mothers. However, the significance of economic incentives explaining the gendered leave division is in general overstated (for example Björnberg 2002). Normatively, men have a larger degree of freedom in *not* choosing care. On the other hand, men have less choice if they want to care. Often fathers' leave uptake tends to be residual: they get what is left when mothers have decided how much leave they themselves want, and some mothers consider the parental leave as their privilege (Sundström and Duvander 2002).

In the public debate, worries are voiced over the potential disadvantageous impact of long leaves on women's labour market opportunities, on their careers and wages (SOU 2005). For example, wages of Norwegian mothers are reduced proportionately with their absence connected to parental leave (NOU 2008). Some argue that women's long parental leave has no positive effect on gender equality in working life; rather the contrary – it contributes to the segmentation of gendered patterns (Björnberg 2002). When women take up most of the leave, this practice becomes an attribute of the 'woman worker', representing a risk for discrimination of women in the labour market. In both Norway and Sweden an increase in complaints from women in connection with pregnancy and parental leave is observed (Gender Equality Ombud 2004; SOU 2005).

During the 2000s, these worries have mounted the pressure on taking *equality-promoting* policies further, particularly in Norway and Sweden (for example SOU 2005, NOU 2008). The main policy proposal is expanding the daddy quota and thus pushing mandate equal sharing of the lengthy leave further. The most influential – and contested – proposal is a three-part division of the *existing* parental leave into one part for the mother, one for the father and one part to be shared as the parents prefer – the so-called 'Icelandic model'. In the public debate 'parental choice' and the 'best interest of the child' are the main points raised against reserving more time for fathers, in both Norway and Sweden. The 'parental choice' argument – that quotas inhibit parents to find the best solution in managing everyday life – is first of all promoted by the political right, parties that also opposed the initial introduction of the daddy quotas on the same ground (Ellingsæter 2007).

The 'best interest of the child' argument against a longer daddy quota typically involves two concerns: that the child gets to spend as long a time as possible at home under parental care, and that the child can be nursed according to the recommendation of health authorities. Regarding the first concern, it is claimed that reserving more time for fathers may result in more children getting a shorter period of time at home, in effect with their mothers (for example Batljan et al. 2004). The child should have 'first priority', thus fathers should be stimulated to take more leave without this being at the cost of 'the best interest of the child'. The other concern, which is at the core of my analysis, is a claim that if more leave is reserved for the father within the existing leave it will prevent mothers from breastfeeding in accordance with the current breastfeeding recommendation. How this claim is articulated in the policy debate and how it eventually affects policy reform, is the question addressed in the following sections.

THE NORWEGIAN BREASTFEEDING REGIME

Breastfeeding is a concern brought into the parental leave debate in Norway only in the 2000s. The direct cause was a change in 2001 in the health authorities' recommended length of intensive breastfeeding. To understand why breastfeeding recommendation is a powerful political force in parental leave reform in Norway, one needs to recognise the extraordinary status of breastfeeding and the profound institutionalisation of breastfeeding recommendations.

An early and active feminist breastfeeding lobby is likely to be significant for the strong public emphasis on breastfeeding. The Norwegian breastfeeding regime can be seen as yet another outcome of 'state feminism'. In the 1950s and 1960s – the golden era of stay-at-home mothers – Norwegian breastfeeding rates were lower than ever (Schiøtz 2003). In 1962, only 22 per cent of mothers were breastfeeding their 3-month-old babies. Nonetheless, infant mortality was declining; mothers had learned to sterilise milk, bottle and teat. In the 1960s the multinational child food producers entered the scene with new milk formulas that in principle made both breastfeeding and sterilising work superfluous. The devastating effects on infant mortality in developing countries are well known. Ammehjelpen (The Breastfeeding Help) was started by Norwegian pioneers in 1968, a voluntary organisation still going strong. Similar organisations have been founded in many other countries. The aim was that women should take back control of infant feeding, and breastfeeding was perceived as a radical, empowering act.

Today Norwegian women have the highest breastfeeding frequency in the Western world – as well as the highest employment rates. In 1998–99, only 1 per cent of Norwegian infants had never been breastfed; similar low rates were also found in the other Nordic countries (Lande et al. 2003). In comparison, rates for the US and the UK were 60 per cent and 66 per cent respectively. Moreover, 80 per cent of Norwegian children were still breastfed at the age of six months, slightly higher than those of the other Nordic countries, but considerably higher than rates in other European countries and the US. Similar figures are reported from 2006 (Helsedirektoratet 2008).

High Norwegian breastfeeding rates did not develop on their own. That children receive breastmilk as the norm, is the result of systematic work on information and persuasion. A significant factor 'in the Norwegian breastfeeding "revolution" is the positive role played by public authorities' (Eide et al. 2003). Since 1976 recommendations about breastfeeding have been part of the state nutrition policy, adapted to recommendations from the World Health Organisation (WHO). Of greatest significance, however, is the *implementation* of policies as an integral part of the institutionalised mother–child health care system. Maternity wards and child health clinics are expected to execute the public breastfeeding policy, and there is active information dissemination to health personnel supporting policy aims. Three out of four children are born in hospitals that are partaking in the 'Mother–child-friendly' initiative in which breastfeeding is promoted by a wide range of specific procedures, and dissemination of information on infant formula is not allowed. Moreover, a national competence centre for breastfeeding was established in 1999 (hereafter the Breastfeeding Centre), promoting breastfeeding and knowledge about mothers' milk, in order to 'strengthen societal conditions that make optimal breastfeeding possible'. Their advocates are highly visible in the public debate. Norway's being at the 'top of the class' is a source of national pride, with expertise in strong demand internationally, generating a pressure to uphold this position.

In 2001, the breastfeeding recommendation was amended, following the WHO. The main difference was that *only breastmilk* should be the source of infant nutrition for the first six months – two months longer than the four months previously recommended. The new recommendation also stated that the infant should receive breastmilk in addition to other nutrition at least until 12 months old.[4] The main argument is short- and long-term health benefits for the child. The new breastfeeding policy is very ambitious compared to mothers' actual nursing practices. In 1998, under the 'old' recommendation, less than half of all children were fed only breastmilk until the age of four months. Data from 2006 show that breastfeeding practices have changed very little since 2001 (Helsedirektoratet 2008: Table 52).[5] In 2006, 46 per cent of the infants were fed only breastmilk at the age of four months, about the same proportion as reported *before* the new recommendation. There had been a minor increase in children who received only breastmilk between the age of four and six months, but at the age of six months, only 9 per cent of children were fed only breastmilk in 2006.

While Norwegian mothers obviously are highly motivated for breastfeeding, the majority do not comply with the recommendation of prolonged intensive breastfeeding. This is in spite of the combination of an extremely supportive (and uncompromising) environment for breastfeeding and mothers' long parental leave. Nonetheless, a state action plan on nutrition has stated a goal of substantially increasing the proportion of infants who are fed only breastmilk at the age of four and six months – to 70 per cent and 20 per cent respectively over the period 2007–2011.[6]

Complaints from mothers about the intense pressure on breastfeeding in the health care system have increased in recent years (Ellingsæter 2005). Some observers declare that Norway is at 'the world's top in breastfeeding hysteria', the downside of the very active propaganda for breastfeeding.[7] The many breastfeeding campaigns over the years do not leave the impression that it is acceptable not to breastfeed, and many women feel that they are not good enough mothers if they do not breastfeed. There is a total lack of information about alternatives to breastfeeding. Bottle-feeding is taboo (Johansen 2007). Some mothers have had to set up an Internet site for parents who bottle-feed, because of lack of information. There is a growing recognition that the implementation of breastfeeding recommendations has become 'too rigid', as expressed by the Norwegian Association of Midwives.[8]

It is generally agreed that breastfeeding is excellent nutrition and that it is important for a child to get mother's milk in the first months after delivery, and thus that a supportive environment for breastfeeding should be facilitated. However, there has been very little public debate among experts on the advantages and disadvantages of prolonged intensive breastfeeding. A few claim that health effects of breastfeeding are greatly exaggerated, and that women must be allowed to decide themselves for how long they breastfeed.[9] 'It is difficult to prove that infant formula is poorer nutrition for infants, and other health effects of mother's milk than infection prevention are very small and difficult to prove.'[10] There are several methodological problems in the study of health effects of breast-feeding.[11] For example, breastfeeding mothers often score high on socio-cultural factors such as health, education, income and intelligence, factors difficult to control for in the study of health effects of breastmilk. Some experts consider the WHO's breastfeeding recommendations irrelevant for the very healthy children in Norway and Sweden. The strong focus on breastfeeding in Norway and Sweden – a source of great worry to mothers – is labelled a kind of 'breastfeeding talibanism'.[12]

DADDY'S CARE OR MOTHER'S MILK?

The seemingly small change in the breastfeeding recommendation has had a huge impact on the political debate, as it causes trouble for a more gender-symmetrical parental leave arrangement. According to the health authorities, the practical implication of the recommendation is as follows: to feed the child only breastmilk for the first six months is difficult to accomplish if the mother is not on 100 per cent leave. In addition comes a period of about two months when the child is gradually introduced to other food and drinks. Thus the mother needs a total of *at least eight months of leave* after the birth.[13]

At the time when the new recommendation was introduced, the paid parental leave arrangement had not been changed since 1993. It consisted of a total of 52 weeks at 80 per cent wage compensation or 42 weeks at 100 per cent compensation, up to a ceiling.[14] Nine of the weeks were reserved for the mother (three weeks before birth and six weeks after) and four weeks reserved for the father – the daddy quota. Thus parents could share at their own discretion a total of 39/29 weeks. If mothers took their own leave and all the leave reserved for sharing, they could spend about nine months (6 weeks + 29 weeks) at 100 per cent compensation before going back to work. In addition came the five weeks of paid annual leave. At work, all breastfeeding mothers were then, as presently, granted the right to a daily unpaid rest of one hour; in the public sector they have the right to two hours' paid rest.

Since the change in the breastfeeding regime, the conflict between expanding the leave take-up of fathers within the existing leave and mothers' opportunity to breastfeed according to the recommendation has been a constantly revolving issue. The articulation of this conflict will be exemplified by interventions from public debates in 2001, 2004 and 2008 respectively.[15] The debate has invoked a wide range of actors, including the public, but here I concentrate on the views of political actors and interest organisations.

The new recommendation stirred public debate right away. In an exchange in 2001 between the Gender Equality Ombud and a representative from the Breastfeeding Centre, two different representatives of 'state feminism' one might say, the main tension was instantly formulated: mothers' prolonged intensive breastfeeding was posed in conflict to increasing daddies' caregiving. The Gender Equality Ombud intervened against the increased pressure on mothers to breastfeed, and a main claim was that it would make it difficult to argue that men should take up more of the parental leave. The Gender Equality Ombud pointed to the double communication originating from public authorities:

it does not seem as if health authorities have thought over which signals the new recommendations are sending beyond the question of infant nutrition. But the recommendations do place clear bearings on the roles of mother, father and having a child together. There are actually other things just as important for children than to get mother's milk as long as possible. For example establishing a good relationship to the father early in life.[16]

The response from the Breastfeeding Centre was that this type of argument is 'old fashioned feminism' and that

there can not be the same tasks for woman and man just after the child has come: It is women who are pregnant and give birth; and irrespective of breastfeeding, the majority are in need of a good leave. Biology is destiny. There are advantages and disadvantages with this for both genders.[17]

It was also claimed that if a mother has a convenient opportunity to breastfeed, but chooses not to, then 'one is actually not a satisfactory mother'.[18]

This Gender Equality Ombud did not support an expansion of the daddy quota within the current parental leave, however, arguing that dividing care requires parents to want it themselves:

> I do not believe in 'forcing' father to the home . . . The ideal would be an addition to the leave earmarked for father . . . My most important argument against binding a larger share of the current leave arrangement to fathers is that we can not assume that all will use it, and the reality will be reduced care for the child.[19]

A heated debate on breastfeeding, parental leave and gender equality surfaced again in 2004 when a couple of young male politicians from the Socialist Left Party suggested a parental leave reform like the 'Icelandic model' – a three-part division of leave. In the public debate, breastfeeding was a main argument for rejecting the proposal. Among the fierce opponents were some young women within the same political party. 'This proposal will not necessarily lead to a more gender equal society. We should rather work for society to accept that women are giving birth and are breastfeeding.'[20] It was also maintained that 'we do not believe that equality means sharing equally – that we can discuss the day that men start giving birth to children'. The underlying conception hence is that women who give birth are more mothers than men ever can be fathers.[21]

The double signals from public authorities were again criticised, this time from the Breastfeeding Helper. They argued that the premise of one year's parental leave arrangement is that the 'parent who can breastfeed must be the one that is to be at home with the child'. The child's right was underscored: 'In this discussion, gender equality interests are set up against the child's right to the best nutritional and relational start that we hitherto know about.'[22] Another feminist interest organisation, The Women's Front of Norway, a leftist women's organisation, took the opposite stance, arguing that half of the current leave should be legislated as the right of fathers, labelling this as a 'culture changing project'.[23]

In 2008, one of the proposals, from a government commission on equal pay, to close the gender pay gap was to reform the parental leave system according to the 'Icelandic model' – a three-part division of the existing leave (NOU 2008). This turned out to be one of the commission's most contested proposals, and a wide range of political actors and interest groups stated their views, both in the heated public debate and in written comments to the public hearing. The commission also proposed other reforms to reduce economic disincentives to fathers' leave take-up, supported by many: to grant the father the right to leave independent of the mother's economic activity before birth and after birth, and to remove the ceiling of wage compensation.[24] Due to space limitations these reforms are not discussed here.

Some influential actors supported the commission's proposal. Some of them did not mention the breastfeeding issue at all, while others actively rejected this as a real obstacle. The main national employer federation (NHO) supported the three-part division, and did not mention breastfeeding: 'The NHO supports the proposal of sharing the parental leave after an Icelandic model. In the NHO's opinion this will strengthen the legitimacy of parental leave for both sexes.'[25] In contrast, another employer association (Spekter) was sceptical, referring to the proposal as 'controversial', mentioning in particular the debate about support for women to breastfeed for the recommended period. They maintained that consequences of the proposal were not fully accounted for.

The Gender Equality Ombud now in office was also supportive, arguing that the further effects of the daddy quota have stagnated and that new measures are needed. In an earlier intervention she rejected breastfeeding as an obstacle:

> A legislated division of leave in three parts is necessary to end discrimination of women in working life . . . Some fear that a division into three will result in children not getting only mothers' milk the first six months. This fear I do not share. A division into three parts implies that women will stay at home at least four to eight months.[26]

Breastfeeding was a concern raised by many actors, and one of the main arguments against a three-part division of leave. Not surprisingly, the Breastfeeding Centre stated that a three-part division of leave will be a clear hindrance for women to breastfeed according to the recommendation: If a 'forced' division of leave in three parts is introduced, this will counteract the possibility to reach the goals set by the action plan on nutrition previously mentioned. Further, it was argued that the division of leave should be set on the basis of the following priorities: 1) The best interest of the child, health benefits for the child from breastmilk, confer the recommendations from the health authorities; 2) Women's different needs for recovery after birth, breastfeeding problems, and their different possibilities and capacities to combine breastfeeding and employment; 3) Promotion of increased equality and pay among parents by increasing fathers' reserved part of leave.

Parliamentary representatives from right-wing parties rejected the proposal basically because it hampers 'parental choice': breastfeeding was not specifically mentioned:

> We do not want to push our youngest children in front of us to promote gender equality. We need to trust that the individual family finds the solutions that are best for their child and situation . . . Families must get to choose themselves as most families have different needs and wishes . . . The parental leave is first of all an arrangement that enable us to care for our newborns until they are one year old.[27]

The Women's Forum of the Conservative Party stated that they are in favour of more equal sharing, but not 'forcing' this upon parents. As an alternative they suggest tax relief for parents who are sharing more equally (inspired by a recent Swedish reform).

Several of those rejecting the commission's proposal came up with alternative models for dividing leave. A four-part division was the most common, consisting of one part for the mother, one part for the father and two parts that can be divided equally between them, in combination with an expansion of the total leave to 52 weeks with 100 per cent wage compensation. Accommodating the breastfeeding recommendation was an important premise of this model. Among those proposing such a model was the largest employee organisation (LO). In addition they proposed paid breastfeeding rests extended to all breastfeeding mothers, and arrangements facilitating breastfeeding at all workplaces.[28] Also the Ombudsman for Children supported a four-part division and emphasised the importance of the breastfeeding recommendation. This would secure fathers' participation in the care of the child from the start, at the same time as it does not harm the child's 'health needs'. The Men's Panel, set up by the Ministry of Gender and Equality in 2007 to give advice on men's perspectives on gender equality, also suggested this model, underlining the breastfeeding recommendation as an important premise.[29]

The red–green majority coalition government ended up in this position too. The Minister of Children and Gender Equality from the Labour Party argued that it is 'good gender equality policy to take care of women who have children'. Breastfeeding was a key concern in her rejection of a three-part division of leave:

> we need a moderate form of [leave] sharing that benefit both children and parents. This way, we can secure women a stronger attachment to the labour market and men more responsibility for the care of their own children. But this must not lead to women only having a maximum of six months of leave. Many women need rest after giving birth, both for their own restitution and for breastfeeding and taking care of the child. They should have the opportunity to do so. At the same time father must stay more at home.[30]

The minister claimed that a three-part division would be particularly hard for women with low education and ordinary jobs, as they more often take the shorter leave at 100 per cent pay and have jobs that are more difficult to combine with continued breastfeeding. The prime minister, also from the Labour Party, supported this view in the public debate, arguing that leave should not 'be taken from mothers'. However, there were other Labour Party members of the parliament who actively supported the proposed three-part division:

> The father gets too little of the leave today . . . He does not get to know his child as well as the mother. This again does something with the division of labour at home. The mother takes the main responsibility for children and is parked in relation to job and career, while the man works more overtime and his career is furthered.[31]

Another parliamentary member, from the same party, maintained that 'one needs to remember that the parental leave is not mother's leave. If father gets one third of the leave then he just gets more of the leave that parents are supposed to share.'

In the time period examined, the initial 4-week daddy quota has been extended three times, which is indicative of the pressure for reform. In 2005 and 2006, one extra week was added to the total leave each year. The first extension was adopted by a minority centre-right government, the second by a majority red–green government. Clearly these extensions do not conflict with the breastfeeding recommendation, and the effect on gender symmetry is minor. In 2008 the red–green government decided to extend the daddy quota further by four weeks; two weeks were placed *within* the current leave, two weeks were *added* to the total leave.[32] This reform is a compromise between increasing gender symmetry minimally and at the same time accommodating the breastfeeding recommendation.

BREASTFEEDING: THE FRONTIER OF GENDER SYMMETRY?

Gender equality is a matter of dispute and a project constantly in the making. The Nordic welfare states are strategic cases for examining these enduring struggles, contributing important knowledge about the persistence of gender norms in the shaping of gender inequality, and how norms are reshaped themselves.

This chapter has disclosed how breastfeeding is articulated as a new and powerful concern influencing policy outcomes. The tension between daddy's care and mother's breastfeeding represents a new challenge to gender equality policies. The 2001 recommendation prolonging mothers' intensive breastfeeding appears as a key explanation of why *equality-promoting* parental leave policies have not progressed much in the 2000s, despite the rather strong consensus that fathers should take up more leave. The breastfeeding recommendation has in effect blocked a more gender-symmetrical parental leave arrangement. The public debate has revolved around the premise that lengthy intensive breastfeeding is critical to children's health. Even many of those supporting a more symmetrical leave emphasise that it still would be possible for mothers to breastfeed according to the recommendation. 'Strong egalitarianism' is quite a step away in parental leave reforms in Norway – at least for the time being.

The discursive field of political strategies is broad, however. At one end are those who want mothers to have all the leave, at the other those who want a legislated fifty-fifty division between the mother and the father. Hence strategies stretch between feminist positions of 'equality' (or 'sameness') and 'difference', that is, strategies where sexual difference is an irrelevant consideration versus strategies based on needs and interests common to women as a group (Scott 1988). However, the majority of strategies constitute various compromises between 'difference' and 'equality' – combining perceived demands arising from the breastfeeding recommendation and the ambition of increasing fathers' caregiving and strengthening mothers' position in the labour market. Moreover, while there is a visible left–right political divide regarding the use of quotas as a political strategy to achieve gender equality, the breastfeeding recommendation divides women (and men) on the left. This situation underpins Scott's (1988) assertion that 'equality' and 'difference' is not necessarily a binary opposition; when looked at closely, arguments of feminists do not usually fall into 'neat compartments', and are instead often attempts to reconcile 'equal rights' with 'difference'.

Improving the social conditions of motherhood, especially working motherhood, has been at the core of Scandinavian 'state feminism'. Helga Hernes, who actually coined the very concept, argues that 'taking biological realities into account and thus differential treatment of women . . . is not equal to difference feminism in a philosophical sense . . . gender equality . . . cannot be obtained *without* differential treatment, partly as a permanent need from biological concerns, and partly as a hopefully time limited tool against discrimination' (Hernes 2004: 293). The critical point, however, is how to conceptualise 'permanent needs from biological concerns' and the differential treatment entailed.

The boundaries of biological motherhood connect to the much-disputed issue of the distinction between natural and cultural gender differences. An essential point is the relationship between women's bodies and social norms. I think Moi's (2005: 38) reasoning is particularly valuable on this issue. Moi argues that the distinction between biological and social gender sometimes is necessary, but it should be irrelevant to a concrete, historical conception of what it means to be a woman or a man in a given society. The kind of essentialism that many feminists worry about is that which argues that the female body inevitably is the origin of and justifies specific cultural and psychological norms. But this is biological determinism. The human body is neither biological nor social gender, neither nature nor culture. Based on Simone de Beauvoir's *The Second Sex*, Moi develops the notion of the body as a *situation*: the body is an outline of the kind of projects it is possible for us to have, but it does not follow from this that individual choice or social or ethical norms can be deduced from the structure of the human body. In the sense that most women can breastfeed, this is part of women's 'bodily situation'. Yet, the fact that women can breastfeed does not imply that they *must* breastfeed. Historical evidence implies that breastfeeding practices certainly do not represent 'nature unfolding'. Breastfeeding practices have been shaped and reshaped by shifting socioeconomic and cultural conditions (Schiøtz 2003). In a historical perspective, it is interesting to note that women have always breastfed *less* than recommended by public authorities (Ellingsæter 2005).

'Woman-friendly' social policies are powerful sites of institutionalising social norms. There has been a new politicisation of motherhood and breastfeeding in recent times (Meyer and Oliveira, 2003). The 'best interest of the child' is increasingly brought into public policy debate, and there is an expanding focus on perfecting and maximising children (Wall 2001). An increasingly important question thus is who gets to interpret the 'best interest of the child'? A hard-line implementation of lengthy intensive breastfeeding in the 'best interest of the child' runs the risk of transforming breastfeeding from women empowerment to a duty under state control. The woman as a subject, with legitimate needs and desires, become diffuse, restricting the subject positions of women (Wall 2001). Prolonged intensive breastfeeding thus is an example of policies that sacrifice the autonomy of mothers and the caregiving potential of fathers – for a perceived benefit to children (see also Bergmann 2008). Breastfeeding is not at odds with gender symmetry in caregiving in the child's first year of life, but some breastfeeding *practices* are.

NOTES

1. At the end of the 2000s, Sweden has the longest total leave, 15 months (68 weeks), while Iceland has the shortest, 9 months (39 weeks). Wage compensation levels are high in

272 *Gender inequalities in the 21st century*

all the countries; Denmark and Norway have the highest (90 per cent and 100 per cent, respectively), Finland the lowest (70 per cent). Wages are usually compensated up to a ceiling. Full compensation is negotiated in some sectors, for example among public sector employees. The eligibility criteria typically require employment/earned income (low thresholds) in the period prior to the receipt of benefits, usually 9 months or less. All five countries have flexible arrangements for take-up (see Ellingsæter 2009).

2. For example, fewer that 4 per cent of Norwegian fathers took any leave by the early 1990s.
3. Although in Sweden the Liberal party was leading in adopting the reform in a period when the social democrats were not in power.
4. Denmark and Sweden also followed up the new WHO recommendation, while Finland decided to keep the previous one.
5. Samples and definitions vary somewhat in the two surveys. The 2006 survey also had a lower response rate (67 compared to 80), and a higher proportion of mothers with high education. If there is a sample bias, it is likely to be in favour of mothers with high breastfeeding rates.
6. http://www.regjeringen.no/upload/HOD/Dokumenter%20FHA/SEM/ Kostholdsplanen/IS-0238%20kortversjon%20eng.pdf.
7. 'På verdenstoppen i ammehysteri', *Dagbladet*, 28 November 2001.
8. http://www.jordmorforeningen.no/tidsskriftet/artikler_tema07_5_1.html.
9. *Smittskydd* no. 3, 2007.
10. 'Ammepresset må dempes – Svensk lege med kraftsalve mot amming', *Aftenposten*, 11 July 2007.
11. A recent meta-study of developed countries found several positive effects of breastfeeding on both the child's and the mother's health, but only 4 per cent of more than 9000 studies reviewed were deemed methodologically adequate (for example including satisfactory definitions of breastfeeding) (see Greve 2007).
12. 'Ammepresset må dempes – Svensk lege med kraftsalve mot amming', *Aftenposten*, 11 July 2007.
13. The Breastfeeding Centre, written comment to the public hearing on the Government commission on equal pay, 25 July 2008.
14. In the public sector wages are fully compensated, which is also the case in many local agreements in the private sector.
15. The analysis is based on newspaper articles extracted from ATEKST, a data base containing 47 national and local newspapers. For 2008 it also includes written comments to the public hearing on the proposal from the Government commission on equal pay (NOU 2008); c.f. http://www.regjeringen.no/nb/dep/bld/dok/Hoyringar/hoerings dok/2008/horing---nou-2008--6-kjonn-og-lonn/horingsuttalelser.html?id=505160.
16. 'Bekymret likestillingsombud – Amme-fokus hemmer likestillingen', *Aftenposten*, 16 November 2001.
17. 'Gammeldags feminisme fra likestillingsombudet', *Aftenposten*, 17 November 2001.
18. *Stavanger Aftenblad*, 20 December 2003.
19. 'Duellen Pupp eller Pappa', *Dagbladet*, 8 March 2003.
20. 'Går mot økt pappakvote', *Klassekampen*, 6 January 2004.
21. 'Ut av ammetåka', *Dagsavisen*, 13 November 2004.
22. 'Deling av svangerskapspermisjon', *Bergens Tidende*, 25 November 2004.
23. 'Nei til lengre permisjon til mor', *Klassekampen*, 10 June 2004.
24. In the late 2000s the father was entitled to the daddy quota if the mother had been employed 50 per cent or more before birth, and entitled to parental leave if the mother was employed/in education 75 per cent or more after the birth.
25. 'NHO vil ha pappa hjem', *Dagsavisen*, 8 February 2008.
26. 'Høyre på feil spor', *Dagbladet*, 26 November 2007.
27. 'Foreldrene vil bestemme selv!', http://hoyre.no, 4 February 2008.
28. http://www.lo.no, 29 September 2008.
29. *Mannspanelets konklusjonsnotat*, 3 March 2008.

30. 'Kvinnesak ennå viktig', *Aftenposten*, 8 March 2008.
31. http://arkiv.nettavisen.no, 19 February 2008.
32. Effective as of 1 July 2009, the total leave is 56 weeks at 80 per cent wage compensation (or 46 weeks at 100 per cent compensation). Nine weeks are still reserved for the mother (3 weeks before and 6 weeks after birth), 10 weeks are reserved for the father, parents can share 37 weeks (or 27 weeks) as they prefer.

REFERENCES

Batljan, I. et al. (2004), *Föräldrapenning, pappornas uttag av dagar, fakta och analys*, Stockholm: Socialdepartmentet.

Bergmann, B. (2008), 'Long leaves, child well-being, and gender equality', *Politics & Society*, **36**(3), 350–59.

Björnberg, U. (2002), 'Ideology and choice between work and care: Swedish family policy for working parents', *Critical Social Policy*, **22**(1), 33–52.

Borchorst, A. (2006), 'The public–private split rearticulated: the abolishment of the Danish daddy leave', in A.L. Ellingsæter and A. Leira (eds), *Politicising Parenthood in Scandinavia*, Bristol: Policy Press, pp. 101–20.

Brighouse, H. and E.O. Wright (2008), 'Strong gender egalitarianism', *Politics & Society*, **36**(3), 360–72.

Crompton, R. (2009), 'The normative and institutional embeddedness of parental employment: its impact on gender egalitarianism in parenthood and employment', in J.C. Gornick and M.K. Meyers (eds), *Gender Equality: Transforming Family Divisions of Labor*, New York: Verso, pp. 365–84.

Deven, F. and P. Moss (2002), 'Leave arrangements for parents: overview and future outlook', *Community, Work & Family*, **5**(3), 237–55.

Eide, I. et al. (2003), *Ammeundersøkelsen 2000*, Oslo: Helsetilsynet.

Ellingsæter, A.L. (2005), 'De "nye" mødrene og remoralisering av moderskapet', *Nytt Norsk Tidsskrift*, no. 4, 374–84.

Ellingsæter, A.L. (2006), 'The Norwegian child care regime and its paradoxes', in A.L. Ellingsæter and A. Leira (eds), *Politicising Parenthood in Scandinavia*, Bristol: Policy Press, pp. 121–44.

Ellingsæter, A.L. (2007), '"Old" and "new" politics of time to care: three Norwegian reforms', *Journal of European Social Policy*, **17**(1), 49–60.

Ellingsæter, A.L. (2009), 'Leave policy in the Nordic welfare states: a "recipe" for high employment/high fertility?', *Community, Work and Family*, **12**(1), 1–19.

Ellingsæter, A.L. and A. Leira (eds) (2006), *Politicising Parenthood in Scandinavia*, Bristol: Policy Press.

Fraser, N. (1994), 'After the family wage: gender equity and the welfare state', *Political Theory*, **22**, 591–618.

Gender Equality Ombud (2004), *Høringsuttalelse. Anmodningsvedtak fra Stortinget til Regjeringen*, 7 July, Oslo.

Gornick, J. and M.K. Meyers (2008), 'Creating gender egalitarian societies: an agenda for social reform', *Politics & Society*, **36**(3), 313–49.

Greve, T. (2007), 'Morsmelkens fordeler og ammingens utfordringer', *Tidsskrift for jordmødre*, no.5, available at http://www.jordmorforeningen.no/tidsskriftet/artikler_tema07_5_1.html.

Helsedirektoratet (2008), *Spedkost – 6 måneder. Landsomfattende kostholdsundersøkelse blant 6 måneder gamle barn*, Oslo: Helsedirektoratet.
Hernes, H. (1987), *Welfare State and Woman Power*, Oslo: Norwegian University Press.
Hernes, H. (2004), 'Statsfeminisme – et personlig tilbakeblikk', *Nytt Norsk Tidsskrift*, no. 3–4, 288–94.
Johansen, A.M.W. (2007), 'Om ammeproblemer og flaskemating', *Tidsskrift for jordmødre*, no.5, available at http://www.jordmorforeningen.no/tidsskriftet/artikler_tema07_5_1.html.
Lande, B. et al. (2003), 'Infant feeding practices and associated factors in the first six months of life: The Norwegian Infant Nutrition Survey', *Acta Pædiatrica*, **92**, 152–61.
Leira, A. (2006), 'Parenthood change and policy reform in Scandinavia, 1970s–2000s', in A.L. Ellingsæter and A. Leira (eds), *Politicising Parenthood in Scandinavia*, Bristol: Policy Press, pp. 27–52.
Mandel, H. and M. Semyonov (2006), 'A welfare state paradox: state interventions and women's employment opportunities in 22 countries', *American Journal of Sociology*, **111**(6), 1910–49.
Meyer, D.E. and D.L. Oliveira (2003), 'Breastfeeding policies and the production of motherhood: a historical-cultural approach', *Nursing Inquiry*, **10**(1), 11–18.
Moi, T. (2005), *Sex, Gender and the Body*, Oxford: Oxford University Press.
Moss, P. and F. Deven (2006), 'Leave policies and research: a cross-national overview', *Marriage & Family Review*, **39**(3/4), 255–85.
NOU (2008), *Kjønn og lønn. Fakta, analyser og virkemidler for likelønn*, Oslo.
Orloff, A.S. (2009), 'Should feminists aim for gender symmetry? Why a dual-earner/dual-caregiver society is not every feminist's utopia', in J.C. Gornick and M.K. Meyers (eds), *Gender Equality: Transforming Family Divisions of Labor*, New York: Verso, pp. 129–57.
Schiøtz, A. (2003), *Folkets Helse – Landets Styrke 1850–2003*, Oslo: Universitetsforlaget.
Scott, J.W. (1988), *Gender and the Politics of History*, New York: Columbia University Press.
SOU (2005), *Reformerad föräldraförsäkring*, SOU 2005:73, Betenkande av Föräldraförsäkringsutredningen, Stockholm: Socialdepartementet.
Sundström, M. and A.Z.E. Duvander (2002), 'Gender division of childcare and the sharing of parental leave among new parents in Sweden', *European Sociological Review*, **18**, 433–47.
Wall, G. (2001), 'Moral constructions of motherhood in breastfeeding discourse', *Gender & Society*, **15**(4), 592–610.

13. A mysterious commodity: capitalism and femininity

Mary Evans

The relationship between gender and capitalism has proved to be fertile ground for discussion and debate. Some of those debates have concerned arguments about the relationship between capitalism and ideological distinctions about gender and sexuality, whilst others have examined the assumption, of both Marx and Engels, that the entry by women into paid production would provide the grounds for our emancipation from familial forms of authority (Merck 2007). The focus of this chapter, however, is the question of the ideology of femininity and of how that ideology is constructed, through ideas about fashion and behaviour appropriate to women (especially in relation to the care of others) in ways which have a central importance to the cultural dynamic of contemporary capitalism.

Those assumptions about Marx which consider him primarily as a student of economic systems obscure those moments in his work when he demonstrates his recognition of the cultural. Indeed, in one of the more vivid passages of Volume One of *Capital* Marx presents an account of a working day in the second half of the nineteenth century which suggests links between the economic and cultural. As becomes clear from the text, the term 'working day' is something of a misnomer since many of the people whose hours of work he is describing work both day and night, often with little break. These hours of work are inevitably a cause of illness and death; Marx writes of one case – that of a young seamstress – who had died, the coroner wrote, of 'overwork' (Marx 1990).

In painting a picture of this young woman's life, and the circumstances of her death, Marx makes some connections which are, I shall suggest, still relevant both to the discussion of women and employment in the twenty-first century and to the ways in which we consider those complex ideas of the 'cultural' and the 'material'. Marx writes:

> The girl worked, on an average, sixteen and a half hours during the season, often thirty hours without a break, whilst her failing labour power was revived by occasional supplies of sherry, port or coffee. It was just now the height of the

season. It was necessary to conjure up in the twinkling of an eye the gorgeous dresses for the noble ladies bidden to the ball in honour of the newly imported Princess of Wales (Marx 1990).

In the passages which follow this comment, Marx goes on to acknowledge that he is not alone in condemning these kinds of exploitative working practices; as he points out, the free traders Cobden and Bright speak of our 'white slaves' who are working (or being worked) to death in a thousand similar places.

In the first decade of the twenty-first century attention has continued to focus on the ways in which human labour is exploited in the manufacture of clothing. Although the focus of much of the attention has now passed from the conditions of work in factories making very expensive clothes for the very rich to factories making inexpensive clothes for a mass market, what remains a driving force for much of this manufacture is the concept of fashion, an idea which is closely related to our changing expectations of femininity. In this chapter I wish to explore some of the possible connections between 'fashion', femininity and capitalism. My contention is that whilst aspects of the formal institutional and legal worlds move slowly closer to androgynous expectations of the 'citizen', many attitudes towards men and women continue to maintain and indeed to develop distinctions of masculinity and femininity. As Scott, and others, have pointed out, there is a considerable cultural lag between social assumptions about gender equality and actual practice in both the private and the public sphere (Crompton and Lyonette 2005; Scott 2006).

The literature on the 'lived' meaning of femininity and masculinity in the UK is now very extensive. For example, Skeggs and McDowell have produced important work on the ways in which individual human beings internalise ideas about appropriate behaviour for women and men (McDowell 1997; Skeggs 2004). In the case of work by both authors it is also emphasised that subjectivities of gender are also subjectivities of class: for working-class young women, for example, the version of femininity which is most likely to be 'lived' is a version which makes explicit its commitment to the care of others. To reject the cultural assumption of a female responsibility for caring is seen, therefore, as an inappropriate choice by sections of the working class. The work by Skeggs and McDowell (and other work, for example by Lawler), thus suggests that there is no one way of 'being' female and that subjectivities of gender are highly nuanced by circumstances of both class and race (Lawler 2000). Work by other writers (for example Duncan) extends the discussion to middle-class women and emphasises that caring is a responsibility shared by middle class as well as working-class women (Duncan and Irwin 2004).

Yet at the same time as we can see how class position produces different ways of 'doing' gender for women, what can also be seen is that in one way or another, women, whatever their position of race or class, are all in some sense (and in this the resonance with the ideas of Butler is clear) 'performing' gender. But whilst this idea is widely referred to, the precise way in which gender is 'performed' is seldom fully explored, although various voices sympathetic to psycho-analysis have continued to explore what Rose has described as the 'difficulty of femininity for women' (Rose 1986). Butler's implicit suggestion that existing ideological constructions of gender should be re-formed into androgyny ignores historical evidence which suggests that when this has happened (most often in times of national emergency) the form that androgyny has taken has been masculinised (Riley 1979; Summerfield 1984).

The argument of this chapter is that the 'performance' of the complex quality of femininity is a crucial part not just of the lives of women but of the social dynamic of capitalism in the early twenty-first century. A considerable body of literature now exists on the history of the development of 'consumer' capitalism, but this literature is seldom considered in the same context as the literature on the politics of gender and the social recognition of inequality (Lury 1996; Lury and Adkins 1999). Yet the various forms of subjectivity within which we live play an essential part in maintaining the consumer spending of the neoliberal state; as any reader of the financial pages of the press will know, 'consumer confidence' is regarded as a crucial part of Western financial prosperity. Marx may have put this in terms of capitalism's constant need to maintain the rate of profit, but both Marxists and neoliberals are agreed that for capitalism to continue to exist so must consumer spending.

The manufacture of goods and 'needs' over and above those necessary for survival has been one of the great transformations of the past two hundred years, a transformation made possible by technological change and by the extension of mass markets. The societies which have emerged from this process of transformation have often been described as 'feminised', although the analysis on which this judgement is based has often been focused on ideological rather than material change. The work of Douglas, for example, which has argued that modernism, especially in literature, allowed a greater place for the exploration of the lives and experiences of women, did not include a detailed discussion of other aspects (particularly employment) of women's lives (Douglas 1977). It is rather more difficult to recognise a 'feminised' society in the comparative distribution of men and women in various public hierarchies of power than in certain cultural shifts. Equally, to speak of a 'feminised' society radically obscures the way in which care work is still largely (although by no means exclusively) performed by women. Judgements about the gender of a society are thus complex; whilst they may seem apt in certain contexts, they have little visible meaning in others.

But in one sense the case could be made for the 'feminisation' of society, a case which does not depend on the equal access of women to equal pay or equal public power but relates to the centrality of the 'feminine' to the economy and to the material world. Society may (or may not) have become 'feminine' but the possibilities of 'femininity' have become recognisable as commodities in late capitalism and as such an idea and a form of human existence which has manifest and extensive meanings that can be exploited and commodified in various forms of labour, including emotional work (Hochschild 1983). In the first sense the exploitation of the biologically female person (what might be described as the 'literal' woman of the social world) has allowed, and continues to allow, extensive industries around dressing and policing the body. In a second, less literal sense, the 'feminine' is an immensely porous form of the articulation and development of certain kinds of socially agreed emotional responses and forms of affectivity. In the first place we can all see, in any urban space, the various locations (hairdressers, clothes shops and so on) concerned with the maintenance of normative orders about the body. In the second context we can also see, although in a less immediately visible way, the re-creation of aspects of city spaces and human relationships as occasions for 'romance' or the fulfilment of other 'feminised' forms of social relations (Frisby 2001: 126).

It is in this context – a context of global neoliberal societies with political commitments to sustained economic growth – that the concept of femininity as a commodity, and as a structurally significant concept of considerable importance, merits attention. Profits do not, we might remind ourselves, maintain themselves, and the ways in which they are maintained should come as no surprise to individuals who have lived through the past sixty years of various forms of material transformation throughout the world. Therborn has commented on the way in which Western, liberal ideas of sexual emancipation have shared a common agenda with consumer capitalism (Therborn 2004). Therborn (and others, for example Weeks) have only positive views about the extension of various forms of civil rights to women and sexual minorities but these authors (and others) have been less energetic in pursuing the connection between liberal agendas of human emancipation and the satisfaction of individual desires with the interests of consumer capitalism (Weeks 2007). In her work on the social implications of the introduction of a market economy in China, Rofel has suggested that an aspect of that process of social change has also involved the creation of what she describes as the 'desiring subject' (Rofel

2007). Again, changes which we might regard as politically positive (more equal gender relations, greater autonomy for women and so on) become part of twenty-first century subjectivity, but so too does that aspect of 'desire' which underpins consumer engagement.

The visible transformation of the appearance of Chinese women, from the androgynous workers of Mao's China to the westernised women (and particularly young women) of contemporary China, vividly demonstrates the potential power of fashion as a location of both aspiration and achievement. To be able to dress in a certain way becomes a symbol of identification with a particular version of the modern world; to support that aspiration it is apparent, from the Western example, that both women and men are willing to commit themselves to considerable amounts of consumer spending and personal debt. 'Dedicated followers of fashion' have become central to the healthy continuation of Western (and increasingly global) consumer demand. Crucial to fashion (whether it be in clothes or other forms of consumer spending) is its relationship with 'femininity', a commodity of increasing concern to those failing retail sectors of the West. Even though a commodity, Marx reminds us, is a mysterious thing, there are two aspects of the commodity of femininity which can be made less than mysterious. The first is the relationship of femininity to social class and the second is the necessity, to capitalism, of instability and diversity in the concept of femininity. In the latter case the interests of capitalism towards women and the feminine differ radically from those regimes, for example in Saudi Arabia, who wish to maintain a stable (not to say rigid) version of the feminine condition.

FEMININITY AND SOCIAL CLASS

An interesting recent example of the importance of social class to visual constructions of femininity involved the decision by Alexandra Shulman, the editor of British *Vogue*, to choose to put on the front cover of that magazine a photograph of Colleen McLoughlin, the then girlfriend of the footballer Wayne Rooney. Shulman herself said that she was amazed by the highly negative comments that she received from some of her readers, many of whom felt that an important location of 'taste' had been undermined by this choice of subject. Yet Shulman herself, when interviewing another footballer's wife, Victoria Beckham (also photographed for *Vogue*'s cover) expressed surprise when meeting Mrs Beckham at 'both her good manners and her degree of interest in a world outside her own' (Shulman 2007).

The above illustrates many of those ideas about 'taste' and 'cultural capital' which Bourdieu has made a central part of sociology. As the editor of *Vogue*, Shulman is clearly perceived by some as the guardian not just of 'good' taste but of an elite, privileged, form of taste, a taste which can distinguish its adherents from those who do not possess it. To bring into this world figures such as Victoria Beckham and, even more so, Colleen McLoughlin, undermines the authority and the value of that taste. What Shulman did, in these editorial decisions, was to bring *Vogue* close to the popular culture of magazines such as *Heat* and remind us how much is at stake in fashion, in particular the importance, in this case, of maintaining the distinctions between the iconic, long-standing status of *Vogue* as an arbiter of taste with other media forms.

The commodities which are advertised in *Vogue* (and featured in the magazine's editorial pages) are all expensive and largely beyond the purchasing power of the majority of the population. These commodities are only mysterious in the sense of those rhetorical questions about the identity of their potential consumers. But what we know of patterns of consumption in Britain (for example, through the extensive work of Savage and his colleagues) is that it is women who are the major purchasers of all clothes (including those for men) and household goods (Savage et al. 2008). It is women who constitute that elusive 'public' whose consumer energy makes or breaks many aspects of the retail trade. Yet, as the case of *Vogue* and McLoughlin illustrates, what women are buying, when they are buying clothes or other goods, are forms of social identity, identities which both separate or relate them to other people. It is not difficult to identify the ways in which women consumers are encouraged to replicate the appearance of significant others (and the 'naming' or endorsement of collections of merchandise by iconic figures demonstrates this). However, it is rather more difficult to show the explicit ways in which fashion can be used as a way of separation from others and, most significantly in a society such as Britain where divisions about class are still apparent in data about higher education, health and social mobility, how visible expressions of femininity are structured by considerations of class. The purchase of expensive goods that can be carried on (or by) the person is one way, as it has always been, of demonstrating wealth, but this form of Veblen's 'conspicuous consumption' has incurred numerous recent difficulties, not the least of which are the association of those items with those of lower social status and the widespread forgery of expensive items of clothing.

In this, it could be that women, as consumers, become resistant to the purchase of a certain form of privileged femininity because the symbolic expressions of that privilege acquire less the status of exclusivity than of parody. (The case of the Burberry scarf is a good example of an 'elite' object becoming an object of parody and social undesirability: once the scarf had been successfully copied and adopted by poor and unfashionable young people, the 'real' object itself became valueless as a commodity, even if it still had 'use-value' as a scarf.) But just as this process is part of the intrinsic dynamic of fashion (this year's clothes render last year's 'unwearable') so it demonstrates something of the dialectic which is involved in fashion, a dialectic in which an object is only desirable as long as it can maintain its positive social identity, an identity which depends upon judgements of taste as well as a degree of material scarcity. To look 'fashionable' thus involves complex decisions (inevitably mediated by cost) about the achievement of an individuality which is recognisable in terms of its association with the identity of a desirable individual or group. The sartorial turmoil at the centre of fashion apparently offers individuals a 'free' space for the definition of self, but central to that definition remains a crucial element of recognition; every 'sign' needs a reader.

These comments about fashion do not directly relate femininity to social class, except in the sense that dress for women in the twenty-first century is as bound by diverse codes (including those of 'respectability' and age suitability) as it ever was. But in suggesting ways in which dress involves questions of social class, it is also possible to begin to see how, in societies (such as that of Britain) which have begun to identify themselves (contrary to considerable sociological evidence) as 'class-less', a paradox evolves in which dress, particularly for women, becomes more important as other signs of social status and social recognition (for example, patterns of recreation) change. We know (as suggested above) that women are the major domestic consumers in all Western economies but we also know that in the majority of those economies women both earn less and have less access to significant social power than men. For women, therefore, the form of social agency which may well be the most generally (and relatively democratically) available, and which is the most homologous with a general culture of individuation, is that of the presentation of self. Precisely because the degree of women's social agency and autonomy is less than that of men, so the visible self has the most potential (and is certainly the most easily exploited) as a source of social and cultural gratification.

A number of authors have contributed in various ways (not all of them explicit) which can assist in further developing the question of the relationship between women's presentation of self, social class and femininity. The first is the now considerable collection of literature, much of it by feminist authors, on emotions and 'feeling'. This literature, as Gorton points out in a recent review article, 'offers a way of thinking about subjectivity that is not tied solely to the psyche' (Gorton 2007). In other words, our actions are guided not just by what we think but also by how we feel and our bodily response to feelings. This is a particularly interesting and revealing comment since, although a distinction is made between 'subjectivity and the psyche', there is little or no suggestion that 'feelings' might be formed by a considerable variety of outside experiences and interests. As Gorton rightly points out, sociological and feminist work on the emotions does not assume that all emotions are necessarily positive, but it does leave unanswered the questions about the origin of 'desire-as-process'. Whilst Gorton emphasises the range of feminist work on the emotions (Ahmed 2006; Berlant 2000) she also makes the valuable distinction between what desire *does* and what desire *is*. If we turn our attention to what desire does then this allows us to consider the social origins and impact of desire and opens up the theoretical space for the discussion of what Andrew Sayer has identified as patterns of 'Class, Moral Worth and Recognition' (Sayer 2007). As Sayer writes:

> we will better understand the implications of class if we probe lay normative responses to it, particularly as regards how people value themselves and others. If we are to understand the significance of class we need to take lay normativity, especially morality, much more seriously than sociology has tended to do; without this we are likely to produce bland, alienated accounts which fail to make sense of why class is a matter of concern and embarrassment to people. (Sayer 2007)

As Sayer says, later in the same paragraph, one of the aspects of the social world which sociologists might study further is the question of 'the different kind of goods which people value' (Sayer 2007). It is clear from empirical evidence that although men have interests in fashion, and certain men with definably male skills become icons of both masculinity and masculine fashion (David Beckham being the most visible, and global, example) that there is a significant gender difference in the goods which women and men value and see as important to their sense of self (Edwards 2006).

Sayer does not, in his discussion, 'gender' the nature of the goods which he is discussing, but like others (including those to whom he refers), he does set out to consider the ways in which we are 'encultured' into certain actions or choices. Again, neither fashion nor gender are part of his argument but what emerges here, as in the various authors discussed by Gorton, is a concern with subjectivity, that very quality which has long been identified with women. What seems to be evolving therefore is both an 'affective turn' in sociology as well as a more general turn to the 'feminine' in the wider culture. The cultural validation of 'feeling' which is part of that aspect of 'femininisation' allows a greater social toleration for the satisfaction of individual desire. As sociologists, we have to recognise the social processes which define and create desires; we also have to recognise that our desires may not all be of our own making and that one of the great recognitions (and long-term relationships) of the twentieth century was that between the female body, fashion and profit. Bringing together the arguments of Sayer and Gorton relates a new emotional culture to a moral culture in which it is possible to see the genesis of the social process of the permission to desire (both relationships and consumer objects) with different aspects of the normative order. Sayer is right to stress those aspects of the moral order which relate to questions about social equality and distributive justice, but at the same time he, in common with some authors of work on emotions, tends to assume that values are necessarily admirable. Nevertheless he makes the important point that 'distributional inequalities in access to valued practices and goods in any case render equality of conditional recognition impossible' (Sayer 2007).

It is at this point that it becomes possible to relate that 'distributional inequality' to women and more specifically to those visual qualities which constitute femininity. Women, since the beginning of the nineteenth century, have been symbolically associated with the 'modern' and the general assumption made that the 'emancipation' of women is one of the features of modernity. This assumption now contributes to global distinctions between 'modern' societies and those which maintain rigidly organised (and enforced) social codes about gender. One of the many differences between generations of Western women is that of the increased number of married women, and women who have children, into the labour force. But although this shift was politically managed during the two world wars in terms of the demands of the state, there remains an important sense in which (as numerous studies about women and occupational mobility demonstrate) women remain a problematic presence in certain contexts. In her study of the City of London, McDowell wrote of a work place where 'The game of femininity is one which is imposed on women by male values and language'. But as she went on to say:

> theorists have shown how the representation of femininity rests on structures of oppression that necessitate the dominated group seeing through the eyes and categories of the dominant culture. In negotiating this alienation of identity, women are led into simulating appearances of femininity through masks and masquerade in an infinite regress. (McDowell 1997: 202)

This 'alienation of identity' is, as Skeggs has suggested, particularly acute in the case of working-class women where individual appearance may be seen to carry the 'signs' of social inferiority and marginality. The ways in which white working-class women dress have long been the subject of feminist attention on both sides of the Atlantic: various authors have pointed out the resolute sexual boldness of media representations of working-class femininity (for example Julia Roberts playing Erin Brockavitch in the film of the same name). What this (hetero)sexual boldness does is to suggest, visually, that class-based distinction between women who work 'as women' (that is in work which is unskilled and badly paid and long associated with the domestic role of women) and women who are employed in middle-class occupations, occupations where women have to some extent neutralised the 'negative' connotations of female gender by the acquisition of 'male' qualifications. Losing or changing the appearance of working-class femininity thus becomes, as the recent British television programme 'Ladette to Lady' (in which working-class young women are 'educated' in the manners and behaviour of the middle class) suggests, an important aspect of aspirational class mobility.

The transition from what Skeggs has described as the unrespectable female 'hen' to respectable female is partly negotiated through clothing, make-up and general demeanour. But there is another form of transformation which has recently acquired considerable attention: that of the physical transformation of the body through cosmetic surgery. The literature on this subject is now considerable and in the work of Davis in particular there is an articulate challenge to the view that cosmetic surgery makes 'victims' out of women (Davis 1995). Views on cosmetic surgery differ, but there are a number of issues which relate the question very directly to questions of class: the first is that cosmetic surgery is almost always elective surgery and as such has to be privately financed. The corollary of this is that cosmetic surgery is highly profitable. The final point is that although, as Davis points out, there is no reason to suppose that women do not freely choose to make the adjustments to their person which they consider the most important, the definition of the 'most important' may be highly susceptible to social pressures and material interests. The female body is no stranger to various forms of physical modification but the belief in the transformation of the body as a means to individual social transformation is arguably a product both of relative social powerlessness and of the strength of material interests. At present cosmetic surgery is a growing, and financially rewarding, form of medical practice largely dependent on female clients.

Cosmetic surgery is, however, only one aspect of that insecurity around the feminine which is so much part of our culture. Hey is amongst those who have argued that the central figure of modernity, the autonomous and independent urban dweller, is a male person, and that the values which this person carries, and which are seen as part of the normative personal order of the twentieth century West, is not gender-neutral (Hey 2002). Some of the complexity in the experience of femininity is reflected in different forms of statistical evidence: on the one hand single women are likely to live longer and more healthy lives than men; on the other the impact of divorce on women and children is generally to impoverish women rather than men. Although much of the latter can be explained by the responsibilities which women carry for the care of children (which restricts their access to paid work), this material nevertheless suggests that the traditional expectations of femininity are still in place. Those expectations, as Smart has pointed out, challenge the theories of Giddens and Beck which argue that individualisation has become the driving force of personal life in the twenty-first century (Smart 2007).

I would suggest, therefore, that femininity remains a porous and malleable concept, and one through which a considerable baggage of class-based values and aspirations can be carried. But it is also a concept which carries a general set of social aspirations, most importantly about 'the modern', even though those aspirations may not be articulated in the interests of women themselves. The history of the Western twentieth century suggests that the meaning of femininity can be made and re-made by powerful dominant interests; at times there may well be a coincidence between those interests and the interests of actual women, but that coincidence is not always reliable.

FEMININITY AND CARING

The demonstration of the relationship between women and responsibility for caring (for children, the sick and the old, both in the home and in the workplace) has been one of the major achievements of second wave feminism. It has resulted in the public recognition and financial reward of this work but, as various writers have pointed out, its impact on various aspects of women's lives remains considerable (Sevenhuijsen 2002). Whilst this impact has now been recorded in terms of the relationship of caring responsibilities to the workplace and the extension of the term 'caring work' to include emotional work, other ways in which 'caring' still structures femininity are being suggested. One instance of this extension of the understanding of the impact of 'caring' is in the work of Evans on working-class girls in a sixth form in east London and their attitudes to higher education (Evans 2009).

In this study of working-class girls considering (and planning for) higher education, two striking features appeared. The first was that for the majority of the young women interviewed a prime motive in higher and/ or professional education was the value that this endeavour might bring to family. Again, the concept of the individual as a 'free' and autonomous subject was found to have little meaning. The young women collectively viewed self-advancement in terms of the improvement of the lives of their families. A second, and closely related point, was that the young women did not wish higher education to act as a barrier or a form of separation between themselves and their families. Thus studying away from home (the typical expectation of middle-class students) was a generally unpopular choice; the value of maintaining local and family links had a greater priority than any individual advantage in leaving home (Crompton 2008; Reay et al. 2001).

These findings involve a small number of individuals in an area of London with highly developed community ties. But what these findings point to, and which have been demonstrated in terms of much larger numbers of informants in the work of Yeandle and her colleagues, is that women do not always see connections and responsibilities to others in the same way as they are presented in the social edicts of governments, however well meaning (Yeandle and Buckner 2007). Far from seeing caring responsibilities as an inhibition on achievement or success in the work force (a view which is clearly tied to models of paid work with well-defined career structures) many women, whilst justifiably resenting the often onerous commitments which they carry, nevertheless see these commitments as part of being human. This important point is further developed by Smart:

> Connectedness is not a normative concept and I am not arguing that connection is a human good, nor that it is invariably nourishing and inevitably desirable. On the contrary, I have highlighted some of the problems of connecting with and relating to others. The point about the idea, however, is that it sets the sociological imagination off on a different intellectual trajectory to the one initiated by the individualisation thesis. (Smart 2007: 189)

Smart, together with other sociologists of the family such as Brannen and Nilsen, goes on to point out that the theoretical consequences of thinking in terms of 'connections' involves a re-thinking (if not rejection) of those theorists (for example Giddens and Ulrich Beck who 'read' the twentieth century as a history of increased individualisation) (Brannen and Nilsen 2005).

CONCLUSION

However the debate about twenty-first century individualisation is resolved, what remains is that the social value of the caring work of 'connectedness' that women do is of fundamental social importance. The structural significance of this work has always been recognised in the

West (whether in terms of rejecting this work, as in second wave feminism or in maintaining it, by any number of conservative pundits throughout the twentieth century). But the contradiction which the performance (or not) of this work poses for the social world as a whole is that whilst the unpaid work is socially necessary, so is the paid work of women. The demonstrable decision by women to refuse to become mothers in those societies which offer little in the way of state provision for childcare (and in Europe Italy is the most notable example here) demonstrates the way in which women's own interpretation of the possibilities of femininity is affected by material factors. It remains to be seen, as E.J. Hobsbawm has suggested, 'if a theoretically libertarian capitalism [can function without] . . . rules of obligation and loyalty inside and outside the traditional family' (Hobsbawm 2005).

This could be read as a call for the revival of the patriarchal family; in this context it is not, but it is a questioning of the social impact of new forms of femininity and masculinity. The latter has not been the subject of this chapter; suffice to say that at present the demands made on women through ideologies about femininity (whether in terms of responsibilities towards others or rigorous demands towards the maintenance of the female body) arguably outweigh those made on men, through ideologies about masculinity. Nevertheless the continuing malleability of femininity, whilst producing various contradictions, also produces a rich vein of those subjectivities which inform and inspire the profitable, if mysterious, world of commodities. Those commodities, as Marx pointed out in 1887, form an essential part of the health of the capitalist economy. Recent concerns about this health, concerns which have often emphasised the profitability of retail sections of the economy, have made visible the relationship of the state to individual *female* subjectivity, a subjectivity which in part consists of concerns about, in the most general sense, personal appearance.

BIBLIOGRAPHY

Ahmed, S. (2006), *Queer Phenomenology: Orientations, Objects, Others*, Durham, NC: Duke University Press.

Beck, U. (1992), *Risk Society*, London: Sage.

Berlant, L. (2000), 'The subject of true feelings: pain, privacy and politics', in S. Ahmed et al. (eds), *Transformation: Thinking Through Feminism*, London: Routledge, pp. 33–47.

Brannen, J. and A. Nilsen (2005), 'Individualisation, choice and structure', *The Sociological Review*, **53**(3), 412–28.

Crompton, R. (2006), *Employment and the Family*, Cambridge: Cambridge University Press.

Crompton, R. (2008), *Class and Stratification*, Cambridge: Polity.
Crompton, R. and C. Lyonette (2005), 'The new gender essentialism – domestic and family "choices" and their relation to attitudes', *British Journal of Sociology*, **56**(4), 601–20.
Davis, K. (1995), *Reshaping the Female Body*, London: Routledge.
Douglas, A. (1977), *The Feminization of American Culture*, New York: Anchor.
Duncan, S. and S. Irwin (2004), 'The social patterning of values and rationalities', *Social Policy and Society*, 3(4), 391–400.
Edwards, T. (1997), *Men in the Mirror: Men's Fashion, Masculinity and Consumer Society*, London: Cassell.
Edwards, T. (2006), *Cultures of Masculinity*, London: Routledge.
Evans, S. (2009), 'Working class girls and higher education', *Sociology*, **43**(2), 340–55.
Frisby, D. (2001), *Cityscapes of Modernity*, Cambridge: Polity.
Giddens, A. (1991), *Modernity and Self Identity in the Late Modern Age*, Cambridge: Polity.
Gorton, K. (2007), 'Theorising emotion and affect', *Feminist Theory*, **8**(3), 333–48.
Hey, V. (2002), 'Horizontal solidarities and molten capitalism', *Discourse*, **23**(2), 227–41.
Hobsbawm, E. (2005), 'The retreat of the male', *London Review of Books*, 4 August pp. 6–9.
Hochschild, A. (1983), *The Managed Heart*, Los Angeles: University of California Press.
Lawler, S. (2000), *Mothering the Self: Mothers, Daughters, Subjects*, London: Routledge.
Lury, C. (1996), *Consumer Culture*, Cambridge: Polity.
Lury, C. and L. Adkins (1999), 'The labour of identity', *Economy and Society*, **28**(4), 598–614.
Marx, K. (1990), *Capital Volume 1*, London: Penguin.
McDowell, L. (1997), *Capital Culture*, Oxford: Blackwell.
Merck, M. (2007), in T. Lovell (ed.), *(Mis)recognition, Social Inequality and Social Justice*, London: Routledge, pp. 49–65.
Reay, D., M. Davies and S.J. Ball (2001), 'Choices of degree or degrees of choice?', *Sociology*, **35**(4) 855–74.
Riley, D. (1979), 'War in the nursery', *Feminist Review*, **2**, 82–108.
Rofel, L. (2007), *Desiring China: Experiments in Neoliberal, Sexual and Public Cultures*, Durham: Duke.
Rose, J. (1986), *Sexuality in the Field of Vision*, London: Verso.
Savage, M., L. Yaojun and A. Warde (2008), 'Social mobility and social capital in contemporary Britain', *British Journal of Sociology*, **59**(3), 391–41.
Sayer, A. (2007), 'Class, moral worth and recognition', in T. Lovell (ed.), *(Mis) recognition,Social Inequality and Social Justice*, London: Routledge.
Scott, J. (2006), 'Families and gender roles: how attitudes are changing', *Arxius*, **15**, 143–54.
Sevenhuijsen, J. (2002), 'A third way? Moralities, ethics and families: an approach through the ethic of care', in A. Carling, S. Duncan and R. Edwards (eds), *Analysing Families*, London: Routledge.
Shulman, A. (2007), 'The Victoria principle', *Vogue*, April 2008, pp. 262–6.
Skeggs, B. (2004), *Class, Self, Culture*, London: Routledge.

Smart, C. (2007), *Personal Life*, Cambridge: Polity.

Summerfield, P. (1984), *Women Workers in the Second World War*, London: Croom Helm.

Therborn, G. (2004), *Between Sex and Power: Family in the World 1900–2000*, London: Routledge.

Ungerson, C. and S. Yeandle (eds) (2006), *Cash for Care in Developed Welfare States*, London: Palgrave Macmillan.

Weeks, J. (2007), *The World We Have Won*, London: Routledge.

Yeandle, S. and L. Buckner (2007), *Carers, Employment and Services: Time for a New Social Contract?*, London: Carers UK.

Index